THE

LOST AND HOSTILE GOSPELS.

THE

LOST AND HOSTILE GOSPELS:

An Essay

ON THE TOLEDOTH JESCHU, AND THE PETRINE AND
PAULINE GOSPELS OF THE FIRST THREE CEN-
TURIES OF WHICH FRAGMENTS REMAIN.

BY

REV. S. BARING-GOULD, M.A.

AUTHOR OF "THE ORIGIN AND DEVELOPMENT OF RELIGIOUS BELIEF,"
"LEGENDARY LIVES OF THE OLD TESTAMENT CHARACTERS,"

WILLIAMS AND NORGATE,

14, HENRIETTA STREET, COVENT GARDEN, LONDON;
AND 20, SOUTH FREDERICK STREET, EDINBURGH.

————

1874.

LONDON:
PRINTED BY C. GREEN AND SON,
178, STRAND.

PREFACE.

It is advisable, if not necessary, for me, by way of preface, to explain certain topics treated of in this book, which do not come under its title, and which, at first thought, may be taken to have but a remote connection with the ostensible subject of this treatise. These are :

1. The outbreak of Antinomianism which disfigured and distressed primitive Christianity.

2. The opposition of the Nazarene Church to St. Paul.

3. The structure and composition of the Synoptical Gospels.

The consideration of these curious and important topics has forced its way into these pages ; for the first two throw great light on the history of those Gospels which have disappeared, and which it is not possible to reconstruct without a knowledge of the religious parties to which they belonged. And these parties were determined by the fundamental question of Law or No-law, as represented by the Petrine and ultra-Pauline Christians. And the third of these topics is necessarily bound up with the consideration of the structure and origin of the Lost Gospels, as the reader will see if he cares to follow me in the critical examination of their extant fragments.

Upon each of these points a few preliminary words will not, I hope, come amiss, and may prevent misunderstanding.

1. The history of the Church, as the history of nations, is not to be read with prejudiced eyes, with penknife in hand to erase facts which fight against foregone conclusions.

English Churchmen have long gazed with love on the Primitive Church as the ideal of Christian perfection, the Eden wherein the first fathers of their faith walked blameless before God, and passionless towards each other. To doubt, to dissipate in any way this pleasant dream, may shock and pain certain gentle spirits. Alas! the fruit of the tree of γνῶσις, if it opens the eyes, saddens also and shames the heart.

History, whether sacred or profane, hides her teaching from those who study her through coloured glasses. She only reveals truth to those who look through the cold clear medium of passionless inquiry, who seek the Truth without determining first the masquerade in which alone they will receive it.

It exhibits a strange, a sad want of faith in Truth thus to constrain history to turn out facts according to order, to squeeze it through the sieve of prejudice. And what indeed is Truth in history but the voice of God instructing the world through the vices, follies, errors of the past?

A calm, patient spirit of inquiry is an attitude of the modern mind alone. To this mind History has made strange disclosures which she kept locked up through former ages.

The world of Nature lay before the men of the past, but they could not, would not read it, save from left to right, or right to left, as their prejudices ran. The wise and learned had to cast aside their formulæ, and sit meekly at the feet of Nature, as little children, before they learned her laws. Nor will History submit to hectoring. Only now is she unfolding the hidden truth in her ancient scrolls.

It is too late to go back to conclusions of an uncritical age, though it was that of our fathers; the time for denying the facts revealed by careful criticism is passed away as truly as is the time for explaining the shadows in the moon by the story of the Sabbath-breaker and his faggot of sticks.

And criticism has put a lens to our eyes, and disclosed to us on the shining, remote face of primitive Christianity rents and craters undreamt of in our old simplicity.

That there was, in the breast of the new-born Church, an element of antinomianism, not latent, but in virulent activity, is a fact as capable of demonstration as any conclusion in a science which is not exact.

In the apostolic canonical writings we see the beginning of the trouble; the texture of the Gospels is tinged by it; the Epistles of Paul on one side, of Jude and Peter on the other, show it in energetic operation; ecclesiastical history reveals it in full flagrance a century later.

Whence came the spark? what material ignited? These are questions that must be answered. We cannot point to the blaze in the sub-apostolic age, and protest that it was an instantaneous combustion, with no smouldering train leading up to it,—to the rank crop of weeds, and argue that they

sprang from no seed. We shall have to look up the stream
to the fountains whence the flood was poured.

The existence of antinomianism in the Churches of Greece
and Asia Minor, synchronizing with their foundation, transpires from the Epistles of St. Paul. It was an open sore in
the life-time of the Twelve; it was a sorrow weighing daily on
the great soul of the Apostle of the Gentiles. It called forth
the indignant thunder of Jude and Peter, and the awful
denunciations in the charges to the Seven Churches.

The apocryphal literature of the sub-apostolic period carries
on the sad story. Under St. John's presiding care, the gross
scandals which defiled Gentile Christianity were purged out,
and antinomian Christianity deserted Asia Minor for Alexandria. There it made head again, as revealed to us by the
controversialists of the third century. And there it disappeared for a while.

Yet the disease was never eradicated. Its poison still
lurked in the veins of the Church, and again and again
throughout the Middle Ages heretics emerged fitfully, true
successors of Nicolas, Cerdo, Marcion and Valentine, shaking
off the trammels of the moral law, and seeking justification
through mystic exaltation or spiritual emotion. The Papacy
trod down these ugly heretics with ruthless heel. But at the
Reformation, when the restraint was removed, the disease
broke forth in a multitude of obscene sects spotting the fair
face of Protestantism.

Nor has the virus exhausted itself. Its baleful workings,
if indistinct, are still present and threatening.

But how comes it that Christianity has thus its dark

shadow constantly haunting it? The cause is to be sought in the constitution of man. Man, moving in his little orbit, has ever a face turned away from the earth and all that is material, looking out into infinity,—a dark, unknown side, about whose complexion we may speculate, but which we can never map. It is a face which must ever remain mysterious, and ever radiate into mystery. As the eye and ear are bundles of nerves through which the inner man goes out into, and receives impressions from, the material world, so is the soul a marvellous tissue of fibres through which man is placed *en rapport* with the spiritual world, God and infinity. It is the existence of this face, these fibres—take which simile you like—which has constituted mystics in every age all over the world: Schamans in frozen Siberia, Fakirs in burning India, absorbed Buddhists, ecstatic Saints, Essenes, Witches, Anchorites, Swedenborgians, modern Spiritualists.

Man, double-faced by nature, is placed by Revelation under a sharp, precise external rule, controlling his actions and his thoughts.

To this rule spirit and body are summoned to do homage. But the spirit has an inherent tendency towards the unlimited, by virtue of its nature, which places it on the confines of the infinite. Consequently it is never easy under a rule which is imposed on it conjointly with the body; it strains after emancipation, strives to assert its independence of what is external, and to establish its claim to obey only the movements in the spiritual world. It throbs sympathetically with the auroral flashes in that realm of mystery, like the flake of gold-leaf in the magnetometer.

To be bound to the body, subjected to its laws, is degrading; to be unbounded, unconditioned, is its aspiration and supreme felicity.

Thus the incessant effort of the spirit is to establish its law in the inner world of feeling, and remove it from the material world without.

Moreover, inasmuch as the spirit melts into the infinite, cut off from it by no sharply-defined line, it is disposed to regard itself as a part of God, a creek of the great Ocean of Divinity, and to suppose that all its emotions are the pulsations of the tide in the all-embracing Spirit. It loses the consciousness of its individuality; it deifies itself.

A Suffee fable representing God and the human soul illustrates this well. "One knocked at the Beloved's door, and a voice from within cried, 'Who is there?' Then the soul answered, 'It is I.' And the voice of God said, 'This house will not hold me and thee.' So the door remained shut. Then the soul went away into a wilderness, and after long fasting and prayer it returned, and knocked once again at the door. And again the voice demanded, 'Who is there?' Then he said, 'It is THOU,' and at once the door opened to him."

Thus the mystic always regards his unregulated wishes as divine revelations, his random impulses as heavenly inspirations. He has no law but his own will; and therefore, in mysticism, there is no curb against the grossest licence.

The existence of that evil which, knowing the constitution of man, we should expect to find prevalent in mysticism, the experience of all ages has shown following, dogging its steps inevitably. So slight is the film that separates religious from sensual passion, that uncontrolled spiritual fervour roars readily into a blaze of licentiousness.

It is this which makes revivalism of every description so dangerous. It is a two-edged weapon that cuts the hand which holds it.

Yet the spiritual, religious element in man is that which is most beautiful and pure, when passionless. It is like those placid tarns, crystal clear and icy cold, in Auvergne and the Eifel, which lie in the sleeping vents of old volcanoes. We love to linger by them, yet never with security, for we know that a throb, a shock, may at any moment convert them into boiling geysirs or raging craters.

So well is this fact known in the Roman Church, that a mystic is inexorably shut up in a convent, or cast out as a heretic.

The more spiritual a religion is, the more apt it is to lurch and let in a rush of immorality ; for its tendency is to substitute an internal for the external law, and the internal impulse is too often a hidden jog from the carnal appetite. In a highly spiritual religion, a written revelation is supplemented or superseded by one which is within.

This was eminently the case with the Anabaptists of the sixteenth century. When plied with texts by the Lutheran divines, they coldly answered that they walked not after the letter, but after the spirit ; that to those who are in Christ Jesus, there is an inner illumination directing their conduct, before which that which is without grew pale and waned. The horrible

licence into which this internal light plunged them is matter
of history.

One lesson history enforces inexorably—that there lies a
danger to morals in placing reliance on the spirit as an independent guide.

The spirit has its proper function and its true security;
its function, the perception of the infinite, the divine; its
security, the observance of the marriage-tie which binds it to
the body.

God has joined body and spirit in sacred wedlock, and
subjected both to a revealed external law; in the maintenance
of this union, and submission to this law, man's safety lies.
The spirit supreme, the body a bond-maid, is no marriage; it
is a concubinage, bringing with it a train of attendant evils.

Man stands, so to speak, at the bisection of two circles,
the material and the spiritual, in each of which he has a
part, and to the centres of each of which he feels a gravitation.   Absorption in either realm is fatal to the well-being
of the entire man.

And this leads us to the consideration of the marvellous
aptitude to human nature of the Incarnation, welding together
into indissoluble union spirit and matter, the infinite and the
finite. The religion which flows from that source cannot dissociate soul from body. Its law is the marriage of that which
is spiritual to that which is material; the soul cannot shake
off the responsibilities of the body; everything spiritual is
clothed, and every material object is a sacrament conveying a
ray of divinity.

There can be no evasion, no abrasion and rupture of the tie by either party, without lesion of the chain which binds to the Incarnation; and it is a fact worthy of note, that mysticism has always a tendency to obscure this fundamental dogma, and that the immoral sects of ancient times and of the present day hang loosely by, or openly deny, this great verity.

St. Paul had a natural bias towards mysticism. His trances and revelations betoken a nature branching out into the spiritual realm; and throughout his letters we see the inevitable consequence—a struggle to displace the centre of obedience, to transfer it from without and enthrone it within, to make the internal revelation the governing principle of action, in the room of submission to an external law.

But, like St. Theresa, who never relinquished her common sense whilst yielding up her spirit to the most incoherent raptures; like Mohammad, who, however he might soar in ecstasy above the moon, never lost sight of the principles which would ensure a very material success; like Ignatius Loyola, who, in the midst of fantastic visions, elaborated a system of government full of the maturest judgment,—so St. Paul never surrendered himself unconditionally to the promptings of his spirit. Like the angel of the Apocalypse, if he stood with one foot in the vague sea, he kept the other on the solid land.

That thorn in the flesh, whose presence he deplored, kept him from forgetting the body and its obligations; the moral disorders breaking out wherever he preached his gospel, warned him in time not to relax too far the restraint imposed

by the law without.   As the revolt of the Anabaptists
checked Luther, so did the excesses of the Gentile Christians
arrest Paul. Both saw and obeyed the warning finger of
Providence signalling a retreat.

Divinely inspired St. Paul was.   But inspiration never
obscures and obliterates human characteristics.   It directs
and utilizes them for its own purpose, leaving free margin
beyond that purpose for the exercise of individual proclivities
uncontrolled.

Paul's natural tendency is unmistakable ; and we may see
evidence of divine guidance in the fact of his having refused
to give the rein to his natural propensities, and of being prepared to turn all his energies to the repairing of those dykes
against the ocean which in a moment of impatience he had
set his hand to tear down.

As Socrates was by nature prone 'to become the most
vicious of men, so was Paul naturally disposed to become the
most dangerous of heresiarchs.   But the moral sense of Socrates mastered his passions and converted him into a philosopher; and the guiding spirit of God made of Paul the
mystic an apostle of righteousness.

Christianity, as the religion of the Incarnation, has its
external form and its internal spirit, and it is impossible to
dissociate one from the other without peril.   Mere formalism
and naked spirituality are alike and equally pernicious.   Formalism, the resolution of religion into ceremonial acts only,
void of spirit, is like the octopus, lacing its thousand filaments
about the soul and drawing it into the abyss ; and mysticism,
pure spirituality, like the magnet mountain in Sinbad's

voyage, draws the nails out of the vessel—the rivets of moral law—and the Christian character goes to pieces.

The history of the Church is the history of her leaning first towards one side, then towards the other, of advance amid perpetual recoils from either peril.

2. The alarm caused in Jerusalem amidst the elder apostles and the Nazarene Church at the immorality which disfigured Pauline Christianity, was not the only cause of the mistrust wherewith they viewed him and his teaching. Other causes existed which I have not touched on in my text, lest I should distract attention from the main points of my argument, but they are deserving of notice here.

And the first of these was the intense prejudice which existed among the Jews of Palestine against Greek modes of thought, manners, culture, even against the Greek language.

The second was the jealousy with which the Palestinian Jews regarded the Alexandrine Jews, their mode of interpreting Scripture, and their system of theology.

St. Paul, an accomplished Greek scholar, brought up at Tarsus amidst Hellenistic Jews, adopted the theology and exegesis in vogue at Alexandria, and on both these accounts excited the suspicion and dislike of the national party at Jerusalem. The Nazarenes were imbued with the prejudices they had acquired in their childhood, in the midst of which they had grown up, and they could not but regard Paul with alarm when he turned without disguise to the Greeks, and introduced into the Church the theological system and scriptural interpretations of a Jewish community they had always regarded as of questionable orthodoxy.

First let us consider the causes which contributed to the creation of the prejudice against the Hellenizers. Judæa had served as the battle-field of the Greek kings of Egypt and Syria. Whether Judæa fell under the dominion of Syria or Egypt it mattered not; Ptolemies and Seleucides alike were intolerable oppressors. But it was especially the latter who excited to its last exasperation the fanaticism of the Jews, and called forth in their breasts an ineffaceable antipathy towards everything that was Greek.

The temple was pillaged by them, the sanctuary was violated, the high-priesthood degraded. Antiochus Epiphanes entertained the audacious design of completely overthrowing the religion of the Jews, of forcibly Hellenizing them. For this purpose he forbade the celebration of the Sabbaths and feasts, drenched the sanctuary with blood to pollute it, the sacrifices were not permitted, circumcision was made illegal. The sufferings of the Jews, driven into deserts and remote hiding-places in the mountains, are described in the first book of the Maccabees.

Yet there was a party disposed to acquiesce in this attempt at changing the whole current of their nation's life, ready to undo the work of Ezra, break with their past, and fling themselves into the tide of Greek civilization and philosophic thought. These men set up a gymnasium in Jerusalem, Græcised their names, openly scoffed at the Law, ignored the Sabbath, and neglected circumcision.[1] At the head of this party stood the high-priests Jason and Menelaus. The author

[1] Joseph. Antiq. xii. 5; 1 Maccab. i. 11—15, 43, 52; 2 Maccab. iv. 9—16.

of the first book of the Maccabees styles these conformists to the state policy, "evil men, seducing many to despise the Law." Josephus designates them as "wicked" and "impious."[1]

The memory of the miseries endured in the persecution of Antiochus did not fade out of the Jewish mind, neither did the party disappear which was disposed to symbolize with Greek culture, and was opposed to Jewish prejudice. Nor did the abhorrence in which it was held lose its intensity.

From the date of the Antiochian persecution, the names of "Greek" or "friend of the Greeks" were used as synonymous with "traitor" and "apostate."

Seventy years before Christ, whilst Hyrcanus was besieging Aristobulus in Jerusalem, the besiegers furnished the besieged daily with lambs for the sacrifice. An old Jew, belonging to the anti-national party, warned Hyrcanus that as long as the city was supplied with animals for the altar, so long it would hold out. On the morrow, in place of a lamb, a pig was flung over the walls. The earth shuddered at the impiety, and the heads of the synagogue solemnly cursed from thenceforth whosoever of their nation should for the future teach the Greek tongue to his sons.[2] Whether this incident be true or not, it proves that a century after Antiochus Epiphanes the Jews entertained a hatred of that Greek culture which they regarded as a source of incredulity and impiety.

The son of Duma asked his uncle Israel if, after having

---

[1] πονήροι, ἀσεβεῖς.—Antiq. xiii. 4, xii. 10.

[2] Baba-Kama, fol. 82; Menachoth, fol. 64; Sota, fol. 49; San-Baba, fol. 90.

learned the whole Law, he might not study the philosophy
of the Greeks. "'The Book of the Law shall not depart out
of thy mouth; but thou shalt meditate therein day and night.'
These are the words of God" (Josh. i. 8), said the old man;
"find me an hour which is neither day nor night, and in
that study your Greek philosophy."[1]

Gamaliel, the teacher of St. Paul, was well versed in Greek
literature; that this caused uneasiness in his day is probable;
and indeed the Gemara labours to explain the fact of his
knowledge of Greek, and apologizes for it.[2]   Consequently
Saul, the disciple of Gamaliel, also a Greek scholar, would be
likely to incur the same suspicion, as one leaning away from
strict Judaism towards Gentile culture.

The Jews of Palestine viewed the Alexandrine Jews with
dislike, and mistrusted the translation into Greek of their
sacred books. They said it was a day of sin and blasphemy
when the version of the Septuagint was made, equal only in
wickedness to that on which their fathers had made the
golden calf.[3]

The loudly-proclaimed intention of Paul to turn to the
Gentiles, his attitude of hostility towards the Law, the abrogation of the Sabbath and substitution for it of the Lord's-
day, his denunciation of circumcision, his abandonment of
his Jewish name for a Gentile one, led to his being identified
by the Jews of Palestine with the abhorred Hellenistic party;
and the Nazarene Christians shared to the full in the national
prejudices.

[1] Menachoth, fol. 99.   [2] Baba-Kama, fol. 63.
[3] Mass. Sopherim, c. i. in Othonis Lexicon Rabbin. p. 329.

The Jews, at the time of the first spread of Christianity, were dispersed over the whole world ; and in Greece and Asia Minor occupied a quarter, and exercised influence, in every town. The Seleucides had given the right of citizenship to these Asiatic Jews, and had extended to them some sort of protection. The close association of these Jews with Greeks necessarily led to the adoption of some of their ideas. Since Ezra, the dominant principle of the Palestinian and Babylonish rabbis had been to create a "hedge of the Law," to constitute of the legal prescriptions a net lacing those over whom it was cast with minute yet tough fibres, stifling spontaneity. Whilst rabbinism was narrowing the Jewish horizon, Greek philosophy was widening man's range of vision. The tendencies of Jewish theology and Greek philosophy were radically opposed. The Alexandrine Jews never submitted to be involved in the meshes of rabbinism. They produced a school of thinkers, of whom Aristobulus was the first known exponent, and Philo the last expression, which sought to combine Mosaism with Platonism, to explain the Pentateuch as the foundation of a philosophic system closely related to the highest and best theories of the Greeks.

In the Holy Land, routine, the uniform repetition of prescribed forms, the absence of all alien currents of thought, tended insensibly to transform religion into formalism, and to identify it with the ceremonies which are its exterior manifestation.

In Egypt, on the other hand, the Alexandrine Jews, ambitious to give to the Greeks an exalted idea of their religion, strove to bring into prominence its great doctrines of the

Unity of the Godhead, of Creation, and Providence.   All se-
condary points were allegorized or slurred over.   As Palestinian rabbinism became essentially ceremonial, Alexandrine
Judaism became essentially spiritual.   The streams of life
and thought in these members of the same race were dia-
metrically opposed.

The Jews settled in Asia Minor, subjected to the same
influences, actuated by the same motives, as the Egyptian
Jews, looked to Alexandria rather than to Jerusalem or
Babylon for guidance, and were consequently involved in the
same jealous dislike which fell on the Jews of Egypt.[1]

There can be no doubt that St. Paul was acquainted with,
and influenced by, the views of the Alexandrine school.   That
he had read some of Philo's works is more than probable.
How much he drew from the writings of Aristobulus the
Peripatetic cannot be told, as none of the books of that learned
but eclectic Jew have been preserved.[2]

In more than one point Paul departs from the traditional
methods of the Palestinian rabbis, to adopt those of the
Alexandrines.   The Jews of Palestine did not admit the
allegorical interpretation of Scripture.   Paul, on two occasions, follows the Hellenistic mode of allegorizing the sacred
text.   On one of these occasions he uses an allegory of Philo,
while slightly varying its application.[3]

---

[1] Philo is not mentioned by name once in the Talmud, nor has a single
sentiment or interpretation of an Alexandrine Jew been admitted into
the Jerusalem or Babylonish Talmud.

[2] Aristobulus wrote a book to prove that the Greek sages drew their
philosophy from Moses, and addressed his book to Ptolemy Philometor.

[3] Gal. iv. 24, 25.

The Palestinian Jews knew of no seven orders of angels; the classification of the celestial hierarchy was adopted by Paul[1] from Philo and his school. The identification of idols with demons[2] was also distinctively Alexandrine.

But what is far more remarkable is to find in Philo, born between thirty and forty years before Christ, the key to most of Paul's theology,—the doctrines of the all-sufficiency of faith, of the worthlessness of good works, of the imputation of righteousness, of grace, mediation, atonement.

But in Philo these doctrines drift purposeless. Paul took them and applied them to Christ, and at once they fell into their ranks and places. What was in suspension in Philo, crystallized in Paul. What the Baptist was to the Judæan Jews, that Philo was to the Hellenistic Jews; his thoughts, his theories, were—

> "In the flecker'd dawning
> The glitterance of Christ."[3]

The Fathers, perplexed at finding Pauline words, expressions, ideas, in the writings of Philo, and unwilling to admit that Paul had derived them from Philo, invented a myth that the Alexandrine Jew came to Rome and was there converted to the Christian faith. Chronology and a critical examination of the writings of the Jewish Plato have burst that bubble.[4]

The fact that Paul was deeply saturated with the philosophy of the Alexandrine Jews has given rise also to two

---

[1] Col. i. 16.   [2] 1 Cor. x. 21.

[3] Dante, Parad. xiv.

[4] See the question carefully discussed in M. F. Delaunay's Moines et Sibylles; Paris, 1874, pp. 28 sq.

obstinate Christian legends,—that Dionysius the Areopagite, author of the Celestial Hierarchy, the Divine Names, &c., was the disciple of St. Paul, and that Seneca the philosopher was also his convert and pupil. Dionysius took Philo's system of the universe and emanations from the Godhead and Christianized them. The influence of Philo on the system of Dionysius *saute aux yeux*, as the French would say. And Dionysius protests, again and again, in his writings that he learned his doctrine from St. Paul.

From a very early age, the Fathers insisted on Seneca having been a convert of St. Paul; they pointed out the striking analogies in their writings, the similarity in their thoughts. How was this explicable unless one had been the pupil of the other? But Seneca, we know, lived some time in Alexandria with his uncle, Severus, prefect of Egypt; and at that time the young Roman, there can be little question, became acquainted with the writings of Philo.[1]

Thus St. Paul, by adopting the mode of Biblical interpretation of a rival school to that dominant in Judæa, by absorbing its philosophy, applying it to the person of Christ and the moral governance of the Church, by associating with Asiatic Jews, known to be infected with Greek philosophic heresies, and by his open invocation to the Gentiles to come into and share in all the plenitude of the privileges of the gospel, incurred the suspicion, distrust, dislike of the believers in Jerusalem, who had grown up in the midst of national prejudices which Paul shocked.

[1] See, on this curious topic, C. Aubertin : Sénèque et St. Paul ; Paris, 1872.

3. It has been argued with much plausibility, that because certain of the primitive Fathers were unacquainted with the four Gospels now accounted Canonical, that therefore those Gospels are compositions subsequent to their date, and that therefore also their authority as testimonies to the acts and sayings of Jesus is sensibly weakened, if not wholly overthrown. It is true that there were certain Fathers of the first two centuries who were unacquainted with our Gospels, but the above conclusions drawn from this fact are unsound.

This treatise will, I hope, establish the fact that at the close of the first century almost every Church had its own Gospel, with which alone it was acquainted. But it does not follow that these Gospels were not as trustworthy, as genuine records, as the four which we now alone recognize.

It is possible, from what has been preserved of some of these lost Gospels, to form an estimate of their scope and character. We find that they bore a very close resemblance to the extant Synoptical Gospels, though they were by no means identical with them.

We find that they contained most of what exists in our three first Evangels, in exactly the same words; but that some were fuller, others less complete, than the accepted Synoptics.

If we discover whole paragraphs absolutely identical in the Gospels of Matthew, Mark, Luke, of the Hebrews, of the Clementines, of the Lord, it goes far to prove that all the Evangelists drew upon a common fund. And if we see that, though using the same material, they arranged it differently, we are forced to the conclusion that this material they incorporated in their biographies existed in *anecdota*, not in a consecutive narrative.

Some, at least, of the Gospels were in existence at the close of the first century; but the documents of which they were composed were then old and accepted.

And though it is indisputable that in the second century the Four had not acquired that supremacy which brought about the disappearance of the other Gospels, and were therefore not quoted by the Fathers in preference to them, it is also certain that all the material out of which both the extant and the lost Synoptics were composed was then in existence, and was received in the Church as true and canonical.

Admitting fully the force of modern Biblical criticism, I cannot admit all its most sweeping conclusions, for they are often, I think, more sweeping than just.

The material out of which all the Synoptical Gospels, extant or lost, were composed, was in existence and in circulation in the Churches in the first century. That material is—the sayings of Christ on various occasions, and the incidents in his life. These sayings and doings of the Lord, I see no reason to doubt, were written down from the mouths of apostles and eye-witnesses, in order that the teaching and example of Christ might be read to believers in every Church during the celebration of the Eucharist.

The early Church followed with remarkable fidelity the customs of the Essenes, so faithfully that, as I have shown, Josephus mistook the Nazarenes for members of the Essene sect; and in the third century Eusebius was convinced that the Therapeutæ, their Egyptian counterparts, were actually primitive Christians.[1]

The Essenes assembled on the Sabbath for a solemn feast, in white robes, and, with faces turned to the East, sang antiphonal hymns, broke bread and drank together of the cup of love. During this solemn celebration the president read portions from the sacred Scriptures, and the exhortations of the elders. At the Christian Eucharist the cere-

---

[1] Euseb. Hist. Eccl. ii. 17. The Bishop of Cæsarea is quoting from Philo's account of the Therapeutæ, and argues that these Alexandrine Jews must have been Christians, because their manner of life, religious customs and doctrines, were identical with those of Christians. "Their meetings, the distinction of the sexes at these meetings, the religious exercises performed at them, *are still in vogue among us at the present day*, and, especially at the commemoration of the Saviour's passion, we, like them, pass the time in fasting and vigil, and in the study of the divine word. All these the above-named author (Philo) has accurately described in his writings, and *are the same customs that are observed by us alone*, at the present day, particularly the vigils of the great Feast, and the exercises in them, and the hymns that are commonly recited among us. He states that, whilst one sings gracefully with a certain measure, the others, listening in silence, join in at the final clauses of the hymns; also that, on the above-named days, they lie on straw spread on the ground, and, to use his own words, abstain altogether from wine and from flesh. Water is their only drink, and the relish of their bread salt and hyssop. Besides this, he describes the grades of dignity among those who administer the ecclesiastical functions committed to them, those of deacons, and the presidencies of the episcopate as the highest. Therefore," Eusebius concludes, "it is obvious to all that Philo, when he wrote these statements, *had in view the first heralds of the gospel, and the original practices handed down from the apostles.*"

monial was identical;[1] Pliny's description of a Christian assembly might be a paragraph from Josephus or Philo describing an Essene or Therapeutic celebration. In place of the record of the wanderings of the Israelites and the wars of their kings being read at their conventions, the president read the journeys of the Lord, his discourses and miracles.

No sooner was a Church founded by an apostle than there rose a demand for this sort of instruction, and it was supplied by the jottings-down of reminiscences of the Lord and his teaching, orally given by those who had companied with him.

Thus there sprang into existence an abundant crop of memorials of the Lord, surrounded by every possible guarantee of their truth. And these fragmentary records passed from one Church to another. The pious zeal of an Antiochian community furnished with the memorials of Peter would borrow of Jerusalem the memorials of James and Matthew. One of the traditions of John found its way into the Hebrew Gospel—that of the visit of Nicodemus; but it never came into the possession of the compiler of the first Gospel or of St. Luke.

After a while, each Church set to work to string the *anecdota* it possessed into a consecutive story, and thus the Synoptical Gospels came into being.

---

[1] It is deserving of remark that the turning to the East for prayer, common to the Essenes and primitive Christians, was forbidden by the Mosaic Law and denounced by prophets. When the Essenes diverged from the Law, the Christians followed their lead.

Of these, some were more complete than others, some were composed of more unique material than the others.

The second Gospel, if we may trust Papias, and I see no reason for doubting his testimony, is the composition of Mark, the disciple of St. Peter, and consists exclusively of the recollections of St. Peter. This Gospel was not co-ordinated probably till late, till long after the disjointed memorabilia were in circulation. It first circulated in Egypt; but in at least one of the Petrine Churches—that of Rhossus—the recollections of St. Peter had already been arranged in a consecutive memoir, and, in A.D. 190, Serapion, Bishop of Antioch, found the Church of Rhossus holding exclusively to this book as a Gospel of traditional authority, received from the prince of the apostles.

The Gospel of St. Matthew, on the other hand, is a diatessaron composed of four independent collections of memorabilia. Its groundwork is a book by Matthew the apostle, a collection of the discourses of the Lord. Whether Matthew wrote also a collection of the acts of the Lord, or contributed disconnected anecdotes of the Lord to Churches of his founding, and these were woven in with his work on the Lord's discourses, is possible, but is conjectural only.

But what is clear is, that into the first Gospel was incorporated much, not all, of the material used by Mark for the construction of his Gospel, viz. the recollections of St. Peter. That the first evangelist did not merely amplify the Mark Gospel appears from his arranging the order of his anecdotes differently; that he did use the same "anecdota" is evidenced by the fact of his using them often word for word.

The Gospel of the Hebrews and the Gospel quoted in the Clementines were composed in precisely the same manner, and of the same materials, but not of all the same.

That the Gospel of St. Matthew, as it stands, was the composition of that apostle, cannot be seriously maintained; yet its authority as a record of facts, not as a record of their chronological sequence, remains undisturbed.

The Gospel of St. Luke went, apparently, through two editions. After the issue of his original Gospel, which, there is reason to believe, is that adopted by Marcion, fresh material came into his hands, and he revised and amplified his book.

That this second edition was not the product of another hand, is shown by the fact that characteristic expressions found in the original text occur also in the additions.

The Pauline character of the Luke Gospel has been frequently commented on. It is curious to observe how much more pronounced this was in the first edition. The third Gospel underwent revision under the influence of the same wave of feeling which moved Luke to write the Christian Odyssey, the Acts, nominally of the Apostles, really of St. Paul. With the imprisonment of Paul the tide turned, and a reconciliatory movement set strongly in. Into this the Apostle of Love threw himself, and he succeeded in directing it.

The Apostolic Church was a well-spring tumultuously

gushing forth its superabundance of living waters ; there was a clashing of jets, a conflict of ripples ; but directly St. John gave to it its definite organization, the flood rushed out between these banks, obedient to a common impulse, the clashing forces produced a resultant, the conflicting ripples blended into rhythmic waves, and the brook became a river, and the river became a sea.

The lost Gospels are no mere literary curiosity, the examination of them no barren study. They furnish us with most precious information on the manner in which all the Gospels were compiled ; they enable us in several instances to determine the correct reading in our canonical Matthew and Luke; they even supply us with particulars to fill lacunæ which exist, or have been made, in our Synoptics.

The poor stuff that has passed current too long among us as Biblical criticism is altogether unworthy of English scholars and theologians. The great shafts that have been driven into Christian antiquity, the mines that have been opened by the patient labours of German students, have not received sufficient attention at our hands. If some of our commentators timorously venture to their mouths, it is only to shrink back again scared at the gnomes their imagination pictures as haunting those recesses, or at the abysses down which they may be precipitated, that they suppose lie open in those passages.

This spirit is neither courageous nor honest. God's truth is helped by no man's ignorance.

It may be that we are dazzled, bewildered by the light and

rush of new ideas exploding around us on every side; but, for all that, a cellar is no safe retreat. The vault will crumble in and bury us.

The new lights that break in on us are not always the lanterns of burglars.

I must ask the reader kindly to correct an error which escaped my eye in correcting the proofs of the first three sheets. On page 1, and in the heading of every even page up to 72, for "Ante-Gospels," read "Anti-Gospels."

S. BARING-GOULD.

EAST MERSEA, COLCHESTER,
  November 2nd, 1874.

CONTENTS.

Part Third.

THE LOST PAULINE GOSPELS.

LOST AND HOSTILE GOSPELS.

PART I.

THE JEWISH ANTE-GOSPELS.

I.

THE SILENCE OF JOSEPHUS.

It is somewhat remarkable that no contemporary, or even early, account of the life of our Lord exists, except from the pens of Christian writers.

That we have none by Roman or Greek writers is not, perhaps, to be wondered at; but it is singular that neither Philo, Josephus, nor Justus of Tiberias, should have ever alluded to Christ or to primitive Christianity.

The cause of this silence we shall presently investigate. Its existence we must first prove.

Philo was born at Alexandria about twenty years before Christ. In the year A.D. 40, he was sent by the Alexandrine Jews on a mission to Caligula, to entreat the Emperor not to put in force his order that his statue should be erected in the Temple of Jerusalem and in all the synagogues of the Jews.

Philo was a Pharisee. He travelled in Palestine, and speaks of the Essenes he saw there; but he says not a

B

word about Jesus Christ or his followers. It is possible
that he may have heard of the new sect, but he probably concluded it was but insignificant, and consisted
merely of the disciples, poor and ignorant, of a Galilean
Rabbi, whose doctrines he, perhaps, did not stay to inquire into, and supposed that they did not differ funda-
mentally from the traditional teaching of the rabbis of
his day.

Flavius Josephus was born A.D. 37—consequently
only four years after the death of our Lord—at Jerusalem. Till the age of twenty-nine, he lived in Jerusalem, and had, therefore, plenty of opportunity of
learning about Christ and early Christianity.

In A.D. 67, Josephus became governor of Galilee, on
the occasion of the Jewish insurrection against the
Roman domination. After the fall of Jerusalem he
passed into the service of Titus, went to Rome, where
he rose to honour in the household of Vespasian and of
Titus, A D 81. The year of his death is not known.
He was alive in A.D. 93, for his biography is carried
down to that date.

Josephus wrote at Rome his " History of the Jewish
War," in seven books, in his own Aramaic language.
This he finished in the year A.D. 75, and then translated it into Greek. On the completion of this work he
wrote his "Jewish Antiquities," a history of the Jews
in twenty books, from the beginning of the world to the
twelfth year of the reign of Nero, A.D. 66. He completed this work in the year A.D. 93, concluding it with
a biography of himself. He also wrote a book against
Apion on the antiquity of the Jewish people. A book in
praise of the Maccabees has been attributed to him, but
without justice. In the first of these works, the larger
of the two, the "History of the Jewish War," he treats
of the very period when our Lord lived, and in it he

makes no mention of him. But in the shorter work, the "Jewish Antiquities," in which he goes over briefly the same period of time treated of at length in the other work, we find this passage:

"At this time lived Jesus, a wise man [if indeed he ought to be called a man]; for he performed wonderful works [he was a teacher of men who received the truth with gladness]; and he drew to him many Jews, and also many Greeks. [This was the Christ.] But when Pilate, at the instigation of our chiefs, had condemned him to crucifixion, they who had at first loved him did not cease; [for he appeared to them on the third day again alive; for the divine prophets had foretold this, together with many other wonderful things concerning him], and even to this time the community of Christians, called after him, continues to exist."[1]

That this passage is spurious has been almost universally acknowledged. One may be, perhaps, accused of killing dead birds, if one again examines and discredits the passage; but as the silence of Josephus on the subject which we are treating is a point on which it will be necessary to insist, we cannot omit as brief a discussion as possible of this celebrated passage.

The passage is first quoted by Eusebius (fl. A.D. 315) in two places,[2] but it was unknown to Justin Martyr (fl. A.D. 140), Clement of Alexandria (fl. A.D. 192),

---

[1] Γίνεται δὲ κατὰ τοῦτον τὸν χρόνον Ἰησοῦς, σοφὸς ἀνήρ, εἴγε ἄνδρα αὐτὸν λέγειν χρή· ἦν γὰρ παραδόξων ἔργων ποιητής, διδάσκαλος ἀνθρώπων τῶν ἡδονῇ τ' ἀληθῆ δεχομένων· καὶ πολλοὺς μὲν Ἰουδαίους, πολλοὺς δὲ καὶ τοῦ Ἑλληνικοῦ ἐπηγάγετο. Ὁ Χριστὸς οὗτος ἦν. Καὶ αὐτὸν ἐνδείξει τῶν πρώτων ἀνδρῶν παρ' ἡμῖν σταυρῷ ἐπιτετιμηκότος Πιλάτου, οὐκ ἐπαύσαντο οἵ γε πρῶτον αὐτὸν ἀγαπήσαντες· ἐφάνη γὰρ αὐτοῖς τρίτην ἔχων ἡμέραν πάλιν ζῶν, τῶν θείων προφητῶν ταῦτά τε καὶ ἄλλα μυρία θαυμάσια περὶ αὐτοῦ εἰρηκότων· εἰς ἔτι νῦν τῶν χριστιανῶν ἀπὸ τοῦδε ὠνομασμένων οὐκ ἐπέλιπε τὸ φῦλον.—Lib. xviii. c. iii. 3.

[2] Hist. Eccl. lib. i. c. 11; Demonst. Evang. lib. iii.

Tertullian (fl. A.D. 193), and Origen (fl. A.D. 230). Such a testimony would certainly have been produced by Justin in his Apology, or in his Controversy with Trypho the Jew, had it existed in the copies of Josephus at his time. The silence of Origen is still more significant. Celsus in his book against Christianity introduces a Jew. Origen attacks the arguments of Celsus and his Jew. He could not have failed to quote the words of Josephus, whose writings he knew, had the passage existed in the genuine text.[1]

Again, the paragraph interrupts the chain of ideas in the original text. Before this passage comes an account of how Pilate, seeing there was a want of pure drinking water in Jerusalem, conducted a stream into the city from a spring 200 stadia distant, and ordered that the cost should be defrayed out of the treasury of the Temple. This occasioned a riot. Pilate disguised Roman soldiers as Jews, with swords under their cloaks, and sent them among the rabble, with orders to arrest the ringleaders.

This was done. The Jews finding themselves set upon by other Jews, fell into confusion; one Jew attacked another, and the whole company of rioters melted away. "And in this manner," says Josephus, "was this insurrection suppressed." Then follows the paragraph about Jesus, beginning, "At this time lived Jesus, a wise man, if indeed one ought to call him a man," &c.

And the passage is immediately followed by, "About this time another misfortune threw the Jews into disturbance; and in Rome an event happened in the temple of Isis which produced great scandal." And then he tells an indelicate story of religious deception which need not be repeated here. The misfortune

---

. [1] He indeed distinctly affirms that Josephus did not believe in Christ, Contr. Cels. i.

which befel the Jews was, as he afterwards relates, that Tiberius drove them out of Rome. The reason of this was, he says, that a noble Roman lady who had become a proselyte had sent gold and purple to the temple at Jerusalem. But this reason is not sufficient. It is clear from what precedes—a story of sacerdotal fraud—that there was some connection between the incidents in the mind of Josephus. Probably the Jews had been guilty of religious deceptions in Rome, and had made a business of performing cures and expelling demons, with talismans and incantations, and for this had obtained rich payment.[1]

From the connection that exists between the passage about the " other misfortune that befel the Jews " and the former one about the riot suppressed by Pilate, it appears evident that the whole of the paragraph concerning our Lord is an interpolation.

That Josephus could not have written the passage as it stands, is clear enough, for only a Christian would speak of Jesus in the terms employed. Josephus was a Pharisee and a Jewish priest; he shows in all his writings that he believes in Judaism.

It has been suggested that Josephus may have written about Christ as in the passage quoted, but that the portions within brackets are the interpolations of a Christian copyist. But when these portions within brackets are removed, the passage loses all its interest, and is a dry statement utterly unlike the sort of notice Josephus would have been likely to insert. He gives colour to his narratives, his incidents are always sketched

---

[1] Juvenal, Satir. vi. 546. "Aere minuto qualiacunque voles Judæi somnia vendunt." The Emperors, later, issued formal laws against those who charmed away diseases (Digest. lib. i. tit. 13, i. 1). Josephus tells the story of Eleazar dispossessing a demon by incantations. De Bello Jud. lib. vii. 6 ; Antiq. lib. viii. c. 2.

with vigour; this account would be meagre beside those
of the riot of the Jews and the rascality of the priests
of Isis. Josephus asserts, moreover, that in his time
there were four sects among the Jews—the Pharisees,
the Sadducees, the Essenes, and the sect of Judas of
Gamala. He gives tolerably copious particulars about
these sects and their teachings, but of the Christian sect
he says not a word. Had he wished to write about it,
he would have given full details, likely to interest his
readers, and not have dismissed the subject in a couple
of lines.

It was perhaps felt by the early Christians that the
silence of Josephus—so famous an historian, and a Jew
—on the life, miracles and death of the Founder of
Christianity, was extremely inconvenient; the fact
could not fail to be noticed by their adversaries. Some
Christian transcriber may have argued, Either Josephus
knew nothing of the miracles performed by Christ,—in
which case he is a weighty testimony against them,—or
he must have heard of Jesus, but not have deemed his
acts, as they were related to him, of sufficient importance
to find a place in his History. Arguing thus, the copyist
took the opportunity of rectifying the omission, written
from the standpoint of a Pharisee, and therefore desig-
nating the Lord as merely a wise man.

But there is another explanation of this interpolation,
which will hardly seem credible to the reader at this
stage of the examination, viz. that it was inserted by a
Pharisee after the destruction of Jerusalem; and this is
the explanation I am inclined to adopt. At that time
there was a mutual tendency to sink their differences,
and unite, in the Nazarene Church and the Jews. The
cause of this will be given further on; sufficient for our
purpose that such a tendency did exist. Both Jew and
Nazarene were involved in the same exile, crushed by

the same blow, united in the same antipathies. The Pharisees were disposed to regret the part they had taken in putting Jesus to death, and to acknowledge that he had been a good and great Rabbi. The Jewish Nazarenes, on their side, made no exalted claims for the Lord as being the incarnate Son of God, and later even, as we learn from the Clementine Homilies, refused to admit his divinity. The question dividing the Nazarene from the Jew gradually became one of whether Christ was to be recognized as a prophet or not; and the Pharisees, or some of them at least, were disposed to allow as much as this.

It was under this conciliatory feeling that I think it probable the interpolation was made, at first by a Jew, but afterwards it was amplified by a Christian. I think this probable, from the fact of its not being the only interpolation of the sort effected. Suidas has an article on the name "Jesus," in which he tells us that Josephus mentions him, and says that he sacrificed with the priests in the temple. He quoted from an interpolated copy of Josephus, and this interpolation could not have been made by either a Gentile or a Nazarene Christian: not by a Gentile, for such a statement would have been pointless, purposeless to him; and it could not have been made by a Nazarene, for the Nazarenes, as will presently be shown, were strongly opposed to the sacrificial system in the temple. The interpolation must therefore have been made by a Jew, and by a Jew with a conciliatory purpose.

It is curious to note the use made of the interpolation now found in the text. Eusebius, after quoting it, says, "When such testimony as this is transmitted to us by an historian who sprang from the Hebrews themselves, respecting John the Baptist and the Saviour, what subterfuge can be left them to prevent them from being covered with confusion ?"[1]

There is one other mention of Christ in the "Antiquities" (lib. xx. c. 9):

" Ananus, the younger, of whom I have related that he had obtained the office of high-priest, was of a rash and daring character ; he belonged to the sect of the Sadducees, which, as I have already remarked, exhibited especial severity in the discharge of justice. Being of such a character, Ananus thought the time when Festus was dead, and Albinus was yet upon the road, a fit opportunity for calling a council of judges, and for bringing before them James, the brother of him who is called Christ, and some others : he accused them as transgressors of the law, and had them stoned to death. But the most moderate men of the city, who also were reckoned most learned in the law, were offended at this proceeding. They therefore sent privately to the king (Agrippa II.), entreating him to send orders to Ananus not to attempt such a thing again, for he had no right to do it. And some went to meet Albinus, then coming from Alexandria, and put him in mind that Ananus was not justified, without his consent, in assembling a court of justice. Albinus, approving what they said, angrily wrote to Ananus, and threatened him with punishment; and king Agrippa took from him his office of high-priest, and gave it to Jesus, the son of Donnæus."

This passage is also open to objection.

According to Hegesippus, a Jewish Christian, who wrote a History of the Church about the year A.D. 170, of which fragments have been preserved by Eusebius, St..James was killed in a tumult, and not by sentence of a court. He relates that James, the brother of Jesus, was thrown down from a wing of the temple, stoned, and finally despatched with a fuller's club. Clement of

---

[1] Hist. Eccl. i. 11.

Alexandria confirms this, and is quoted by Eusebius accordingly.

Eusebius quotes the passage from Josephus, without noticing that the two accounts do not agree. According to the statement of Hegesippus, St. James suffered alone; according to that of Josephus, several other victims to the anger or zeal of Ananus perished with him.

It appears that some of the copies of Josephus were tampered with by copyists, for Theophylact says, " The wrath of God fell on them (the Jews) when their city was taken; and Josephus testifies that these things happened to them on account of the death of Jesus." But Origen, speaking of Josephus, says, " This writer, though he did not believe Jesus to be the Christ, inquiring into the cause of the overthrow of Jerusalem and the demolition of the temple .... says, ' These things befel the Jews in vindication of James, called the Just, who was the brother of Jesus, called the Christ, forasmuch as they killed him who was a most righteous man.' "[1] Josephus, as we have seen, says nothing of the sort; consequently Origen must have quoted from an interpolated copy. And this interpolation suffered further alteration, by a later hand, by the substitution of the name of Jesus for that of James.

It is therefore by no means unlikely that the name of James, the Lord's brother, may have been inserted in the account of the high-handed dealing of Ananus in place of another name.

However, it is by no means impossible to reconcile

---

[1] Contr. Cels. i. 47 ; and again, ii. 13 : " This (destruction), as Josephus writes, ' happened upon account of James the Just, the brother of Jesus, called the Christ ;' but in truth on account of Christ Jesus, the Son of God."

the two accounts. The martyrdom of St. James is an historical fact, and it is likely to have taken place during the time when Ananus had the power in his hands.

For fifty years the pontificate had been in the same family, with scarcely an interruption, and Ananus, or Hanan, was the son of Annas, who had condemned Christ. They were Sadducees, and as such were persecuting. St. Paul, by appealing to his Pharisee principles, enlisted the members of that faction in his favour when brought before Ananias.[1]

The apostles based their teaching on the Resurrection, the very doctrine most repugnant to the Sadducees; and their accounts of visions of angels repeated among the people must have irritated the dominant faction who denied the existence of these spirits. It can hardly be matter of surprise that the murder of James should have taken place when Ananus was supreme in Jerusalem. If that were the case, Josephus no doubt mentioned James, and perhaps added the words, "The brother of him who is called Christ;" or these words may have been inserted by a transcriber in place of "of Sechania," or Bar-Joseph.

This is all that Josephus says, or is thought to have said, about Jesus and the early Christians.

At the same time as Josephus, there lived another Jewish historian, Justus of Tiberias, whom Josephus mentions, and blames for not having published his History of the Wars of the Jews during the life of Vespasian and Titus. St. Jerome includes Justus in his Catalogue of Ecclesiastical Writers, and Stephen of Byzantium mentions him.

His book, or books, have unfortunately been lost, but

---

[1] Acts xxiii.

Photius had read his History, and was surprised to find that he, also, made no mention of Christ. "This Jewish historian," says he, "does not make the smallest mention of the appearance of Christ, and says nothing whatever of his deeds and miracles."[1]

[1] Bibliothec. cod. 33.

II

THE CAUSE OF THE SILENCE OF JOSEPHUS.

IT is necessary to inquire, Why this silence of Philo, Josephus and Justus? at first so inexplicable.

It can only be answered by laying before the reader a picture of the Christian Church in the first century. A critical examination of the writings of the first age of the Church reveals unexpected disclosures.

1. It shows us that the Church at Jerusalem, and throughout Palestine and Asia Minor, composed of converted Jews, was to an *external* observer indistinguishable from a modified Essenism.

2. And that the difference between the Gentile Church founded by St. Paul, and the Nazarene Church under St. James and St. Peter, was greater than that which separated the latter from Judaism *externally*, so that to a superficial observer their inner connection was unsuspected.

This applies to the period from the Ascension to the close of the first century,—to the period, that is, in which Josephus and Justus lived, and about which they wrote.

1. Our knowledge of the Essenes and their doctrines is, unfortunately, not as full as we could wish. We are confined to the imperfect accounts of them furnished by Philo and Josephus, neither of whom knew them thoroughly, or was initiated into their secret doctrines.

The Essenes arose about two centuries before the birth

of Christ, and peopled the quiet deserts on the west of the Dead Sea, a wilderness to which the Christian monks afterwards seceded from the cities of Palestine.   They are thus described by the elder Pliny :

"On the western shore of that lake dwell the Essenes, at a sufficient distance from the water's edge to escape its pestilential exhalations—a race entirely unique, and, beyond every other in the world, deserving of wonder ; men living among palm-trees, without wives, without money.   Every day their number is replenished by a new troop of settlers, for those join them who have been visited by the reverses of fortune, who are tired of the world and its style of living. Thus happens what might seem incredible, that a community in which no one is born continues to subsist through the lapse of centuries." [1]

From this first seat of the Essenes colonies detached themselves, and settled in other parts of Palestine; they settled not only in remote and solitary places, but in the midst of villages and towns.   In Samaria they flourished.[2]   According to Josephus, some of the Essenes were willing to act as magistrates, and it is evident that such as lived in the midst of society could not have followed the strict rule imposed on the solitaries.   There must therefore have been various degrees of Essenism, some severer, more exclusive than the others; and Josephus distinguishes four such classes in the sect.   Some of the Essenes remained celibates, others married.   The more exalted and exclusive Essenes would not touch one of the more lax brethren.[3]

---

[1] Plin. Hist. Nat. v. 17 ; Epiphan. adv. Hæres. xix. 1.

[2] Epiphan. adv. Hæres. x.

[3] For information on the Essenes, the authorities are, Philo, Περὶ τοῦ πάντα σπουδαῖον εἶναι ἐλεύθερον, and Josephus, De Bello Judaico, and Antiq.

The Essenes had a common treasury, formed by
throwing together the property of such as entered into
the society, and by the earnings of each man's labour.[1]

They wore simple habits—only such clothing as was
necessary for covering nakedness and giving protection
from the cold or heat.[2]

They forbad oaths, their conversation being "yea, yea,
and nay, nay."[3]

Their diet was confined to simple nourishing food,
and they abstained from delicacies.[4]

They exhibited the greatest respect for the constituted
authorities, and refrained from taking any part in the
political intrigues, or sharing in the political jealousies,
which were rife among the Jews.[5]

They fasted, and were incessant at prayer, but without the ostentation that marked the Pharisees.[6]

They seem to have greatly devoted themselves to the
cure of diseases, and, if we may trust the derivation of
their name given by Josephus, they were called Essenes
from their being the healers of men's minds and
bodies.[7]

If now we look at our blessed Lord's teaching, we
find in it much in common with that of the Essenes.
The same insisting before the multitude on purity of
thought, disengagement of affections from the world,
disregard of wealth and clothing and delicate food, pur-
suit of inward piety instead of ostentatious formalism.

---

[1] Compare Luke x. 4; John xii. 6, xiii. 29; Matt. xix. 21; Acts ii.
44, 45, iv. 32, 34, 37.

[2] Compare Matt. vi. 28—34; Luke xii. 22—30.

[3] Compare Matt. v. 34.

[4] Compare Matt. vi. 25, 31; Luke xii. 22, 23.

[5] Compare Matt. xv. 15—22.

[6] Compare Matt. vi. 1—18.

[7] From אסא, meaning the same as the Greek Therapeutæ.

His miracles of healing also, to the ordinary observer, served to identify him with the sect which made healing the great object of their study.

But these were not the only points of connection between him and the Essenes. The Essenes, instead of holding the narrow prejudices of the Jews against Samaritans and Gentiles, extended their philanthropy to all. They considered that all men had been made in the image of God, that all were rational beings, and that therefore God's care was not confined to the Jewish nation, salvation was not limited to the circumcision.[1]

The Essenes, moreover, exhibited a peculiar veneration for light. It was their daily custom to turn their faces devoutly towards the rising of the sun, and to chant hymns addressed to that luminary, purporting that his beams ought to fall on nothing impure.

If we look at the Gospels, we cannot fail to note how incessantly Christ recurs in his teaching to light as the symbol of the truth he taught,[2] as that in which his disciples were to walk, of which they were to be children, which they were to strive to obtain in all its purity and brilliancy.

The Essenes, moreover, had their esoteric doctrine; to the vulgar they had an exoteric teaching on virtue and disregard of the world, whilst among themselves they had a secret lore, of which, unfortunately, we know nothing certain. In like manner, we find our Lord speaking in parables to the multitude, and privately revealing their interpretation to his chosen disciples. " Unto you it is given to know the mysteries of the kingdom of God, but to others in parables ; that seeing

[1] Compare Luke x. 25—37 ; Mark vii. 26.

[2] Matt. iv. 16, v. 14, 16, vi. 22 ; Luke ii. 32, viii. 16, xi. 23, xvi. 8 John i. 4—9, iii. 19—21, viii. 12, ix. 5, xi. 9, 10, xii. 35—46.

they might not see, and hearing they might not understand."[1]

The Clementines, moreover, preserve a saying of our Lord, contained in the Gospel in use among the Ebionites, "Keep the mysteries for me, and for the sons of my house."[2]

The Essenes, though showing great veneration for the Mosaic law, distinguished between its precepts, for some they declared were interpolations, and did not belong to the original revelation; all the glosses and traditions of the Rabbis they repudiated, as making the true Word of none effect.[3] Amongst other things that they rejected was the sacrificial system of the Law. They regarded this with the utmost horror, and would not be present at any of the sacrifices. They sent gifts to the Temple, but never any beast, that its blood might be shed. To the ordinary worship of the Temple, apart from the sacrifices, they do not seem to have objected. The Clementine Homilies carry us into the very heart of Ebionite Christianity in the second, if not the first century, and show us what was the Church of St. James and St. Peter, the Church of the Circumcision, with its peculiarities and prejudices intensified by isolation and opposition. In that curious book we find the same hostility to the sacrificial system of Moses, the same abhorrence of bloodshedding in the service of God. This temper of mind can only be an echo of primitive Nazarene Christianity, for in the second century the Temple and its sacrifices were no more.

Primitive Jewish Christianity, therefore, reproduced what was an essential feature of Essenism—a rejection of the Mosaic sacrifices.

---

[1] Luke viii. 10 ; Mark iv. 12 ; Matthew xiii. 11—15.
[2] Clem. Homil. xix. 20.
[3] Compare Matt. xv. 3, 6.

In another point Nazarene Christianity resembled Essenism, in the poverty of its members, their simplicity in dress and in diet, their community of goods. This we learn from Hegesippus, who represents St. James, Bishop of Jerusalem, as truly an ascetic as any mediæval monk; and from the Clementines, which make St. Peter feed on olives and bread only, and wear but one coat. The name of Ebionite, which was given to the Nazarenes, signified "the poor."

There was one point more of resemblance, or possible resemblance, but this was one not likely to be observed by those without. The Therapeutæ in Egypt, who were apparently akin to the Essenes in Palestine, at their sacred feasts ate bread and salt. Salt seems to have been regarded by them with religious superstition, as being an antiseptic, and symbolical of purity.[1]

Perhaps the Essenes of Judæa also thus regarded, and ceremonially used, salt. We have no proof, it is true; but it is not improbable.

Now one of the peculiarities of the Ebionite Church in Palestine, as revealed to us by the Clementines, was the use of salt with the bread in their celebrations of the Holy Communion.[2]

But if Christ and the early Church, by their teaching and practice, conformed closely in many things to the doctrine and customs of the Essenes, in some points they differed from them. The Essenes were strict Sabbatarians. On the seventh day they would not move a vessel from one place to another, or satisfy any of the wants of nature. Even the sick and dying, rather than

---

[1] The reference to salt as an illustration by Christ (Matt. v. 13; Mark ix. 49, 50; Luke xiv. 84) deserves to be noticed in connection with this.

[2] Clem. Homil. xiv. 1: "Peter came several hours after, and breaking bread for the Eucharist, and putting salt upon it, gave it first to our mother, and after her, to us, her sons."

break the Sabbath, abstained from meat and drink on
that day. Christ's teaching was very different from this;
he ate, walked about, taught, and performed miracles on
the Sabbath. But though he relaxed the severity of observance, he did not abrogate the institution ; and the
Nazarene Church, after the Ascension, continued to venerate and observe the Sabbath as of divine appointment.
The observance of the Lord's-day was apparently due
to St. Paul alone, and sprang up in the Gentile churches[1]
in Asia Minor and Greece of his founding. When the
churches of Peter and Paul were reconciled and fused
together at the close of the century, under the influence
of St. John, both days were observed side by side ; and
the Apostolical Constitutions represent St. Peter and St.
Paul in concord decreeing, "Let the slaves work five
days; but on the Sabbath-day and the Lord's-day let
them have leisure to go to church for instruction and
piety. We have said that the Sabbath is to be observed
on account of the Creation, and the Lord's-day on
account of the Resurrection."[2]

After the Ascension, the Christian Church in Jerusalem attended the services in the Temple[3] daily, as did
the devout Jews. There is, however, no proof that they
assisted at the sacrifices. They continued to circumcise
their children; they observed the Mosaic distinction of
meats ; they abstained from things strangled and from
blood.[4]

The doctrine of the apostles after the descent of the
Holy Ghost was founded on the Resurrection. They
went everywhere preaching the Resurrection ; they
claimed to be witnesses to it, they declared that Jesus
had risen, they had seen him after he had risen, that

---

[1] Acts xx. 7 ; 1 Cor. xvi. 2 ; Rev. i. 9.
[2] Const. Apost. lib. viii. 33.
[3] Acts ii. 46, iii. 1, v. 42.   [4] Acts xv.

therefore the resurrection of all men was possible.[1] The doctrine of the Resurrection was held most zealously by the Pharisees ; it was opposed by the Sadducees. This vehement proclamation of the disputed doctrine, this production of evidence which overthrew it, irritated the Sadducees then in power. We are expressly told that they "came upon them (the apostles), being grieved that they taught the people, and preached through Jesus the Resurrection." This led to persecution of the apostles. But the apostles, in maintaining the doctrine of the Resurrection, were fighting the battles of the Pharisees, who took their parts against the dominant Sadducee faction,[2] and many, glad of a proof which would overthrow Sadduceeism, joined the Church.[3]

We can therefore perfectly understand how the Sadducees hated and persecuted the apostles, and how the orthodox Pharisees were disposed to hail them as auxiliaries against the common enemy. And Sadduceeism was at that time in full power and arrogance, exercising intolerable tyranny.

Herod the Great, having fallen in love with Mariamne, daughter of a certain Simon, son of Boethus of Alexandria, desired to marry her, and saw no other means of ennobling his father-in-law than by elevating him to the office of high-priest (B.C. 28). This intriguing family maintained possession of the high-priesthood for thirty-five years. It was like the Papacy in the house of Tusculum, or the primacy of the Irish Church in that of the princes of Armagh. Closely allied to the reigning family, it lost its hold of the high-priesthood on the deposition of Archelaus, but recovered it in A.D. 42. This family, called Boethusim, formed a sacerdotal

----

[1] Acts i. 22, iv. 2, 33, xxiii. 6.

[2] Acts xxiii. 7.   [3] Acts xv. 5.

nobility, filling all the offices of trust and emolument
about the Temple, very worldly, supremely indifferent
to their religious duties, and defiantly sceptical. They
were Sadducees, denying angel, and devil, and resurrection; living in easy self-indulgence; exasperating the
Pharisees by their heresy, grieving the Essenes by their
irreligion.

In the face of the secularism of the ecclesiastical rulers,
the religious zeal of the people was sure to break out in
some form of dissent.

John the Baptist was the St. Francis of Assisi, the
Wesley of his time. If the Baptist was not actually an
Essene, he was regarded as one by the indiscriminating
public eye, never nice in detecting minute dogmatic differences, judging only by external, broad resemblances
of practice.

The ruling worldliness took alarm at his bold denunciations of evil, and his head fell.

Jesus of Nazareth seemed to stand forth occupying
the same post, to be the mouthpiece of the long-brooding
discontent; and the alarmed party holding the high-
priesthood and the rulership of the Sanhedrim compassed
his death. To the Sadducean Boethusim, who rose into
power again in A.D. 42, Christianity was still obnoxious,
but more dangerous; for by falling back on the grand
doctrine of Resurrection, it united with it the great sect
of the Pharisees.

Under these circumstances the Pharisees began to
regret the condemnation and death of Christ as a mistake
of policy. Under provocation and exclusion from office,
they were glad to unite with the Nazarene Church in
combating the heretical sect and family which mono-
polized the power, just as at the present day in Germany
Ultramontanism and Radicalism are fraternizing. Jerusalem fell, and Sadduceeism fell with it, but the link

which united Pharisaism and Christianity was not broken as yet; if the Jewish believers and the Pharisees had not a common enemy to fight, they had a common loss to deplore; and when they mingled their tears in banishment, they forgot that they were not wholly one in faith. Christianity had been regarded by them as a modified Essenism, an Essenism gravitating towards Pharisaism, which lent to Pharisaism an element of strength and growth in which it was naturally deficient —that zeal and spirituality which alone will attract and quicken the popular mind into enthusiasm.

Whilst the Jewish Pharisees and Jewish Nazarenes were forgetting their differences and approximating, the great and growing company of Gentile believers assumed a position of open, obtrusive indifference at first, and then of antagonism, to the Law, not merely to the Law as accepted by the Pharisee, but to the Law as winnowed by the Essene.

The apostles at Jerusalem were not disposed to force the Gentile converts into compliance with all the requirements of that Law, which they regarded as vitiated by human glosses; but they maintained that the converts must abstain from meats offered to idols, from the flesh of such animals as had been strangled, and from blood.[1] If we may trust the Clementines, which represent the exaggerated Judaizing Christianity of the ensuing century, they insisted also on the religious obligation of personal cleanliness, and on abstention from such meats as had been pronounced unclean by Moses.

To these requirements one more was added, affecting the relations of married people; these were subjected to certain restrictions, the observance of new moons and sabbaths.

"This," says St. Peter, in the Homilies,[2] " is the rule of

---

[1] Acts xv. 29. [2] Clem. Homil. vii. 8.

divine appointment. To worship God only, and trust only in the Prophet of Truth, and to be baptized for the remission of sins, to abstain from the table of devils, that is, food offered to idols, from dead carcases, from animals that have been suffocated or mangled by wild beasts, and from blood; not to live impurely; to be careful to wash when unclean; that the women keep the law of purification; that all be sober-minded, given to good works, refrain from wrong-doing, look for eternal life from the all-powerful God, and ask with prayer and continual supplication that they may win it."

These simple and not very intolerable requirements nearly produced a schism. St. Paul took the lead in rejecting some of the restraints imposed by the apostles at Jerusalem. He had no patience with their minute prescriptions about meats: "Touch not, taste not, handle not, which all are to perish with the using."[1] It was inconvenient for the Christian invited to supper to have to make inquiries if the ox had been knocked down, or the fowl had had its neck wrung, before he could eat. What right had the apostles to impose restrictions on conjugal relations? St. Paul waxed hot over this. "Ye observe days and months and times and years. I am afraid of you, lest I have bestowed upon you labour in vain."[2] "Let no man judge you in meat or in drink, or in respect of an holiday, or of the new moons, or of the sabbath-days."[3] It was exactly these sabbaths and new moons on which the Nazarene Church imposed restraint on married persons.[4] As for meat offered in sacrifice to idols, St. Paul relaxed the order of the apostles assembled in council. It was no matter of importance whether

---

[1] Col. ii. 21.

[2] Gal. iv. 10. When it is seen in the Clementines how important the observance of these days was thought, what a fundamental principle it was of Nazarenism, I think it cannot be doubted that it was against this that St. Paul wrote.

[3] Col. ii. 16.   [4] Clement. Homil. xix. 22.

men ate sacrificial meat or not, for "an idol is nothing
in the world." Yet with tender care for scrupulous
souls, he warned his disciples not to flaunt their liberty
in the eyes of the sensitive, and offend weak consciences.
He may have thus allowed, in opposition to the apostles
at Jerusalem, because his common sense got the better
of his prudence. But the result was the widening of
the breach that had opened at Antioch when he with-
stood Peter to the face.

The apostles had abolished circumcision as a rite to
be imposed on the Gentile proselytes, but the children
of Jewish believers were still submitted by their parents,
with the consent of the apostles, to the Mosaic institution. This St. Paul would not endure. He made it a
matter of vital importance. " Behold, I, Paul, say unto
you, that if ye be circumcised, Christ shall profit you
nothing. For I testify again to every man that is circumcised, that he is a debtor to do the whole law. Christ
is become of no effect unto you, whosoever of you are
justified by the law; ye are fallen from grace."[1] In a
word, to submit to this unpleasant, but otherwise harmless ceremony, was equivalent to renouncing Christ,
losing the favour of God and the grace of the Holy
Spirit. It was incurring damnation. The blood of
Christ, his blessed teaching, his holy example, could
"profit nothing" to the unfortunate child which had
been submitted to the knife of the circumciser.

The contest was carried on with warmth. St. Paul,
in his Epistle to the Galatians, declared his independence of the Jewish-Christian Church; his Gospel was
not that of Peter and James. Those who could not
symbolize with him he pronounced "accursed." The
pillar apostles, James, Cephas and John, had given, indeed, the right hand of fellowship to the Apostle of

[1] Gal. v. 2—4.

the Gentiles, when they imposed on his converts from
heathenism the light rule of abstinence from sacrificial
meats, blood and fornication; but it was with the understanding that he was to preach to the Gentiles exclusively, and not to interfere with the labours of St. Peter
and St. James among the Jews. But St. Paul was im-
patient of restraint; he would not be bound to confine
his teaching to the uncircumcision, nor would he allow
his Jewish converts to be deprived of their right to that
full and frank liberty which he supposed the Gospel to
proclaim.

Paul's followers assumed a distinct name, arrogated
to themselves the exclusive right to be entitled " Christians," whilst they flung on the old apostolic community
of Nazarenes the disdainful title of " the Circumcision."

An attempt was made to maintain a decent, superficial
unity, by the rival systems keeping geographically separate. But such a compromise was impossible. Wherever
Jews accepted the doctrine that Christ was the Messiah
there would be found old-fashioned people clinging to
the customs of their childhood respecting Moses, and
reverencing the Law; to whom the defiant use of meats
they had been taught to regard as unclean would be
ever repulsive, and flippant denial of the Law under
which the patriarchs and prophets had served God must
ever prove offensive. Such would naturally form a
Judaizing party,—a party not disposed to force their
modes of life and prejudices on the Gentile converts, but
who did not wish to dissociate Christianity from Mosaism,
who would view the Gospel as the sweet flower that had
blossomed from the stem of the Law, not as an axe laid
at its root.

But the attempt to reconcile both parties was impossible at that time, in the heat, intoxication and extravagance of controversy. In the Epistle to the Galatians

we see St. Paul writing in a strain of fiery excitement against those who interfered with the liberty of his converts, imposing on them the light rule of the Council of Jerusalem. The followers of St. Peter and St. James are designated as those who " bewitch" his converts, "remove them from the grace of Christ to another Gospel;" who " trouble" his little Church in its easy liberty, "would pervert the gospel of Christ." To those only who hold with him in complete emancipation of the believer from vexatious restraints, " to as many as walk according to this rule," will he accord his benediction, " Peace and mercy."

He assumed a position of hostility to the Law. He placed the Law on one side and the Gospel on the other; here restraint, there liberty; here discipline, there freedom. A choice must be made between them; an election between Moses and Christ. There was no conciliation possible. To be under the Law was not to be under grace; the Law was a " curse," from which Christ had redeemed man. Paul says he had not known lust but by the Law which said, Thou shalt not covet. Men under the Law were bound by its requirements, as a woman is bound to a husband as long as he lives, but when the husband is dead she is free,—so those who accept the Gospel are free from the Law and all its requirements. The law which said, Thou shalt not covet, is dead. Sin was the infraction of the law. But the law being dead, sin is no more. " Until the law, sin was in the world, but sin is not imputed where there is no law." " Where no law is, there is no transgression." " Now we are delivered from the law, that being dead wherein we were held."

· Such an attack upon what was reverenced and observed by the Jewish Christians, and such doctrine which seemed to throw wide the flood-gates of immorality, naturally excited alarm and indignation among those who followed the more temperate teaching of Peter and James and John.

The converts of St. Paul, in their eagerness to manifest their emancipation from the Law, rolled up ceremonial and moral restrictions in one bundle, and flung both clean away.

The Corinthians, to show their freedom under the Gospel, boasted their licence to commit incest "such as was not so much as named among the Gentiles." [1] Nicolas, a hot Pauline, and his followers "rushed headlong into fornication without shame;" [2] he had the effrontery to produce his wife and offer her for promiscuous insult before the assembled apostles; [3] the later Pauline Christians went further. The law was, it was agreed, utterly bad, but it was promulgated by God; therefore the God of the Law was not the same deity as the God of the Gospel, but another inferior being, the Demiurge, whose province was rule, discipline, restraint, whereas the God of the Gospel was the God of absolute freedom and unrestrained licence.

They refused to acknowledge any Scriptures save the Gospel of St. Luke, or rather the Gospel of the Lord, another recension of that Gospel, drawn up by order of St. Paul, and the Epistles of the Apostle of the Gentiles.

But even in the first age the disorders were terrible. St. Paul's Epistles give glimpses of the wild outbreak of antinomianism that everywhere followed his preaching, — the drunkenness which desecrated the Eucharists, the backbitings, quarrellings, fornication, lasciviousness, which called forth such indignant denunciation from the great apostle.

[1] 1 Cor. v. 1.
[2] Euseb. Hist. Eccl. iii. 29.　　　　[3] Ibid.

Yet he was as guiltless of any wish to relax the restraints of morality as was, in later days, his great counterpart Luther. Each rose up against a narrow formalism, and proclaimed the liberty of the Christian from obligation to barren ceremonial; but there were those in the first, as there were those in the sixteenth century, with more zeal than self-control, who found "Justification by Faith only" a very comfortable doctrine, quite capable of accommodating itself to a sensual or careless life.

St. Paul may have seen, and probably did see, that Christianity would never make way if one part of the community was to be fettered by legal restrictions, and the other part was to be free. According to the purpose apparent in the minds of James and Peter, the Jewish converts were to remain Jews, building up Christian faith on the foundation of legal prescriptions, whilst the Gentile converts were to start from a different point. There could be no unity in the Church under this system—all must go under the Law, or all must fling it off. The Church, starting from her cradle with such an element of weakness in her constitution, must die prematurely.

He was right in his view. But it is by no means certain that St. Peter and St. James were as obstinately opposed to the gradual relaxation of legal restrictions, and the final extinction or transformation of the ceremonial Law, as he supposed.

In the heat and noise of controversy, he no doubt used unguarded language, said more than he thought, and his converts were not slow to take him *au pied de la lettre.*

The tone of Paul's letters shows conclusively that not for one moment would he relax moral obligation. With the unsuspiciousness of a guileless spirit, he never suspected that his words, taken and acted upon as a practical system, were capable of becoming the charter of antinomianism. Yet it was so. No sooner had he begun to denounce the Law, than he was understood to mean the whole Law, not merely its ceremonial part. When he began to expatiate on the freedom of Grace, he was understood to imply that human effort was overridden. When he proclaimed Justification by Faith only, it was held that he swept away for ever obligation to keep the Commandments.

The results were precisely the same in the sixteenth century, when Luther re-affirmed Paulinism, with all his warmth and want of caution. At first he proclaimed his doctrines boldly, without thought of their practical application. When he saw the results, he was staggered, and hasted to provide checks, and qualify his former words:

" Listen to the Papists," he writes; " the sole argument they use against us is that no good result has come of my doctrine. And, in fact, scarce did I begin to preach my Gospel before the country burst into frightful revolt; schisms and sects tore the Church; everywhere honesty, morality, and good order fell into ruin; every one thought to live independently, and conduct himself after his own fancy and caprices and pleasure, as though the reign of the Gospel drew with it the suppression of all law, right and discipline. Licence and all kinds of vices and turpitudes are carried in all conditions to an extent they never were before. In those days there was some observance of duty, the people especially were decorous; but now, like a wild horse without rein and bridle, without constraint or decency, they rush on the accomplishment of their grossest lusts." [1]

---

[1] " Lies der Papisten Bücher, höre ihre Predigen, so wirst du finden, dass diess ihr einziger Grund ist, darauf sie stehen wider uns pochen und trotzen, da sie vorgeben, es sei nichts Gutes aus unserer Lehre gekommen. Denn alsbald, da unser Evangelium anging und sie hören liess, folgte der

Gaspard Schwenkfeld saw the result of this teaching, and withdrew from it into what he considered a more spiritual sect, and was one of the founders of Anabaptism, a reaction against the laxity and licentiousness of Lutheranism. " This doctrine," said he, "is dangerous and scandalous ; it fixes us in impiety, and even encourages us in it." [1]

The Epistles of St. Paul exhibit him grappling with this terrible evil, crying out in anguish against the daily growing scandals, insisting that his converts should leave off their " rioting and drunkenness, chambering and wantonness, strife and envying ;" that their bodies were temples of the Spirit of God, not to be defiled with impurity ; that it was in vain to deceive themselves by boasting their faith and appealing to the freedom of Grace. "Neither fornicators, nor idolaters, nor adulterers, nor effeminate, nor abusers of themselves with mankind, nor thieves, nor coveters, nor drunkards, nor revilers, nor extortioners, shall inherit the kingdom of God."

And he holds himself up to his Corinthian converts as an example that, though professing liberty, they should walk orderly : " Be ye followers of me, even as I also am of Christ." [2]

gräuliche Aufruhr, es erhuben sich in der Kirche Spaltung und Sekten, es ward Ehrbarkeit, Disziplin und Zucht zerrüttet, und Jedermann wolte vogelfrei seyn und thun, was ihm gelüstet nach allem seinen Muthwillen und Gefallen, als wären alle Gesetze, Rechte und Ordnung gans aufhoben, wie es denn leider allzu wahr ist.   Denn der Muthwille in allen Ständen, mit allerlei Laster, Sünden und Schanden ist jetzt viel grösser denn zuvor, da die Leute, und sonderlich der Pöbel, doch etlichermassen in Furcht und in Zaum gehalten waren, welches nun wie ein zaumlos Pferd lebt und thut Alles, was es nur gelüstet ohne allen Scheu."—Ed. Walch, v. 114.   For a very full account of the disorders that broke out on the preaching of Luther, see Döllinger's Die Reformation in ihre Entwicklung.   Regensb. 1848.

[1] Epistolas, 1528, ii. 192.   [2] 1 Cor. xi. 1.

But apparently all his efforts could only control the most exuberant manifestations of antinomianism, like the incest at Corinth.

The grave Petrine Christians at Jerusalem were startled at the tidings that reached them from Asia Minor and Greece. It was necessary that the breach should be closed. The Church at Jerusalem was poor; a collection was ordered by St. Paul to be made for its necessities. He undertook to carry the money himself to Jerusalem, and at the same time, by conforming to an insignificant legal custom, to recover the regard and confidence of the apostles.

This purpose emerges at every point in the history of St. Paul's last visit to Jerusalem. But it was too late. The alienation of parties was too complete to be salved over with a gift of money and appeased by shaven crowns.[1]

When St. Paul was taken, he made one ineffectual effort to establish his relation to Judaism, by an appeal to the Pharisees. But it failed. He was regarded with undisguised abhorrence by the Jews, with coldness by the Nazarenes. The Jews would have murdered him. We do not hear that a Nazarene visited him.

Further traces of the conflict appear in the Epistles. The authenticity of the Epistle to the Hebrews has been doubted, disputed, and on weighty grounds. It is saturated with Philonism, whole passages of Philo re-appear in the Epistle to the Hebrews, yet I cannot doubt that it is by St. Paul. When the heat of contest was somewhat abated, when he saw how wofully he had been misunderstood by his Jewish and Gentile converts in the matter of the freedom of the Gospel; when he learned how that even the heathen, not very nice about morals,

---

[1] Acts xxi. 23, 24.

spoke of the scandals that desecrated the assemblies of
the Pauline Christians,—then no doubt he saw that it
was necessary to lay down a plain, sharp line of demar-
cation between those portions of the Law which were
not binding, and those which were.   Following a train
of thought suggested by Philo, whose works he had just
read, he showed that the ceremonial, sacrificial law was
symbolical, and that, as it typified Christ, the coming of
the One symbolized abrogated the symbol.   But the
moral law had no such natural limit, therefore it was
permanent.   Yet he was anxious not to be thought to
abandon his high views of the dignity of Faith ; and the
Epistle to the Hebrews contains one of the finest passages of his writing, the magnificent eulogy on Faith in
the 11th chapter.   St. Paul, like Luther, was not a clear
thinker, could not follow a thread of argument uninter-
ruptedly to its logical conclusion.   Often, when he saw
that conclusion looming before him, he hesitated to
assert it, and proceeded to weaken the cogency of his
former reasoning, or diverged to some collateral or irre-
levant topic.

The Epistle to the Hebrews is, I doubt not, a reflex
of the mind of Paul under the circumstances indicated.

This Epistle, there can be little question, called forth
the counterblast of the Epistle of James, the Lord's
brother.   But the writer of that Epistle exhibits an
unjust appreciation of the character of St. Paul.   Paul
was urged on by conviction, and not actuated by vanity.
Yet the exasperation must have been great which called
forth the indignant exclamation, " Wilt thou know, O
vain man, that faith without works is dead !"[1]

The second of the Canonical Epistles attributed to

---

[1] James ii. 20.

St. Peter,[1] if not the expression of the opinion of the Prince of the Apostles himself, represents the feelings of Nazarene Christians of the first century. It cautions those who read the writings of St. Paul, " which they that are unlearned and unstable wrest, as they do also the other Scriptures, unto their own destruction."

The Nicolaitans, taking advantage of the liberty accorded them in one direction, assumed it in another. In the letter to the Church of Pergamos, in the Apocalypse, they are denounced as " eating things sacrificed to idols, and committing fornication."[2] They are referred to as the followers of Balaam, both in that Epistle and in the Epistles of Jude and the 2nd of St. Peter. This is because Balaam has the same significance as Nicolas.[3] Jude, the brother of James, writes of them : " Certain men are crept in unawares . . . . ungodly men turning the grace of our God into lasciviousness . . . . who defile the flesh, despise dominion, and speak evil of dignities," i. e. of the apostles ; " these speak evil of those things which they know not ; but what they know naturally, as brute beasts, in those things they corrupt themselves. But, beloved, remember ye the words which were spoken before of the apostles of our Lord Jesus Christ ; how that they told you there should be mockers in the last time, who should walk after their own ungodly lusts. These be they who separate themselves, sensual, having not the Spirit."

And St. Peter wrote in wrath and horror : " It had been better not to have known the way of righteous-

---

[1] It is included by Eusebius in the Antilegomena, and, according to St. Jerome, was rejected as a spurious composition by the majority of the Christian world.

[2] Rev. ii. 1, 14, 15.

[3] בִּלְעָם, destruction of the people, from בָּלַע, to swallow up, and עַם, people = Νικόλαος.

ness, than, after they have known it, to turn from the holy commandment delivered unto them." [1]

The extreme Pauline party went on their way; Marcion, Valentine, Mark, were its successive high-priests and prophets. It ran from one extravagance to another, till it sank into the preposterous sect of the Cainites; in their frantic hostility to the Law, canonizing Cain, Esau, Pharaoh, Saul, all who are denounced in the Old Testament as having resisted the God of the Law, and deifying the Serpent, the Deceiver, as the God of the Gospel who had first revealed to Eve the secret of liberty, of emancipation from restraint.

But disorders always are on the surface, patent to every one, and cry out for a remedy. Those into which the advanced Pauline party had fallen were so flagrant, so repugnant to the good sense and right feelings of both Jew and Gentile believers, that they forced on a reaction. The most impracticable antinomians on one side, and obstructive Judaizers on the other, were cut off, or cut themselves off, from the Church; and a temper of mutual concession prevailed among the moderate. At the head of this movement stood St. John.

The work of reconciliation was achieved by the Apostle of Love. A happy compromise was effected. The Sabbath and the Lord's-day were both observed, side by side. Nothing was said on one side about distinction in meats, and the sacred obligation of washing; and on the other, the Gentile Christians adopted the Psalms of David and much of the ceremonial of the Temple into their liturgy. The question of circumcision was not mooted. It had died out of exhaustion, and the doctrine of Justification was accepted as a harmless opinion, to be constantly corrected by the moral law and common sense.

[1] 2 Pet. ii. 21.

A similar compromise took place at the English Reformation. In deference to the dictation of foreign reformers, the Anglican divines adopted their doctrine of Justification by Faith only into the Articles, but took the wise precaution of inserting as an antidote the Decalogue in the Communion Office, and of ordering it to be written up, where every one might read, in the body of the church.

The compromise effected by the influence and authority of St. John was rejected by extreme partizans on the right and the left. The extreme Paulines continued to refuse toleration to the Law and the Old Testament. The Nazarene community had also its impracticable zealots who would not endure the reading of the Pauline Epistles.

The Church, towards the close of the apostolic age, was made up of a preponderance of Gentile converts; in numbers and social position they stood far above the Nazarenes.

Under St. John, the Church assumed a distinctively Gentile character. In its constitution, religious worship, in its religious views, it differed widely from the Nazarene community in Palestine.

With the disappearance from its programme of distinction of meats and circumcision, its connection with Judaism had disappeared. But Nazarenism was not confined to Palestine. In Rome, in Greece, in Asia Minor, there were large communities, not of converted Jews only, but of proselytes from Gentiledom, who regarded themselves as constituting the Church of Christ. The existence of this fact is made patent by the Clementines and the Apostolic Constitutions. St. Peter's successors in the see of Rome have been a matter of perplexity. It has impressed itself on ecclesiastical students that Linus and Cletus ruled simultaneously. I have

little doubt it was so. The Judaizing Church was strong
in Rome. Probably each of the two communities had
its bishop set over it, one by Paul, the other by Peter.

Whilst the "Catholic" Church, the Church of the
compromise, grew and prospered, and conquered the
world, the narrow Judaizing Church dwindled till it ex-
pired, and with its expiration ceased conversion from
Judaism. This Jewish Church retained to the last its
close relationship with Mosaism. Circumstances, as has
been shown, drew the Jewish believer and the Pharisee
together.

When Jerusalem fell, the Gentile Church passed without a shudder under the Bethlehem Gate, whereon an
image of a swine had been set up in mockery; contem-
plated the statue of Hadrian on the site of the Temple
without despair, and constituted itself under a Gentile
bishop, Mark, in Ælia Capitolina.

But the old Nazarene community, the Church of
James and Symeon, clinging tightly to its old traditions,
crouched in exile at Pella, confounded by the Romans
in common banishment with the Jew. The guards
thrust back Nazarene and Jew alike with their spears,
when they ventured to approach the ruins of their pros-
trate city, the capital of their nation and of their faith.

The Church at Jerusalem under Mark was, to the
Nazarene, alien; its bishop an intruder. To the Nazarene, the memory of Paul was still hateful. The Clementine Recognitions speak of him with thinly-disguised
aversion, and tell of a personal contest between him,
when the persecutor Saul, and St. James their bishop,
and of his throwing down stairs, and beating till nearly
dead, the brother of the Lord. In the very ancient
apocryphal letter of St. Peter to St. James, belonging to
the same sect, and dating from the second century, Paul
is spoken of as the "enemy preaching a doctrine at once

foolish and lawless." [1] The Nazarene Christians, as
Irenæus and Theodoret tell us, regarded him as an apos-
tate.[2] They would not receive his Epistles or the
Gospel of St. Luke drawn up under his auspices.

In the Homilies, St. Peter is made to say :

" Our Lord and Prophet, who hath sent us, declared that
the Wicked One, having disputed with him forty days, and
having prevailed nothing against him, promised that he
would send apostles among his subjects to deceive. Wherefore, above all, remember to shun apostle or teacher or prophet who does not first accurately compare his preaching with
[that of] James, who was called the Brother of my Lord, and
to whom was entrusted the administration of the Church of
the Hebrews at Jerusalem. And that, even though he come
to you with credentials ; lest the wickedness which prevailed
nothing when disputing forty days with our Lord should
afterwards, like lightning falling from heaven upon earth,
send a preacher to your injury, preaching under pretence of
truth, like this Simon [Magus], and sowing error." [3]

The reader has but to study the Clementine Homilies

---

[1] Τοῦ ἐχθροῦ ἀνθρώπου ἄνομον τίνα καὶ φλυαρώδη διδασκαλιάν.—
Clem. Homil. xx. ed. Dressel, p. 4. The whole passage is sufficiently
curious to be quoted. St. Peter writes : "There are some from among
the Gentiles who have rejected my legal preaching, attaching themselves to
certain lawless and trifling preaching of the man who is my enemy. And
these things some have attempted while I am still alive, to transform my
words by certain various interpretations, in order to the dissolution of the
Law ; as though I also myself were of such a mind, but did not freely proclaim it, which God forbid ! For such a thing were to act in opposition to
the law of God, which was spoken by Moses, and was borne witness to by
our Lord in respect of its eternal continuance ; for thus he spoke : The
heavens and the earth shall pass away, but one jot or one tittle shall in no
wise pass from the law."

[2] "Apostolum Paulum recusantes, apostatam eum legis dicentes."—
Iren. Adv. Hæres. i. 26. Τὸν δὲ ἀπόστυλον ἀποστάτην καλοῦσι.—
Theod. Fabul. Hæret. ii. 1.

[3] Hom. xi. 35.

and Recognitions, and his wonder at the silence of Josephus and Justus will disappear.

Those curious books afford us a precious insight into the feelings of the Nazarenes of the first and second centuries, showing us what was the temper of their minds and the colour of their belief. They represent St. James as the supreme head of the Church. He is addressed by St. Peter, " Peter to James, the Lord and Bishop of the Holy Church, under the Father of all." St. Clement calls him " the Lord and Bishop of bishops, who rules Jerusalem, the Holy Church of the Hebrews, and the Churches everywhere excellently founded by the providence of God."

Throughout the curious collection of Homilies, Christianity is one with Judaism. It is a reform of Mosaism. It bears the relation to Judaism that the Anglican Church of the last three centuries, it is pretended, bears to the Mediæval Church in England. Everything essential was retained; only the traditions of the elders, the glosses of the lawyers, were rejected.

Christianity is never mentioned by name. A believer is called, not a Christian, but a Jew. Clement describes his own conversion: " I betook myself to the holy God and Law of the Jews, putting my faith in the well-assured conclusion that the Law has been assigned by the righteous judgment of God." [1]

Apion the philosopher, is spoken of as hating the Jews; the context informs us that by Jews is meant those whom we should call Christians.

Moses is the first prophet, Jesus the second. Like their spiritual ancestors the Essenes, the Nazarenes protested that the Law was overlaid with inventions of a later date; these Jesus came to efface, that he might re-edit the Law in its ancient integrity. The original

[1] Hom. iv. 22.

Law, as given by God and written by Moses, was lost; it was found again after 300 years, lost again, and then re-written from memory by Ezra. Thus it came to pass that the Old Revelation went through various editions, which altered its meaning, and left it a compound of truths and errors.[1] It was the mark of a good and wise Jew, instructed by Jesus, to distinguish between what was true and what was false in the Scriptures.

Thus the Nazarene thought himself a Hebrew of the Hebrews, as an Anglican esteems himself a better Catholic than the Catholics. The Nazarenes would have resented with indignation the imputation that they were a sect alien from the commonwealth of Israel, and, like all communities occupying an uneasy seat between two stools, were doubly, trebly vehement in their denunciation of that sect to which they were thought to bear some relation. They repudiated "Christianity,"[2] as a high Anglican repudiates Protestantism; they held aloof from a Pauline believer, as an English Churchman will stand aloof from a Lutheran.

And thus it came to pass that the Jewish historians of the first century said nothing about Christ and the Church he founded.

And yet St. Paul had wrought a work for Christ and the Church which, humanly speaking, none else could have effected.

The Nazarene Church was from its infancy prone to take a low view of the nature of Christ. The Jewish converts were so infected with Messianic notions that they could look on Jesus Christ only as the Messiah, not as incarnate God. They could see in him a prophet, "one like unto Moses," but not one equal to the Father.

[1] Clem. Homil. ii. 38—40, 48, iii. 50, 51.

[2] Of course I mean the designation given to the Pauline sect, not the religion of Christ.

The teaching of the apostles seemed powerless at the time to lift the faith of their Jewish converts to high views of the Lord's nature and mission. Their Judaic prejudice strangled, warped their faith. Directly the presence of the apostles was withdrawn, the restraint on this downward gravitation was removed, and Nazarenism settled into heresy on the fundamental doctrine of Christianity. To Gentiles it was in vain to preach Messianism. Messianism implied an earnest longing for a promised deliverer. Gentiles had no such longing, had never been led to expect a deliverer.

The apostle must take other ground. He took that of the Incarnation, the Godhead revealing the Truth to mankind by manifestation of itself among men, in human flesh.

The apostles to the circumcision naturally appealed to the ruling religious passion in the Jewish heart—the passion of hope for the promised Messiah. The Messiah was come. The teaching of the apostles to the circumcision necessarily consisted of an explanation of this truth, and efforts to dissipate the false notions which coloured Jewish Messianic hopes, and interfered with their reception of the truth that Jesus was the one who had been spoken of by the prophets, and to whose coming their fathers had looked.

To the Gentiles, St. Paul preached Christ as the revealer to a dark and ignorant world of the nature of God, the purpose for which He had made man, and the way in which man might serve and please God. The Jews had their revelation, and were satisfied with it. The Gentiles walked in darkness; they had none; their philosophies were the gropings of earnest souls after light. The craving of the Gentile heart was for a revelation. Paul preached to them the truth manifested to the world through Christ.

Thus Pauline teaching on the Incarnation counteracted the downward drag of Nazarene Messianism, which, when left to itself, ended in denying the Godhead of Christ.

If for a century the churches founded by St. Paul were sick with moral disorders, wherewith they were inoculated, the vitality of orthodox belief in the Godhead of Christ proved stronger than moral heresy, cast it out, and left only the scars to tell what they had gone through in their infancy.

Petrine Christianity upheld the standard of morality, Pauline Christianity bore that of orthodoxy.

St. John, in the cool of his old age, was able to give the Church its permanent form. The Gentile converts had learned to reverence the purity, the uprightness, the truthfulness of the Nazarene, and to be ashamed of their excesses; and the Nazarene had seen that his Messianism supplied him with nothing to satisfy the inner yearning of his nature. Both met under the apostle of love to clasp hands and learn of one another, to confess their mutual errors, to place in the treasury of the Church, the one his faith, the other his ethics, to be the perpetual heritage of Christianity.

Some there were still who remained fixed in their prejudices, self-excommunicated, monuments to the Church of the perils she had gone through, the Scylla and Charybdis through which she had passed with difficulty, guided by her Divine pilot.

I have been obliged at some length to show that the early Christian Church in Palestine bore so close a resemblance to the Essene sect, that to the ordinary superficial observer it was indistinguishable from it. And also, that so broad was the schism separating the Nazarene Church consisting of Hebrews, from the Pauline Church consisting of Gentiles, that no external observer who had 'not examined the doctrines of these communities would suppose them to be two forms of the same faith, two religions sprung from the same loins. Their connection was as imperceptible to a Jew, as would be that between Roman Catholicism and Wesleyanism to-day.

Both Nazarene and Jew worshipped in the same temple, observed the same holy days, practised the same rites, shrank with loathing from the same food, and mingled their anathemas against the same apostate, Paul, who had cast aside at once the law in which he had been brought up, and the Hebrew name by which he had been known.

The silence of Josephus and Justus under these circumstances is explicable. They have described Essenism ; that description covers Nazarenism as it appeared to the vulgar eye. If they have omitted to speak of Jesus and his death, it is because both wrote at the time when Nazarene and Pharisee were most closely united in sympathy, sorrow and regret for the past. It was not a time to rip up old wounds, and Justus and Josephus were both Pharisees.

That neither should speak of Pauline Christianity is also not remarkable. It was a Gentile religion, believed in only by Greeks and Romans ; it had no open *observable* connection with Judaism. It was to them but another of those many religions which rose as mushrooms, to fade away again on the soil of the Roman world, with which the Jewish historians had little interest and no concern.

If this explanation which I have offered is unsatisfactory, I know not whither to look for another which can throw light to the strange silence of Philo, Josephus and Justus.

It is thrown in the teeth of Christians, that history,

apart from the Gospels, knows nothing of Christ; that the silence of contemporary, and all but contemporary, Jewish chroniclers, invalidates the testimony of the inspired records.

The reasons which I have given seem to me to explain this silence plausibly, and to show that it arose, not from ignorance of the acts of Christ and the existence of the Church, but from a deliberate purpose.

III.

CELSUS was one of the four first controversial opponents of Christianity. His book has been lost, with the exception of such portions as have been preserved by Origen.

Nothing for certain is known of Celsus. Origen endeavours to make him out to be an Epicurean, as prejudice existed even among the heathen against this school of philosophy, which denied, or left as open questions, the existence of a God, Providence, and the Eternity of the Soul. He says in his first book that he has heard there had existed two Epicureans of the name of Celsus, one who lived in the reign of Nero (✝ A.D. 68), the other under Hadrian (✝ A.D. 138), and it is with this latter that he has to do. But it is clear from passages of Celsus quoted by Origen, that this antagonist of Christianity was no Epicurean, but belonged to that school of Eclectics which based its teaching on Platonism, but adopted modifications from other schools. Origen himself is obliged to admit in several passages of his controversial treatise that the views of Celsus are not Epicurean, but Platonic; but he pretends that Celsus disguised his Epicureanism under a pretence of Platonism. Controversialists in the first days of Christianity were as prompt to discredit their opponents by ungenerous, false accusation, as in these later days.

We know neither the place nor the date of the birth of Celsus. That he lived later than the times of Hadrian

is clear from his mention of the Marcionites, who only
arose in A.D. 142, and of the Marcellians, named after
the woman Marcella, who, according to the testimony
of Irenæus,[1] first came to Rome in the time of Pope
Anicetus, after A.D. 157. As Celsus in two passages remarks that the Christians spread their doctrines secretly,
because they were forbidden under pain of death to
assemble together for worship, it would appear that he
wrote his book Λόγος ἀληθής during the reign of Marcus
Aurelius (between 161—180), who persecuted the Christians. We may therefore put the date of the book approx-
imately at A.D. 176.

The author is certainly the Celsus to whom Lucian
dedicated his writing, " Alexander the False Prophet."
Of the religious opinions of Celsus we are able to form a
tolerable conception from the work of Origen. " If the
Christians only honoured One God," says he,[2] " then the
weapons of their controversy with others would not be
so weak; but they show to a man, who appeared not
long ago, an exaggerated honour, and are of opinion that
they are not offending the Godhead, when they show to
one of His servants the same reverence that they pay
to God Himself." Celsus acknowledges, with the Plato-
nists, One only, eternal, spiritual God, who cannot be
brought into union with impure matter, the world. All
that concerns the world, he says, God has left to the
dispensation of inferior spirits, which are the gods of
heathendom. The welfare of mankind is at the disposal
of these inferior gods, and men therefore do well to
honour them in moderation; but the human soul is called
to escape the chains of matter and strain after perfect
purity; and this can only be done by meditation on the
One, supreme, almighty God. "God," says he,[3] " has

[1] Adv. Hæres. i. 24.   [2] Origen, Contr. Cels. lib. viii.
[3] Ibid. lib. vi.

not made man in His image, as Christians affirm; for
God has not either the appearance of a man, nor indeed
any visible form." In the fourth Book he remarks, in
opposition to the Christian doctrine of the Incarnation,
" I will appeal to that which has been held as true in
all ages,—that God is good, beautiful, blessed, and possesses in Himself all perfections. If He came down
among men, He must have altered His nature; from a
good God, He must have become bad; from beautiful,
ugly; from blessed, unhappy; and His perfect Being
would have become one of imperfection. Who can tolerate
such a change ? Only transitory things alter their conditions; the intransitory remain ever the same. Therefore it is impossible to conceive that God can have been
transformed in such a manner."

It is remarkable that Celsus, living in the middle of
the second century, and able to make inquiries of aged
Jews whose lives had extended from the first century,
should have been able to find out next to nothing about
Jesus and his disciples, except what he read in the
Gospels. This is proof that no traditions concerning
Jesus had been preserved by the Jews, apart from those
contained in the Gospels, Canonical and Apocryphal.

Origen's answer to Celsus is composed of eight Books.
In the first Book a Jew·speaks, who is introduced by
Celsus as addressing Jesus himself; in the second Book
this Jew addresses those of his fellow-countrymen who
have embraced Christianity; in the other six Books
Celsus speaks for himself. Origen extracts only short
passages from the work of Celsus, and then labours to
demolish the force of the argument of the opponent of
Christianity as best he can.

The arguments of Celsus and the counter-arguments
of Origen do not concern us here. All we have to deal

with are those traditions or slanders detailed to Celsus
by the Jews, which he reproduces. That Celsus was
in communication with Jews when he wrote the two
first Books is obvious, and the only circumstances he
relates which concern the life of our Lord he derived
from his Jewish informants. "The Jew (whom Celsus
introduces) addresses Jesus, and finds much fault. In
the first place, he charges him with having falsely proclaimed himself to be the Son of a Virgin; afterwards,
he says that Jesus was born in a poor Jewish village,
and that his mother was a poor woman of the country,
who supported herself with spinning and needlework;
that she was cast off by her betrothed, a carpenter; and
that after she was thus rejected by her husband, she
wandered about in disgrace and misery till she secretly
gave birth to Jesus. Jesus himself was obliged from
poverty and necessity to go down as servant into Egypt,
where he learnt some of the secret sciences which are
in high honour among the Egyptians; and he placed
such confidence in these sciences, that on his return to
his native land he gave himself out to be a God."

Origen adds: "The carpenter, as the Jew of Celsus
declares, who was betrothed to Mary, put the mother
of Jesus from him, because she had broken faith with
him, in favour of a soldier named Panthera."

Again: "Celsus relates from the Gospel of Matthew
the flight of Christ into Egypt; but he denies all that
is marvellous and supernatural in it, especially that an
angel should have appeared to Joseph and ordered him
to escape. Instead of seeking whether the departure of
Jesus from Judæa and his residence in Egypt had not
some spiritual meaning, he has made up a fable concerning it. He admits, indeed, that Jesus may have
wrought the miracles which attracted such a multitude

of people to him, and induced them to follow him as
the Messiah; but he pretends that these miracles were
wrought, not by virtue of his divine power, but of his
magical knowledge. Jesus, says he, had a bad education; later he went into Egypt and passed into service
there, and there learnt some wonderful arts. When he
came back to his fatherland, on account of these arts,
he gave himself out to be a God."[1]

"The Jew brought forward by Celsus goes on to say, 'I
could relate many things more concerning Jesus, all
which are true, but which have quite a different character from what his disciples relate touching him; but
I will not now bring these forward.' And what are
these facts," answers Origen, "which are not in agreement with the narratives of the Evangelists, and which
the Jew refrains from mentioning? Unquestionably, he
is using only a rhetorical expression; he pretends that
he has in his store abundance of munitions of war to
discharge against Jesus and his doctrine, but in fact he
knows nothing which can deceive the hearer with the
appearance of truth, *except those particulars which he has
culled from the Gospels themselves.*"[2]

This is most important evidence of the utter ignorance
of the Jews in the second century of all that related to
the history of our Lord. Justus and Josephus had been
silent. There was no written narrative to which the
Jew might turn for information; his traditions were
silent. The fall of Jerusalem and the dispersion of the
Jews had broken the thread of their recollections.

It is very necessary to bear this in mind, in order to
appreciate the utter worthlessness of the stories told of
our Saviour in the Talmud and the Toledoth Jeschu. An
attempt has been made to bolster up these late fables,

---

[1] Contra Cels. lib. i.   [2] *Ibid.* lib. ii.

and show that they are deserving of a certain amount of confidence.[1]

But it is clear that the religious movement which our Lord originated in Palestine attracted much less attention at the time than has been usually supposed. The Sanhedrim at first regarded his teaching with the contempt with which, in after times, Leo X. heard of the preaching of Luther. "It is a schoolman's proposition," said the Pope. "A new rabbinical tradition," the elders probably said. Only when their interests and fears were alarmed, did they interfere to procure the condemnation of Christ. And then they thought no more of their victim and his history than they did later of the history of James, the Lord's brother. The preaching and death of Jesus led to no tumultuous outbreak against the Roman government, and therefore excited little interest. The position of Christ as the God-man was not forced on them by the Nazarenes. The Jews noticed the virtues of these men, but ignored their peculiar tenets, till traditions were lost; and when the majesty of Christ, incarnate God, shone out on the world which turned to acknowledge him, they found that they had preserved no records, no recollections of the events in the history of Jesus. That he was said by Christians to have been born of a Virgin, driven into Egypt by King Herod—that he wrought miracles, gathered disciples, died on the cross and rose again—they heard from the Christians; and these facts they made use of to pervert them into fantastic fables, to colour them with malignant inventions. The only trace of independent tradition is in the mention made of Panthera by the Jew produced by Celsus.

[1] Amongst others, Clemens : Jesus von Nazareth, Stuttgart, 1850; Von der Alme: Die Urtheile heidnischer und jüdischer Schriftsteller, Leipzig, 1864.

It is perhaps worthy of remark that St. Epiphanius,
who wrote against heresies at the end of the fourth century, gives the genealogy of Jesus thus :[1]

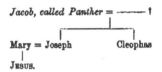

It shows that in the fourth century the Jewish stories
of Panthera had made such an impression on the Christians, that his name was forced into the pedigree of Jesus.

Had any of the stories found in the Toledoth Jeschu
existed in the second century, we should certainly have
found them in the book of Celsus.

Origen taunts the Jew with knowing nothing of Christ
but what he had found out from the Gospels. He would
not have uttered that taunt had any anti-Christian apocryphal biographies of Christ existed in his day. The
Talmud, indeed, has the tale of Christ having studied
magic in Egypt. Whence this legend, as well as that of
Panthera, came, we shall see presently.

[1] Adv. Hær. lib. iii.; Hær. lxviii. 7.

IV

THE TALMUD.

THE Talmud (*i.e.* the Teaching) consists of two parts, the Mischna and the Gemara.

The Mischna (*i.e.* δευτέρωσις, Second Law, or Recapitulation) is a collection of religious ordinances, interpretations of Old Testament passages, especially of Mosaic rules, which have been given by various illustrious Rabbis from the date of the founding of the second Temple, therefore from about B.C. 400 to the year A.D. 200. These interpretations, which were either written or orally handed down, were collected in the year A.D. 219 by the Rabbi Jehuda the Holy, at Tiberias, on the Sea of Galilee, into a book to which he gave the name of Mischna, the Recapitulation of the Law. At that time the Jewish Sanhedrim and the Patriarch resided at Tiberias. After the destruction of Jerusalem in A.D. 70, the Sanhedrim, which consisted of seventy-one persons, assembled at Jamnia, the ancient Philistine city of Jabne; but on the insurrection of the Jews under Barcochab, A.D. 135, it took up its quarters at Tiberias. There the Sanhedrim met under a hereditary Patriarch of the family of Gamaliel, who bore the title of Nasi, Chief, till A.D. 420, when the last member of the house of Gamaliel died, and the Patriarchate and Sanhedrim departed from Tiberias.

The Mischna is made up of six Orders (Sedarim), which together contain sixty-three Tractates. The first Order or Seder is called Iesaïm, and treats of agriculture. The second, Moed, treats of festivals. The third, Naschim, deals with the rights of women. The fourth, Nezikim, or Jechnoth, treats of cases of law. The fifth, Kodaschim, of holy things. The sixth, Taharoth, of impurity and purifications.

The Orders of Kodaschim and Taharoth are incomplete. The Jerusalem Talmud consists of only the first four, and the tract Nidda, which belongs to the Order Taharoth.

Now it is deserving of remark, that many of the Rabbis whose sayings are recorded in the Mischna lived in the time of our Lord, or shortly after, and yet that not the smallest reference is made to the teaching of Jesus, nor even any allusion to him personally. Although the Mischna was drawn up beside the Sea of Galilee, at Tiberias, near where Jesus lived and wrought miracles and taught, neither he nor his followers are mentioned once throughout the Mischna.

There must be a reason why the Mischna, as well as Josephus and Justus of Tiberias, is silent respecting Jesus of Nazareth. The reason I have already given. The followers of Jesus were regarded as belonging to the sect of the Essenes. Our Lord's teaching made no great impression on the Jews of his time. It was so radically unlike the pedantry and puerilities of their Rabbis, that they did not acknowledge him as a teacher of the Law. He had preached Essene disengagement from the world, conquest of passion. Only when Essene enthusiasm was thought to threaten the powerful families which held possession of and abused the pontifical office, had the high-priest and his party taken alarm, and obtained the condemnation and death of Jesus. Their alarm died away, the political situation altered, the new Essenianism ceased to be suspected, and Nazarene Christianity took its place among the parties of

Judaism, attracting little notice and exciting no active hostility.

The Mischna was drawn up at the beginning of the third century, when Christianity was spreading rapidly through the Roman empire, and had excited the Roman emperors to fierce persecution of those who professed it. Yet Jehuda the Holy says not a word about Christ or Christianity.

He and those whose sayings he quotes had no suspicion that this religion, which was gaining ground every day among the Gentiles, had sprung from the teaching of a Jew. Christianity ruffled not the surface of Jewdom. The harmless Nazarenes were few, and were as strict observers of the Law as the straitest Pharisees.

And if Christianity was thus a matter of indifference to the Jews, no wonder that every recollection of Jesus of Nazareth, every tradition of his birth, his teaching, his death, had died away, so that, even at the close of the second century, Origen could charge his Jew opponent with knowing nothing of Jesus save what he had learned from the Gospels.

The Mischna became in turn the subject of commentary and interpretation by the Rabbis. The explanations of famous Rabbis, who taught on the Mischna, were collected, and called Gemara (the Complement), because with it the collection of rabbinical expositions of the Law was completed.

There are two editions of the Gemara, one made in Palestine and called the Jerusalem Gemara, the other made at Babylon.

The Jerusalem Gemara was compiled about A.D. 390, under the direction of the Patriarch of Tiberias. But there was a second Jewish Patriarchate at Babylon, which lasted till A.D. 1038, whereas that of Tiberias was extinguished, as has been already said, in A.D. 420.

Among the Babylonish Jews, under the direction of their Patriarch, an independent school of commentators on the Mischna had arisen. Their opinions were collected about the year A.D. 500, and compose the Babylonish Gemara. This latter Gemara is held by modern Jews in higher esteem than the Jerusalem Gemara.

The Mischna, which is the same to both Gemaras, together with one of the commentaries and glosses, called Mekilta and Massektoth, form either the Jerusalem or the Babylonish Talmud.

All the Jewish historians who speak of the compilation of the Gemara of Babylon, are almost unanimous on three points: that the Rabbi Ashi was the first to begin the compilation, but that death interrupted him before its completion; that he had for his assistant another doctor, the Rabbi Avina; and that a certain Rabbi Jose finished the work seventy-three years after the death of Rabbi Ashi. Rabbi Ashi is believed to have died A.D. 427, consequently the Babylonish Talmud was completed in A.D. 500.

St. Jerome (d. 420) was certainly acquainted with the Mischna, for he mentions it by name.[1]

St. Ephraem (d. 378) says:

"The Jews have had four sorts of traditions which they call Repetitions (δευτερώσεις). The first bear the name of Moses the Prophet; they attribute the second to a doctor named Akiba or Bar Akiba. The third pass for being those of a certain Andan or Annan, whom they call also Judas; and they maintain that the sons of Assamonæus were the authors of the fourth. It is from these four sources that all those doctrines among them are derived, which, however futile they

---

[1] "Quantæ traditiones Pharisæorum sint, quas hodie vocant δευτερώσεις et quam aniles fabulæ, evolvere nequeo : neque enim libri patitur magnitudo, et pleraque tam turpia sunt ut erubescam dicere."

may be, by them are esteemed as the most profound science, and of which they speak with ostentation." [1]

From this it appears that St. Ephraem was acquainted not only with the Mischna, but with the Gemara, then in process of formation.

Both the Jerusalem and the Babylonish Gemara, in their interpretations of the Mischna, mention Jesus and the apostles, or, at all events, have been supposed to do so. At the time when both Gemaras were drawn up, Christianity was the ruling religion in the Roman empire, and the Rabbis could hardly ignore any longer the Founder of the new religion. But their statements concerning Jesus are untrustworthy, because so late. Had they occurred in the Mischna, they might have deserved attention.

But before we consider the passages containing allusions to Jesus, it will be well to quote a very singular anecdote in the Jerusalem Gemara: [2]

"It happened that the cow of a Jew who was ploughing the ground began to low. An Arab (or a traveller) who was passing, and who understood the language of beasts, on hearing this lowing said to the labourer, 'Son of a Jew! son of a Jew! loose thine ox and set it free from the plough, for the Temple is fallen.' But as the ox lowed a second time, he said, 'Son of a Jew! son of a Jew! yoke thy ox, join her to the plough, for the Messiah is born.' 'What is his name?' asked the Jew. 'כובדס, the Consoler,' replied the Arab. 'And what is the name of his father?' asked the Jew. 'Hezekiah,' answered the Arab. 'And whence comes he?' 'From the royal palace of Bethlehem Juda.' Then the Jew sold his ox and his plough, and becoming a seller of children's clothes went to Bethlehem, where he found the mother of the Consoler afflicted, because that, on the day he was born, the

[1] Hæres. xiii.   [2] Beracoth, xi. a.

Temple had been destroyed. But the other women, to console her, said that her son, who had caused the ruin of the Temple, would speedily rebuild it. Some days after, she owned to the seller of children's clothes that the Consoler had been ravished from her, and that she knew not what had become of him. Rabbi Bun observes thereupon that there was no need to learn from an Arab that the Messiah would appear at the moment of the fall of the Temple, as the prophet Isaiah had predicted this very thing in the two verses, x. 34 and xi. 1, on the ruin of the Temple, and the cessation of the daily sacrifice, which took place at the siege by the Romans, or by the impious kingdom."

This is a very curious story, and its appearance in the Talmud is somewhat difficult to understand.

We must now pass on to those passages which have been supposed to refer to our Lord.

In the Babylonish Gemara [1] it is related that when King Alexander Jannæus persecuted the Rabbis, the Rabbi Jehoshua, son of Parachias, fled with his disciple Jesus to Alexandria in Egypt, and there both received instruction in Egyptian magic. On their way back to Judæa, both were hospitably lodged by a woman. Next day, as Jehoshua and his disciple were continuing their journey, the master praised the hospitality of their hostess, whereupon his disciple remarked that she was not only a hospitable but a comely woman.

Now as it was forbidden to Rabbis to look with admiration on female beauty, the Rabbi Jehoshua was so angry with his disciple, that he pronounced on him excommunication and a curse. Jesus after this separated from his master, and gave himself up wholly to the study of magic.

The name Jesus is Jehoshua Græcised. Both mas-

---

[1] Tract. Sanhedrim, fol. 107, and Sota, fol. 47.

ter and pupil in this legend bore the same name, but
that of the pupil is in the Talmud abbreviated into
Jeschu.

This story is introduced in the Gemara to illustrate
the obligation incumbent on a Rabbi to keep custody
over his eyes. It bears no signs of having been forced
in so as to give expression to antipathy against Jeschu.

That this Jeschu is our blessed Lord is by no means
evident. On the contrary, the balance of probability is
that the pupil of Jehoshua Ben Perachia was an entirely different person.

This Jehoshua, son of Perachia, is a known historical
personage. He was one of the Sanhedrim in the reign
of Alexander Jannæus. He began to teach as Rabbi in
the year of the world 3606, or B.C. 154. Alexander
Jannæus, son of Hyrcanus, was king of the Jews in
B.C. 106. The Pharisees could not endure that the
royal and high-priestly functions should be united in
the same person; they therefore broke out in revolt.
The civil war caused the death of some 50,000, according to Josephus. When Alexander had suppressed the
revolt, he led 800 prisoners to the fortress of Bethome,
and crucified them before the eyes of his concubines at
a grand banquet he gave.

The Pharisees, and those of the Sanhedrim who had
not fallen into his hands, sought safety in flight. It was
then probably that Jehoshua, son of Perachia, went down
into Egypt and was accompanied by Jeschu.

Jehoshua was buried at Chittin, but the exact date
of his death is not known.[1]

Alexander Jannæus died B.C. 79, after a reign of
twenty - seven years, whilst besieging the castle of
Ragaba on the further side of Jordan.

It will be seen at once that the date of the Talmudic

[1] Bartolocci : Bibliotheca Maxima Rabbinica, sub. nom.

Jeschu is something like a century earlier than that of the Jesus of the Gospels.

Moreover, it cannot be said that Jewish tradition asserts their identity. On the contrary, learned Jewish writers have emphatically denied that the Jeschu of the Talmud is the Jesus of the Gospels.

In the " Disputation " of the Rabbi Jechiels with Nicolas, a convert, occurs this statement : " This (which is related of Jesus and the Rabbi Joshua, son of Perachia) contains no reference to him whom Christians honour as a God ;" and then he points out that the impossibility of reconciling the dates is enough to prove that the disciple of Joshua Ben Perachia was a person altogether distinct from the Founder of Christianity.

The Rabbi Lippmann[1] gives the same denial, and shows that Jesus of the Gospels was a contemporary of Hillel, whereas the Jeschu of the anecdote lived from two to three generations earlier.

The Rabbi Salman Zevi entered into the question with great care in a pamphlet, and produced ten reasons for concluding that the Jeschu of the Talmud was not the Jesus, son of Mary, of the Evangelists.[2]

We can see now how it was that the Jew of Celsus brought against our Lord the charge of having learned magic in Egypt. He had heard in the Rabbinic schools the anecdote of Jeschu, pupil of Jehoshua, son of Perachia,—an anecdote which could scarcely fail to be narrated to all pupils. He at once concluded that this Jeschu was the Jesus of the Christians, without troubling himself with the chronology.

In the Mischna, Tract. Sabbath, fol. 104, it is forbidden to make marks upon the skin. The Babylonish Gemara

[1] Sepher Nizzachon, n. 337.

[2] Eisenmenger : Neuentdecktes Judenthum, I. pp. 231-7. Königsberg, 1711.

observes on this passage: " Did not the son of Stada
mark the magical arts on his skin, and bring them with
him out of Egypt ?" This son of Stada is Jeschu, as
will presently appear.

In the Mischna of Tract. Sanhedrim, fol. 43, it is ordered
that he who shall be condemned to death by stoning
shall be led to the place of execution with a herald
going before him, who shall proclaim the name of the
offender, and shall summon those who have anything to
say in mitigation of the sentence to speak before the
sentence is put in execution.

On this the Babylonish Gemara remarks, " There exists
a tradition: On the rest-day before the Sabbath they
crucified Jeschu. For forty days did the herald go before
him and proclaim aloud, He is to be stoned to death
because he has practised evil, and has led the Israelites
astray, and provoked them to schism. Let any one who
can bring evidence of his innocence come forward and
speak! But as nothing was produced which could establish his innocence, he was crucified on the rest-day of
the Passah (i.e. the day before the Passover)."

The Mischna of Tract. Sanhedrim, fol. 67, treats of the
command in Deut. xiii. 6—11, that any Hebrew who
should introduce the worship of other gods should be
stoned with stones. On this the Gemara of Babylon
relates that, in the city of Lydda, Jeschu was heard
through a partition endeavouring to persuade a Jew to
worship idols; whereupon he was brought forth and
crucified on the eve of the Passover. " None of those
who are condemned to death by the Law are spied upon
except only those (seducers of the people). How are
they dealt with? They light a candle in an inner
chamber, and place spies in an outer room, who may
watch and listen to him (the accused). But he does not
see them. Then he whom the accused had formerly

endeavoured to seduce says to him, ' Repeat, I pray you, what you told me before in private.' Then, should he do so, the other will say further, ' But how shall we leave our God in heaven and serve idols ? ' Now should the accused be converted and repent at this saying, it is well; but if he goes on to say, That is our affair, and so and so ought we to do, then the spies must lead him off to the house of judgment and stone him. This is what was done to the son of Stada at Lud, and they hung him up on the eve of the Passover."[1] And the Tract. Sanhedrim says, " It is related that on the eve of the Sabbath they crucified Jeschu, a herald going before him," as has been already quoted; and then follows the comment: " Ula said, Will you not judge him to have been the son of destruction, because he is a seducer of the people ? For the Merciful says (Deut. xiii. 8), Thou shalt not spare him, neither shalt thou conceal him. But I, Jesus, am heir to the kingdom. Therefore (the herald) went forth proclaiming that he was to be stoned because he had done an evil thing, and had seduced the people, and led them into schism. And (Jeschu) went forth to be stoned with stones because he had done an evil thing, and had seduced the people and led them into schism."

The Babylonish Gemara to the Mischna of Tract. Sabbath gives the following perplexing account of the parents of Jeschu :[2] " They stoned the son of Stada in Lud (Lydda), and crucified him on the eve of the Pass-over. This Stada's son was Pandira's son. Rabbi Chasda said Stada's husband was Pandira's master, namely Paphos, son of Jehuda. But how was Stada his mother ? His (i.e. Pandira's) mother was a woman's hair-dresser. As they say in Pombeditha (the Babylonish school by the Euphrates), this one went astray (S'tath-da) from her husband."

[1] Tract. Sabbath, fol. 67.   [2] Ibid. fol. 104.

The Gloss or Paraphrase on this is: "Stada's son was not the son of Paphos, son of Jehuda; No. As Rabbi Chasda observed, Paphos had a servant named Pandira. Well, what has that to do with it? Tell us how it came to pass that this son was born to Stada. Well, it was on this wise. Miriam, the mother of Pandira, used to dress Stada's hair, and .... Stada became a mother by Pandira, son of Miriam. As they say in Pombeditha, Stada by name and Stada by nature."[1]

The obscurity of the passage arises from various causes. R. Chasda is a punster, and plays on the double meaning of "Baal" for "husband" and "master." There is also ambiguity in the pronoun "his;" it is difficult to say to whom it always refers. The Paraphrase is late, and is a conjectural explanation of an obscure passage.

It is clear that the Jeschu of the Talmud was the son of one Stada and Pandira. But the name Pandira having the appearance of being a woman's name,[2] this led to additional confusion, for some said that Pandira was his mother's name.

The late Gloss does not associate Stada with the blessed Virgin. It gives the name of Miriam or Mary

---

[1] The passage is not easy to understand. I give three Latin translations of it, one by Cl. Schickardus, the second quoted from Scheidius (Loca Talm. i. 2). "Filius Satdæ, filius Pandeiræ fuit. Dixit Raf Chasda: Amasius Pandeiræ, maritus Paphos filius Jehudæ fuit. At quomodo mater ejus Satda? Mater ejus Mirjam, comptrix mulierum fuit." "Filius Stadæ filius Pandiræ est. Dixit Rabbi Chasda: Maritus seu procus matris ejus fuit Stada, iniens Pandiram. Maritus Paphus filius Judæ ipse est, mater ejus Stada, mater ejus Maria," &c. Lightfoot, Matt. xxvii. 56, thus translates it: "Lapidârunt filium Satdæ in Lydda, et suspenderunt eum in vesperâ Paschatis. Hic autem filius Satdæ fuit filius Pandiræ. Dixit quidem Rabb Chasda, Maritus (matris ejus) fuit Satda, maritus Pandira, maritus Papus filius Judæ: sed tamen dico matrem ejus fuisse Satdam, Mariam videlicet, plicatricem capillorum mulierum: sicut dicunt in Panbeditha, Declinavit ista a marito suo."

[2] פנדירה‎. As a man's name it occurs in 2 Targum, Esther vii.

to be the mother of Pandira, the father of Jeschu. The
Jew of Celsus says that the mother of Jesus was a poor
needlewoman, who also span for her livelihood. He probably recalled what was said of Miriam, the mother of
Panthera and grandmother of Jeschu, and applied it
to St. Mary the Virgin, misled by the obscurity of the
saying of Chasda, which was orally repeated in the Rabbinic schools.

The Jerusalem Gemara to Tract. Sabbath says : " The
sister's son of Rabbi Jose swallowed poison, or something
deadly. There came to him a man and conjured him in
the name of Jeschu, son of Pandeira, and he was healed
or made easy. But when he went forth it was said to
him, How hast thou healed him ? He answered, by
using such and such words. Then he (R. Jose) said to
him, It had been better for him to have died than to
have heard this name. And so it was with him (*i.e.* the
boy died)."

In another place :[1] " Eleasar, the son of Damah, was
bitten by a serpent. There came to him James, a man
of the town of Sechania, to cure him in the name of
Jeschu, son of Pandeira ; but the Rabbi Ismael would
not suffer it, but said, It is not permitted to thee, son
of Damah. But he (James) said, Suffer me, and I will
bring an argument against thee which is lawful. But
he would not suffer him."

The Gemara to Tract. Sanhedrim, fol. 43, mentions five
disciples of Jeschu Ben-Stada, namely, Matthai, Nakai,
Netzer, Boni and Thoda. It says :—

" Jeschu had five disciples, Matthai, Nakai, Nezer and Boni,
and also Thoda. They brought Matthai (to the tribunal) to
pronounce sentence of death against him. He said, Shall Matthai suffer when it is written (Ps. xlii. 3), מתי When shall

[1] Avoda Sava, fol. 27.

I come to appear before the presence of God? They replied,
Shall not Matthai die when it is written, מרי When shall
he die and his name perish? They produced Nakai. He
said, Shall Nakai נקאי die? Is it not written, The innocent
ונקי slay thou not? (Exod. xxiii. 7). They answered him,
Shall not Nakai die when it is written, In the secret places
does he murder the innocent? (Ps. x. 8). When they brought
forth Netzer, he said unto them, Shall Netzer נצר be slain?
Is it not written (Isa. xi. 1), A branch ונצר shall grow out
of his roots? They replied, Shall not Netzer die because it
is written (Isa. xiv. 19), Thou art cast out of thy grave like
an abominable branch? They brought forth Boni בוני. He
said, Shall Boni die the death when it is written (Ex. iv. 22),
בני My son, my firstborn, is Israel? They replied, Shall not
Boni die the death when it is written (Ex. v. 23), So I will
slay thy son, thy firstborn son? They led out Thoda תודה.
He said, Shall Thoda die when it is written (Ps. c. 1), A
psalm לתודה of thanksgiving? They replied, Shall not Thoda
die when it is written (Ps. l. 23), He that sacrificeth praise,
he honoureth me?"

This is all that the Gemara tells us about Jeschu,
son of Stada or Pandira. It behoves us now to consider
whether he can have been the same person as our Lord.

That there really lived such a person as Jeschu Ben-
Pandira, and that he was a disciple of the Rabbi Jehoshua Ben-Perachia, I see no reason to doubt.

That he escaped from Alexander Jannæus with his
master into Egypt, and there studied magical arts; that
he returned after awhile to Judæa, and practised his
necromantic arts in his own country, is also not improbable. Somewhat later the Jews were famous, or in-
famous, throughout the Roman world as conjurors and
exorcists. Egypt was the head-quarters of magical
studies.

That Jeschu, son of Pandira, was stoned to death, in

accordance with the Law, for having practised magic, is also probable. The passages quoted are unanimous in stating that he was stoned for this offence. The Law decreed this as the death sorcerers were to undergo.

In the Talmud, Jeschu is first stoned and then crucified. The object of this double punishment being attributed to him is obvious. The Rabbis of the Gemara period had begun—like the Jew of Celsus—to confuse Jesus son of Mary with Jeschu the sorcerer. Their tradition told of a Jeschu who was stoned ; Christian tradition, of a Jesus who was crucified. They combined the punishments and fused the persons into one. But this was done very clumsily. It is possible that more than one Jehoshua has contributed to form the story of Jeschu in the Talmud. For his mother Stada is said to have been married to Paphos, son of Jehuda. Now Paphos Ben-Jehuda is a Rabbi whose name recurs several times in the Talmud as an associate of the illustrious Rabbi Akiba, who lived after the destruction of Jerusalem, and had his school at Bene-Barah. To him the first composition of the Mischna arrangements is ascribed. As a follower of the pseudo-Messiah Barcochab, in the war of Trajan and Hadrian, he sealed a life of enthusiasm with a martyr's death, A.D. 135, at the capture of Bether. When the Jews were dispersed and forbidden to assemble, Akiba collected the Jews and continued instructing them in the Law. Paphus remonstrated with him on the risk. Akiba answered by a parable. " A fox once went to the river side, and saw the fish flying in all directions. What do you fear ? asked the fox. The nets spread by the sons of men, answered the fish. Ah, my friends, said the fox, come on shore by me, and so you will escape the nets that drag the water." A few days after, Akiba was in prison, and Paphus also. Paphus said, " Blessed art thou, Rabbi Akiba, because thou art imprisoned for the words of the Law, and woe is me who am imprisoned for matters of no importance." [1]

We naturally wonder how it is that Stada, the mother of Jeschu, who was born about B.C. 120, should be represented as the wife of Paphus, son of Jehuda, who died about A.D. 150, two centuries and a half later.

It is quite possible that this Paphus lost his wife, who eloped from him with one Pandira, and became mother of a son named Jehoshua. The name of Jehoshua or Jesus is common enough.

In Gittin, Paphus is again mentioned. "There is who finds a fly in his cup, and he takes it out, and will not drink of it. And this is what did Paphus Ben-Jehuda, who kept the door shut upon his wife, and nevertheless she ran away from him." [2]

Mary, the plaiter of woman's hair, occurs in Chajigah. "Rabbi Bibai, when the angel of death at one time stood before him, said to his messenger, Go, and bring hither Mary, the women's hair-dresser. And the young man went," &c. [3]

·According to the Toledoth Jeschu, as we shall see presently, Mary's instructor is the Rabbi Simon Ben Schetach. She is visited and questioned by the Rabbi Akiba. This visitation by Akiba is given in the Talmudic tract, Calla, [4] and thence the author of the Toledoth Jeschu drew it.

"As once the Elders sat at the gate, there passed two boys before them. One uncovered his head, the other did not. Then said the Rabbi Elieser, The latter is certainly a Mamser; but the Rabbi Jehoshua [5] said, He is a Ben-hannidda. Akiba said, He is both a Mamser and a Ben-hannidda. They said to him, How canst thou

---

[1] Talmud, Tract. Beracoth, ix. fol. 61, b.   [2] Gittin, fol. 90, a.
[3] Chajigah, fol. 4, b.   [4] Calla, fol. 18, b.
[5] Son of Levi, according to the Toledoth Jeschu of Huldrich.

oppose the opinion of thy companions? He answered, I will prove what I have said. Then he went to the boy's mother, who was sitting in the market selling fruit, and said to her, My daughter, if you will tell me the truth I will promise you eternal life. She said to him, Swear to me. And he swore with his lips, but in his heart he did not ratify the oath." Then he learned what he desired to know, and came back to his companions and told them all.[1]

We have here corroborative evidence that this Stada and her son Jeschu lived at the time of Akiba and Paphus, that is, after the fall of Jerusalem, in the earlier part of the second century.

I think that probably the story grew up thus:

A certain Jehoshua, in the reign of Alexander Jannæus, went down into Egypt, and there learnt magic. He returned to Judæa, where he practised it, but was arrested at Lydda and executed by order of the Sanhedrim, by being stoned to death.

But who was this Jehoshua? Tradition was silent. However, there was a floating recollection of a Jehoshua born of one Stada, wife of Paphus, son of Jehuda, the companion of Akiba. The two Jehoshuas were confounded together. Thus stood the story when Origen wrote against Celsus in A.D. 176.

By A.D. 500 it had grown considerably. The Jew of Celsus had already fused Jesus of Nazareth with the other two Jehoshuas. This led to the Rabbis of the Gemara relating that Jehoshua was both stoned and crucified.

I do not say that this certainly is the origin of the story as it appears in the Talmud, but it bears on the

---

[1] In the apocryphal Gospel of Thomas, Jesus as a boy behaves without respect to his master and the elders; thence possibly this story was derived.

face of it strong likelihood that it is.   Jehoshua who
went into Egypt could not have been stoned to death
after the destruction of Jerusalem and the revolt of Barcochab, for then the Jews had not the power of life and
death in their hands. The execution must have taken
place long before ; yet the Rabbis whose names appear in
connection with the story—always excepting Jehoshua
son of Perachia—all belong to the second century after
Christ.

The solution I propose is simple, and it explains what
otherwise would be inexplicable.

If it be a true solution, it proves that the Jews in
A.D. 500, when the Babylonian Gemara was completed,
had no traditions whatever concerning Jesus of Nazareth.

We shall see next how the confusion that originated
in the Talmud grew into the monstrous romance of the
Toledoth Jeschu, the Jewish counter-Gospel of the
Middle Ages.

V

THE COUNTER-GOSPELS.

IN the thirteenth century it became known among the Christians that the Jews were in possession of an anti-evangel. It was kept secret, lest the sight of it should excite tumults, spoliation and massacre. But of the fact of its existence Christians were made aware by the account of converts.

There are, in reality, two such anti-evangels, each called Toldoth Jeschu, not recensions of an earlier text, but independent collections of the stories circulating among the Jews relative to the life of our Lord.

The name of Jesus, which in Hebrew is Joshua or Jehoshua (the Lord will sanctify) is in both contracted into Jeschu by the rejection of an *A in,* ישׁו for ישׁוע.

The Rabbi Elias, in his Tischbi, under the word Jeschu, says, "Because the Jews will not acknowledge him to be the Saviour, they do not call him Jeschua, but reject the *Ain* and call him Jeschu." And the Rabbi Abraham Perizol, in his book Maggers Abraham, c. 59, says, "His name was Jeschua; but as Rabbi Moses, the son of Majemoun of blessed memory, has written it, and as we find it throughout the Talmud, it is written Jeschu. They have carefully left out the *Ain,* because he was not able to save himself."

The Talmud in the Tract. Sanhedrim[1] says, "It is not lawful to name the name of a false God." On this account the Jews, rejecting the mission of our Saviour,

[1] Fol. 114.

refused to pronounce his name without mutilating it.
By omitting the *Ain*, the Cabbalists were able to give a
significance to the name. In its curtailed form it is
composed of the letters Jod, Schin, Vau, which are
taken to stand for יסח שסי וזכרונו jimmach schemo
vezichrono, "His name and remembrance shall be extinguished." This is the reason given by the Toledoth
Jeschu.

Who were the authors of the books called Toledoth
Jeschu, the two counter-Gospels, is not known.

Justin Martyr, who died A.D. 63, speaks of the blas-
phemous writings of the Jews about Jesus;[1] but that
they contained traditions of the life of the Saviour can
hardly be believed in presence of the silence of Josephus
and Justus, and the ignorance of the Jew of Celsus.
Origen says in his answer, that "though innumerable
lies and calumnies had been forged against the vener-
able Jesus, none had dared to charge him with any
intemperance whatever."[2] He speaks confidently, with
full assurance. If he had ever met with such a calumny,
he would not have denied its existence, he would have
set himself to work to refute it. Had such calumnious
writings existed, Origen would have been sure to know
of them. We may therefore be quite satisfied that none
such existed in his time, the middle of the third
century.

The Toledoth Jeschu comes before us with a flourish
of trumpets from Voltaire. "Le Toledos Jeschu," says
he, "est le plus ancien écrit Juif qui nous ait été trans-
mis contre notre religion. C'est une vie de Jesus Christ,
toute contraire à nos Saints Evangiles : elle parait être
du premier siècle, et même écrite avant les evangiles."[3]

---

[1] Justin Mart. Dialog. cum Tryph. c. 17 and 108.

[2] Cont. Cels. lib. iii.

[3] Lettres sur les Juifs. Œuvres, I. 69, p. 36.

A fair specimen of reckless judgment on a matter of importance, without having taken the trouble to examine the grounds on which it was made! Luther knew more of it than did Voltaire, and put it in a very different place :—

" The proud evil spirit carries on all sorts of mockery in this book. First he mocks God, the Creator of heaven and earth, and His Son Jesus Christ, as you may see for yourself, if you believe as a Christian that Christ is the Son of God. Next he mocks us, all Christendom, in that we believe in such a Son of God. Thirdly, he mocks his own fellow Jews, telling them such disgraceful, foolish, senseless affairs, as of brazen dogs and cabbage-stalks and such like, enough to make all dogs bark themselves to death, if they could understand it, at such a pack of idiotic, blustering, raging, nonsensical fools. Is not that a masterpiece of mockery which can thus mock all three at once? The fourth mockery is this, that whoever wrote it has made a fool of himself, as we, thank God, may see any day."

Luther knew the book, and translated it, or rather condensed it, in his " Schem Hamphoras." [1]

There are two versions of the Toledoth Jeschu, differing widely from one another. The first was published by Wagenseil, of Altdorf, in 1681. The second by Huldrich at Leyden in 1705. Neither can boast of an antiquity greater than, at the outside, the twelfth century. It is difficult to say with certainty which is the earlier of the two. Probably both came into use about the same time; the second certainly in Germany, for it speaks of Worms in the German empire.

According to the first, Jeschu (Jesus) was born in the year of the world 4671 (B.C. 910), in the reign of Alex-

[1] Luther's Works, Wittemberg, 1556, T. V. pp. 509—535. The passage quoted is on p. 513.

ander Jannæus (B.C. 106—79)! He was the son of
Joseph Pandira and Mary, a widow's daughter, the
sister of Jehoshua, who was affianced to Jochanan, disciple of Simeon Ben Schetah; and Jeschu became the
pupil of the Rabbi Elchanan. Mary is of the tribe of
Juda.

According to the second, Jeschu was born in the reign
of Herod the Proselyte, and was the son of Mary,
daughter of Calpus, and sister of Simeon, son of Calpus,
by Joseph Pandira, who carried her off from her husband,
Papus, son of Jehuda. Jeschu was brought up by
Joshua, son of Perachia, in the days of the illustrious
Rabbi Akiba! Mary is of the tribe of Benjamin.

The anachronisms of both accounts are so gross as to
prove that they were drawn up at a very late date, and
by Jews singularly ignorant of the chronology of their
history.

In the first, Mary is affianced to Jochanan, disciple of
Simeon Ben Schetah. Now Schimon or Simeon, son of
Scheta, is a well-known character. He is said to have
strangled eighty witches in one day, and to have been
the companion of Jehudu Ben Tabai. He flourished
B.C. 70.

In the second life we hear of Mary being the sister
of Simeon Ben Kalpus (Chelptu). He also is a well-
known Rabbi, of whom many miracles are related. He
lived in the time of the Emperor Antoninus, before
whom he stood as a disciple, when an old man (circ.
A.D. 160).

In this also the Rabbi Akiba is introduced. Akiba
died A.D. 135. Also the Rabbi Jehoshua Ben Levi.
Now this Rabbi's date can also be fixed with tolerable
accuracy. He was the teacher of the Rabbi Jochanan,
who compiled the Jerusalem Talmud. His date is
A.D. 220.

We have thus, in the two lives of Jeschu, the following personages introduced as contemporaries:

I.	II.
Jeschu born (date given), B.C. 910.	Herod the Great, B.C. 70—4.
Alexander Jannæus, B.C. 106—79.	R. Jehoshua Ben Perachia, c. B.C. 90.
R. Simeon Ben Schetach, B.C. 70.	R. Akiba, A.D. 135.
	R. Papus Ben Jehuda, c. A.D. 140.
	R. Jehoshua Ben Levi, c. A.D. 220.

The second Toledoth Jeschu closes with, "These are the words of Jochanan Ben Zaccai;" but it is not clear whether it is intended that the book should be included in "The words of Jochanan," or whether the reference is only to a brief sentence preceding this statement, "Therefore have they no part or lot in Israel. The Lord bless his people Israel with peace." Jochanan Ben Zaccai was a priest and ruler of Israel for forty years, from A.D. 30 or 33 to A.D. 70 or 73. He died at Jamnia, near Jerusalem (Jabne of the Philistines), and was buried at Tiberias.

Nor are these anachronisms the only proofs of the ignorance of the composers of the two anti-evangels. In the first, on the death of King Alexander Jannæus, the government falls into the hands of his wife Helena, who is represented as being "also called Oleina, and was the mother of King Mumbasius, afterwards called Hyrcanus, who was killed by his servant Herod."

The wife of Alexander Jannæus was Alexandra, not Helena; she reigned from B.C. 79 to B.C. 71. She was the mother of Hyrcanus and Aristobulus; but was quite distinct from Oleina, mother of Mumbasius, and Mumbasius was a very different person from Hyrcanus. Oleina was a queen of Adiabene in Assyria.

The first Life refers to the Talmud: "This is the same

Mary who dressed and curled women's hair, mentioned several times in the Talmud."

Both give absurd anecdotes to account for monks wearing shaven crowns; both reasons are different.

In the first Life, the Christian festivals of the Ascension "forty days after Jeschu was stoned," that of Christmas, and the Circumcision "eight days after," are spoken of as institutions of the Christian Church.

In the VIIIth Book of the Apostolical Constitutions, the festivals of the Nativity and the Ascension are spoken of,[1] consequently they must have been kept holy from a very early age. But it was not so with the feast of the Circumcision.

The 1st of Jannary was a great day among the heathen. In the Homilies of the Fathers down to the eighth century, the 1st of January is called the "Feast of Satan and Hell," and the faithful are cautioned against observing it. All participation in the festivities of that day was forbidden by the Council "in Trullo," in A.D. 692, and again in the Council of Rome, A.D. 744.

Pope Gelasius (A.D. 496) forbade all observance of the day, according to Baronius,[2] in the hope of rooting out every remembrance of the pagan ceremonies which were connected with it. In ancient Sacramentaries is a mass on this day, "de prohibendo ab idolis." Nevertheless, traces of the celebration of the Circumcision of Christ occur in the fourth century; for Zeno, Bishop of Verona (d. A.D. 380), preached a sermon on it. In the ancient Mozarabic Kalendar, in the Martyrology wrongly attributed to St. Jerome, and in the Gelasian Sacramentary, the Circumcision is indicated on January 1. But though noted in the Kalendars, the day was, for the reason of its being observed as a heathen festival, not

[1] Lib. viii. 33.   [2] Martyrol. Rom. ad. 1 Januar.

treated by the Church as a festival till very late. Litanies and penitential offices were appointed for it.

The notice in the Toledoth Jeschu, therefore, points to a time when the feast was observed with outward demonstration of joy, and the sanction of the Church accorded to other festivities.

The Toledoth Jeschu adopts the fable of the Sanhedrim and King having sent out an account of the trial of Jesus to the synagogues throughout the world to obtain from them an expression of opinion. The synagogue of Worms remonstrated against the execution of Christ. "The people of Girmajesa (Germany) and all the neighbouring country round Girmajesa which is now called Wormajesa (Worms), and which lies in the realm of the Emperor, and the little council in the town of Wormajesa, answered the King (Herod) and said, Let Jesus go, and slay him not! Let him live till he falls and perishes of his own accord."

The synagogues of several cities in the Middle Ages did, in fact, produce apocryphal letters which they pretended had been written by their forefathers remonstrating with the Jewish Sanhedrim at Jerusalem, and requesting that Jesus might be spared. An epistle was produced by the Jews of Ulm in A.D. 1348, another by the Jews of Ratisbon about the same date, from the council at Jerusalem to their synagogues.[1] The Jews of Toledo pretended to possess similar letters in the reign of Alfonso the Valiant, A.D. 1072. These letters probably served to protect them from feeling the full stress of persecution which oppressed the Jews elsewhere.

The most astonishing ignorance of Gospel accounts of Christ and the apostles is observable in both anti-evangels. Matthias and Matthew are the same, so are

[1] Fabricius, Codex Apocryph. N.T. ii. p. 493.

John the Baptist and John the Apostle, whilst Thaddæus is said to be "also called Paul," and Simon Peter
is confounded with Simon Magus.[1]

These are instances of the confusion of times and persons into which these counter-Gospels have fallen, and
they are sufficient to establish their late and worthless
character.

The two anti-Gospels are clearly not two editions of
an earlier text. The only common foundation on which
both were constructed was the mention of Jeschu, son
of Panthera, in the Talmud. Add to this such distorted
versions of Gospel stories as circulated among the Jews
in the Middle Ages, and we have the constituents of
both counter-Gospels. Both exhibit a profound ignorance of the sacred text, but a certain acquaintance with
prominent incidents in the narrative of the Evangelists,
not derived directly from the Gospels, but, as I believe,
from miracle-plays and pictorial and sculptured representations such as would meet the eye of a mediæval
Jew at every turn.

We have not to cast about far for a reason which shall
account for the production of these anti-evangels.

The persecution to which the Jews were subjected in
the Middle Ages from the bigotry of the rabble or the
cupidity of princes, fanned their dislike for Christianity
into a flame of intense mortal abhorrence of the Founder
of that religion whose votaries were their deadliest foes.
The Toledoth Jeschu is the utterance of this deep-seated
hatred,—the voice of an oppressed people execrating him
who had sprung from the holy race, and whose blood
was weighing on their heads.

And it is not improbable that the Gospel record of
the patient, loving life of Jesus may have exerted an

---

[1] Whereas the bitter conflict of Simon Peter and Simon Magus was a
subject well known in early Christian tradition.

influence on the young who ventured, with the daring
curiosity of youth, to explore those peaceful pages.
What answer had the Rabbis to make to those of their
own religion who were questioning and wavering ? They
had no counter-record to oppose to the Gospels, no tradition wherewith to contest the history written by the
Evangelists. The notices in the Talmud were scanty,
incomplete. It was open to dispute whether these
notices really related to Christ Jesus.

Under such circumstances, a book which professed to
give a true account of Jesus was certain to be hailed and
accepted without too close a scrutiny as to its authenticity ; much as in the twelfth century Joseph Ben
Gorion's "Jewish War" was assumed to be authentic.

The Toledoth Jeschu or "Birth of Jesus" boldly identified the Jesus of the Gospels with the Jeschu of the
Talmud, and attempted to harmonize the Rabbinic and
the Christian stories.

There is a certain likeness between the two counter-
Gospels, but this arises solely from each author being
actuated by the same motives as the other, and from
both deriving from common sources,—the Talmud and
Jewish misrepresentations of Gospel events.

But if there be a likeness, there is sufficient dissimi-
larity to make it evident that the two authors wrote
independently, and had no common written text to
amplify and adorn.

VI

THE FIRST TOLEDOTH JESCHU.

WE will take first the WAGENSEIL edition of the TOLEDOTH JESCHU,[1] and give an outline of the story, only suppressing the most offensive particulars, and commenting on the narrative as we proceed. Wagenseil's Toledoth Jeschu begins as follows:

"In the year of the world 4671, in the days of King Jannæus, a great misfortune befel Israel. There arose at that time a scape-grace, a wastrel and worthless fellow, of the fallen race of Judah, named Joseph Pandira. He was a well-built man, strong and handsome, but he spent his time in robbery and violence. His dwelling was at Bethlehem, in Juda. And there lived near him a widow with her daughter, whose name was Mirjam; and this is the same Mirjam who dressed and curled women's hair, who is mentioned several times in the Talmud."

It is remarkable that the author begins with the very phrase found in Josephus. He calls the appearance of our Lord "a great misfortune which befel Israel." Josephus, after the passage which has been intruded into his text relative to the miracles and death of Christ, says, "About this time another great misfortune set the Jews in commotion;" from which it appears as if Josephus regarded the preaching of Christ as a great misfortune. That he made no such reference has been already shown.

[1] Wagenseil: Tela ignea Satanæ. Hoc est arcani et horribiles Judæorum adversus Christum Deum et Christianam religionem libri anecdoti; Altdorf, 1681.

The author also places the birth of Jesus, in accordance with the Talmud, in the reign of Alexander Jannæus, who reigned from B.C. 106 to B.C. 79. He reckons from the creation of the world, and gives the year as 4671 (B.C. 910). This manner of reckoning was only introduced among the Jews in the fourth century after Christ, and did not become common till the twelfth century.

The Wagenscil Toledoth goes on to say that the widow engaged Mirjam to an amiable, God-fearing youth, named Jochanan (John), a disciple of the Rabbi Simeon, son of Shetach (fl. B.C. 70); but he went away to Babylon, and she became the mother of Jeschu by Joseph Pandira. The child was named Joshua, after his uncle, and was given to the Rabbi Elchanan to be instructed in the Law.

One day Jeschu, when a boy, passed before the Rabbi Simeon Ben Shetach and other members of the Sanhedrim without uncovering his head and bowing his knee. The elders were indignant. Three hundred trumpets were blown, and Jeschu was excommunicated and cast out of the Temple. Then he went away to Galilee, and spent there several years.

" Now at this time the unutterable Name of God was engraved in the Temple on the corner-stone. For when King David dug the foundations, he found there a stone in the ground on which the Name of God was engraved, and he took it and placed it in the Holy of Holies.

" But as the wise men feared lest some inquisitive youth should learn this Name, and be able thereby to destroy the world, which God avert ! they made, by magic, two brazen lions, which they set before the entrance to the Holy of Holies, one on the right, the other on the left.

" Now if any one were to go within, and learn the holy Name, then the lions would begin to roar as he came out, so that, out of alarm and bewilderment, he would lose his presence of mind and forget the Name.

"And Jeschu left Upper Galilee, and came secretly to Jerusalem, and went into the Temple and learned there the holy writing; and after he had written the incommunicable Name on parchment, he uttered it, with intent that he might feel no pain, and then he cut into his flesh, and hid the parchment with its inscription therein. Then he uttered the Name once more, and made so that his flesh healed up again.

"And when he went out at the door, the lions roared, and he forgot the Name. Therefore he hasted outside the town, cut into his flesh, took the writing out, and when he had sufficiently studied the signs he retained the Name in his memory."

It is scarcely necessary here to point out the amazing ignorance of the author of the Toledoth Jeschu in making David the builder of the Temple, and in placing the images of lions at the entrance to the Holy of Holies. The story is introduced because Jeschu, son of Stada, in the Talmud is said to have made marks on his skin. But the author knew his Talmud very imperfectly. The Babylonian Gemara says, "Did not the son of Stada mark the magical arts on his skin, and bring them with him out of Egypt?" The story in the Talmud which accounted for the power of Jeschu to work miracles was quite different from that in the Toledoth Jeschu. In the Talmud he has power by bringing out of Egypt, secretly cut on his skin, the magic arts there privately taught; in the Toledoth he acquires his power by learning the incommunicable Name and hiding it under his flesh.

However, the author says, "He could not have penetrated into the Holy of Holies without the aid of magic; for how would the holy priests and followers of Aaron have suffered him to enter there? This must certainly have been done by the aid of magic." But the author gives no account of how Jeschu learned magic. That we ascertain from the Huldrich text, where we are told that Jeschu spent many years in Egypt, the head-quarters of those who practised magic.

Having acquired this knowledge, Jeschu went into Galilee and proclaimed himself to have been the creator of the world, and born of a virgin, according to the prophecy of Isaiah (vii. 14). As a sign of the truth of his mission, he said :

" Bring me here a dead man, and I will restore him to life. Then all the people hasted and dug into a grave, but found nothing in it but bones.

" Now when they told him that they had found only bones, he said, Bring them hither to me.

" So when they had brought them, he placed the bones together, and surrounded them with skin and flesh and muscles, so that the dead man stood up alive on his feet.

" And when the people saw this, they wondered greatly; and he said, Do ye marvel at this that I have done? Bring hither a leper, and I will heal him.

" So when they had placed a leper before him, he gave him health in like manner, by means of the incommunicable Name. And all the people that saw this fell down before him, prayed to him and said, Truly thou art the Son of God !

" But after five days the report of what had been done came to Jerusalem, to the holy city, and all was related that Jeschu had wrought in Galilee. Then all the people rejoiced greatly; but the elders, the pious men, and the company of the wise men, wept bitterly. And the great and the little Sanhedrim mourned, and at length agreed that they would send a deputation to him.

" For they thought that, perhaps, with God's help, they might overpower him, and bring him to judgment, and condemn him to death.

" Therefore they sent unto him Ananias and Achasias, the noblest men of the little council; and when they had come to him, they bowed themselves before him reverently, in order to

deceive him as to their purpose. And he, thinking that they
believed in him, received them with smiling countenance, and
placed them in his assembly of profligates.

"They said unto him, The most pious and illustrious
among the citizens of Jerusalem sent us unto thee, to hear if
it shall please thee to go to them; for they have heard say
that thou art the Son of God.

"Then answered Jeschu and said, They have heard aright.
I will do all that they desire, but only on condition that both
the great and lesser Sanhedrim and all who have despised my
origin shall come forth to meet me, and shall honour and receive me as servants of their Lord, when I come to them.

"Thereupon the messengers returned to Jerusalem and related all that they had heard.

"Then answered the elders and the righteous men, We
will do all that he desires. Therefore these men went again
to Jeschu, and told him that it should be even as he had
said.

"And Jeschu said, I will go forthwith on my way! And
it came to pass, when he had come as far as Nob,[1] nigh unto
Jerusalem, that he said to his followers, Have ye here a good
and comely ass?

"They answered him that there was one even at hand.
Therefore he said, Bring him hither to me.

"And a stately ass was brought unto him, and he sat upon
it, and rode into Jerusalem. And as Jeschu entered into the
city, all the people went forth to meet him. Then he cried,
saying, Of me did the prophet Zacharias testify, Behold thy
King cometh unto thee, righteous and a Saviour, poor, and
riding on an ass, and a colt the foal of an ass!

"Now when they heard this, all wept bitterly and rent
their clothes.. And the most righteous hastened to the Queen.
She was the Queen Helena, wife of King Jannæus, and she

---

[1] Nob was a city of Benjamin, situated on a height near Jerusalem, on
one of the roads which led from the north to the capital, and within sight
of it, as is certain from the description of the approach of the Assyrian
army in Isaiah (x. 28—32).

reigned after her husband's death.   She was also called
Oleina, and had a son, King Mumbasus, otherwise called
Hyrcanus, who was slain by his servant Herod.[1]

" And they said to her, He stirreth up the people; therefore is he guilty of the heaviest penalty.   Give unto us full
power, and we will take him by subtlety.

" Then the Queen said, Call him hither before me, and I
will hear his accusation.   But she thought to save him out
of their hands because he was related to her.   But when the
elders saw her purpose, they said to her, Think not to do
this, Lady and Queen! and show him favour and good; for
by his witchcraft he deceives the people.   And they related
to her how he had obtained the incommunicable Name. . . .

" Then the Queen answered, In this will I consent unto
you; bring him hither that I may hear what he saith, and
see with my eyes what he doth; for the whole world speaks
of the countless miracles that he has wrought.

" And the wise men answered, This will we do as thou
hast said.   So they sent and summoned Jeschu, and he came
and stood before the Queen."

In the sight of Queen Helena, Jeschu then healed a
leper and raised a dead man to life.

" Then Jeschu said, Of me did Isaiah prophesy: The
lame shall leap as a hart, and the tongue of the dumb shall
sing.

" So the Queen turned to the wise men and said, How say
ye that this man is a magician?   Have I not seen with my
eyes the wonders he has wrought as being the Son of God?

" But the wise men answered and said, Let it not come
into the heart of the Queen to say so; for of a truth he is a
wizard.

" Then the Queen said, Away with you, and bring no such
accusations again before me!

[1] Herod put Alexander Hyrcanus to death B.C. 30.   Alexandra, the
mother of Hyrcanus, reigned after the death of Jannæus, from B.C. 79 to
B.C. 71.

"Therefore the wise men went forth with sad hearts, and one turned to another and said, Let us use subtlety, that we may get him into our hands. And one said to another, If it seems right unto you, let one of us learn the Name, as he did, and work miracles, and perchance thus we shall secure him. And this counsel pleased the elders, and they said, He who will learn the Name and secure the Fatherless One shall receive a double reward in the future life.

"And thereupon one of the elders stood up, whose name was Judas, and spake unto them, saying, Are ye agreed to take upon you the blame of such an action, if I speak the incommunicable Name? for if so, I will learn it, and it may happen that God in His mercy may bring the Fatherless One into my power.

"Then all cried out with one voice, The guilt be on us; but do thou make the effort and succeed.

"Thereupon he went into the Holiest Place, and did what Jeschu had done. And after that he went through the city and raised a cry, Where are those who have proclaimed abroad that the Fatherless is the Son of God? Cannot I, who am mere flesh and blood, do all that Jeschu has done?

"And when this came to the ears of the Queen, Judas was brought before her, and all the elders assembled and followed him. Then the Queen summoned Jeschu, and said to him, Show us what thou hast done last. And he began to work miracles before all the people.

"Thereat Judas spake to the Queen and to all the people, saying, Let nothing that has been wrought by the Fatherless make you wonder, for were he to set his nest between the stars, yet would I pluck him down from thence!

"Then said Judas, Moses our teacher said:

"If thy brother, the son of thy mother, or thy son, or thy daughter, or the wife of thy bosom, or thy friend, which is as thine own soul, entice thee secretly, saying, Let us go and serve other gods, which thou hast not known, thou, nor thy fathers;

"Namely, of the gods of the people which are round about

you, nigh unto thee, or far off from thee, from the one end of
the earth even unto the other end of the earth;

"Thou shalt not consent unto him, nor hearken unto him;
neither shall thine eye pity him, neither shalt thou spare,
neither shalt thou conceal him:

"But thou shalt surely kill him; thine hand shall be first
upon him to put him to death, and afterwards the hand of
all the people.

"And thou shalt stone him with stones, that he die; because he hath sought to thrust thee away from the Lord thy
God, which brought thee out of the land of Egypt, from the
house of bondage.

"But the Fatherless One answered, Did not Isaias prophesy of me? And my father David, did he not speak of
me? The Lord said unto me, Thou art my Son; this day
have I begotten thee. Desire of me, and I will give thee
the heathen for thine inheritance and the uttermost part of
the earth for thy possession. Thou shalt rule them with a
rod of iron, and break them in pieces like a potter's vessel.
And in like manner he speaks in another place, The Lord said
unto my Lord, Sit thou on my right hand, till I make thine
enemies my footstool! And now, behold! I will ascend to
my Heavenly Father, and will sit me down at His right hand.
Ye shall see it with your eyes, but thou, Judas, shalt not
prevail!

"And when Jeschu had spoken the incommunicable Name,
there came a wind and raised him between heaven and earth.
Thereupon Judas spake the same Name, and the wind raised
him also between heaven and earth. And they flew, both of
them, around in the regions of the air; and all who saw it
marvelled.

"Judas then spake again the Name, and seized Jeschu, and
thought to cast him to the earth. But Jeschu also spake the
Name, and sought to cast Judas down, and they strove one
with the other."

Finally Judas prevails, and casts Jeschu to the ground,
and the elders seize him, his power leaves him, and he

is subjected to the tauntings of his captors. Then sentence of death was spoken against him.

" But when Jeschu found his power gone, he cried and said, Of me did my father David speak, For thy sake are we killed all the day long; we are counted as sheep for the slaughter.

" Now when the disciples of Jeschu saw this, and all the multitude of sinners who had followed him, they fought against the elders and wise men of Jerusalem, and gave Jeschu opportunity to escape out of the city.

" And he hasted to Jordan; and when he had washed therein his power returned, and with the Name he again wrought his former miracles.

" Thereafter he went and took two millstones, and made them swim on the water; and he seated himself thereon, and caught fishes to feed the multitudes that followed him."

Before going any further, it is advisable to make a few remarks on what has been given of this curious story.

The Queen Helena is probably the mother of Constantine, who went to Jerusalem in A.D. 326 to see the holy sites, and, according to an early legend, discovered the three crosses on Calvary. There are several incidents in the apocryphal story which bear a resemblance to the incidents in the Toledoth Jeschu.

The Empress Helena favours the Christians against the Jews. Where three crosses are found, a person suffering from " a grievous and incurable disease" is applied to the crosses, and recovers on touching the true one. Then the same experiment is tried with a dead body, with the same success.[1] According to the Apocryphal Acts of St. Cyriacus, a Jew named Judas was brought before the Empress, and ordered to point out where the

---

[1] Sozomen, Hist. Eccl. ii. 1.

cross was buried. Judas resisted, but was starved in a well till he revealed the secret. The resemblance between the stories consists in the names of Helena and Judas, and the miracles of healing a leper, and raising a dead man to life.

According to the Apocryphal Acts of St. Cyriacus, Judas was the grandson of Zacharias, and nephew of St. Stephen the protomartyr.[1]

It is remarkable that Jeschu should be made to quote two passages in the Psalms as prophecies of himself, both of which are used in this manner in the New Testament: Ps. ii. 7, in Acts xiii. 33, and again Heb. i. 5, and v. 5 ; and Ps. cx. 1, in St. Matthew xxii. 44, and the corresponding passages in St. Mark and St. Luke ; also in Acts ii. 34, in 1 Cor. xv. 25, and Heb. i. 13.

The scene of the struggle in the air is taken from the contest of St. Peter with Simon Magus, and reminds one of the contest in the Arabian Nights between the Queen of Beauty and the Jin in the story of the Second Calender.

The putting forth from land on a millstone on the occasion of the miraculous draught of fishes is probably a perversion of the incident of Jesus entering into the boat of Peter—the stone—before the miracle was performed, according to St. Luke, v. 1—8. In the Toledoth Jeschu there are two millstones which our Lord sets afloat, and he mounts one, and then the fishes are caught ; in St. Luke's Gospel there are two boats.

" He saw two ships standing by the lake. . . . . And he entered into one of the ships, which was Simon's, and prayed him that he would thrust out a little from the land. And he sat down and taught the people out of the ship. Now when he had left speaking, he said unto Simon, Launch out into the deep, and let down your nets for a draught."

[1] Acta Sanct. Mai. T. I. pp. 445—451.

It was standing on the swimming-stone, according to
the Huldrich version, that Jeschu preached to the people,
and declared to them his divine mission.

The story goes on. The Sanhedrim, fearing to allow
Jeschu to remain at liberty, send Judas after him to
Jordan. Judas pronounces a great incantation, which
obliges the Angel of Sleep to seal the eyes of Jeschu and
his disciples. Then, whilst they sleep, he comes and
cuts from the arm of Jeschu a scrap of parchment on
which the Name of Jehovah is written, and which was
concealed under the flesh. Jeschu awakes, and a spirit
appears to him and vexes him sore. Then he feels that
his power is gone, and he announces to his disciples
that his hour is come when he must be taken by his
enemies.

The disciples, amongst whom is Judas, who, unob-
served, has mingled with them, are sorely grieved; but
Jeschu encourages them, and bids them believe in him,
and they will obtain thrones in heaven. Then he goes
with them to the Paschal Feast, in hopes of again being
able to penetrate into the Holy of Holies, and reading
again the incommunicable Name, and of thus recovering
his power. But Judas forewarns the elders, and as Jeschu
enters the Temple he is attacked by armed men. The
Jewish servants do not know Jeschu from his disciples.
Accordingly Judas flings himself down before him, and
thus indicates whom they are to take. Some of the disciples offer resistance, but are speedily overcome, and
take to flight to the mountains, where they are caught
and executed.

" But the elders of Jerusalem led Jeschu in chains into the
city, and bound him to a marble pillar, and scourged him,
and said, Where are now all the miracles thou hast wrought?
And they plaited a crown of thorns and set it on his head.
Then the Fatherless was in anguish through thirst, and he

cried, saying, Give me water to drink! So they gave him
acid vinegar; and after he had drunk thereof he cried, Of
me did my father David prophesy, They gave me gall to
eat, and in my thirst they gave me vinegar to drink.[1] But
they answered, If thou wert God, why didst thou not know
it was vinegar before tasting of it? Now thou art at the
brink of the grave, and changest not. But Jeschu wept and
said, My God, my God! why hast thou forsaken me? And
the elders said, If thou be God, save thyself from our hands.
But Jeschu answered, saying, My blood is shed for the redemption of the world, for Isaiah prophesied of me, He was
wounded for our transgression and bruised for our iniquities;
our chastisement lies upon him that we may have peace, and
by his wounds we are healed.[2] Then they led Jeschu forth
before the greater and the lesser Sanhedrim, and he was sen-
tenced to be stoned, and then to be hung on a tree. And it
was the eve of the Passover and of the Sabbath. And they
led him forth to the place where the punishment of stoning
was wont to be executed, and they stoned him there till he
was dead. And after that, the wise men hung him on the
tree; but no tree would bear him; each brake and yielded.
And when even was come the wise men said, We may not,
on account of the Fatherless, break the letter of the law
(which forbids that one who is hung should remain all night
on the tree). Though he may have set at naught the law,
yet will not we. Therefore they buried the Fatherless in the
place where he was stoned. And when midnight was come,
the disciples came and seated themselves on the grave, and
wept and lamented him. Now when Judas saw this, he took
the body away and buried it in his garden under a brook.
He diverted the water of the brook elsewhere; but when the
body was laid in its bed, he brought its waters back again
into their former channel.

"Now on the morrow, when the disciples had assembled
and had seated themselves weeping, Judas came to them and
said, Why weep you? Seek him who was buried. And

---

[1] Ps. lxix. 22.   [2] Isa. liii. 5.

they dug and sought, and found him not, and all the company cried, He is not in the grave; he is risen and ascended into heaven, for, when he was yet alive, he said, He would raise him up, Selah !"

When the Queen heard that the elders had slain Jeschu and had buried him, and that he was risen again, she ordered them within three days to produce the body or forfeit their lives. In sore alarm, the elders seek the body, but cannot find it. They therefore proclaim a fast.

"Now there was amongst them an elder whose name was Tanchuma; and he went forth in sore distress, and wandered in the fields, and he saw Judas sitting in his garden eating. Then Tanchuma drew near to him, and said to him, What doest thou, Judas, that thou eatest meat, when all the Jews fast and are in grievous distress?

"Then Judas was astonished, and asked the occasion of the fast. And the Rabbi Tanchuma answered him, Jeschu the Fatherless is the occasion, for he was hung up and buried on the spot where he was stoned; but now is he taken away, and we know not where he is gone. And his worthless disciples cry out that he is ascended into heaven. Now the Queen has condemned us Israelites to death unless we find him.

"Judas asked, And if the Fatherless One were found, would it be the salvation of Israel? The Rabbi Tanchuma answered that it would be even so.

"Then spake Judas, Come, and I will show you the man whom ye seek; for it was I who took the Fatherless from his grave. For I feared lest his disciples should steal him away, and I have hidden him in my garden and led a waterbrook over the place.

"Then the Rabbi Tanchuma hasted to the elders of Israel, and told them all. And they came together, and drew him forth, attached to the tail of a horse, and brought him before the Queen, and said, See! this is the man who, they say, has ascended into heaven!

" Now when the Queen saw this, she was filled with shame, and answered not a word.

" Now it fell out, that in dragging the body to the place, the hair was torn off the head; and this is the reason why monks shave their heads. It is done in remembrance of what befel Jeschu.

" And after this, in consequence thereof, there grew to be strife between the Nazarenes and the Jews, so that they parted asunder; and when a Nazarene saw a Jew he slew him. And from day to day the distress grew greater, during thirty years. And the Nazarenes assembled in thousands and tens of thousands, and hindered the Israelites from going up to the festivals at Jerusalem. And then there was great distress, such as when the golden calf was set up, so that they knew not what to do.

" And the belief of the opposition grew more and more, and spread on all sides. Also twelve godless runagates separated and traversed the twelve realms, and everywhere in the assemblies of the people uttered false prophecies.

" Also many Israelites adhered to them, and these were men of high renown, and they strengthened the faith in Jeschu. And because they gave themselves out to be messengers of him who was hung, a great number followed them from among the Israelites.

" Now when the wise men saw the desperate condition of affairs, one said to another, Woe is unto us! for we have deserved it through our sins. And they sat in great distress, and wept, and looked up to heaven and prayed.

" And when they had ended their prayer, there rose up a very aged man of the elders, by name Simon Cephas, who understood prophecy, and he said to the others, Hearken to me, my brethren! and if ye will consent unto my advice, I will separate these wicked ones from the company of the Israelites, that they may have neither part nor lot with Israel. But the sin do ye take upon you.

"Then answered they all and said,.The sin be on us ; declare unto us thy counsel, and fulfil thy purpose.

"Therefore Simon, son of Cephas, went into the Holiest Place and wrote the incommunicable Name, and cut into his flesh and hid the parchment therein. And when he came forth out of the Temple he took forth the writing, and when he had learned the Name he betook himself to the chief city of the Nazarenes,[1] and he cried there with a loud voice, Let all who believe in Jeschu come unto me, for I am sent by him to you !

"Then there came to him multitudes as the sand on the sea-shore, and they said to him, Show us a sign that thou art sent ! And he said, What sign ? They answered him, Even the signs that Jeschu wrought when he was alive."

Accordingly he heals a leper and restores a dead man to life. And when the people saw this, they submitted to him, as one sent to them by Jeschu.

"Then said Simon Cephas to them, Yea, verily, Jeschu did send me to you, and now swear unto me that ye will obey me in all things that I command you.

"And they swore to him, We will do all things that thou commandest.

"Then Simon Cephas said, Ye know that he who hung on the tree was an enemy to the Israelites and the Law, because of the prophecy of Isaiah, Your new moons and festivals my soul hateth.[2] And that he had no pleasure in the Israelites, according to the saying of Hosea, Ye are not my people.[3] Now, although it is in his power to blot them in the twinkling of an eye from off the face of the earth, yet will he not root them out, but will keep them ever in the midst of you as a witness to his stoning and hanging on the tree. He endured these pains and the punishment of death, to redeem your souls from hell. And now he warns and commands you

---

[1] Rome. Simon Cephas is Simon Peter, but the miraculous power attributed to him perhaps belongs to the story of Simon Magus.

[2] Isa. i, 14.   [3] Hosea i. 9.

to do no harm to any Jew. Yea, even should a Jew say to a Nazarene, Go with me a mile, he shall go with him twain; or should a Nazarene be smitten by a Jew on one cheek, let him turn to him the other also, that the Jews may enjoy in this world their good things, for in the world to come they must suffer their punishment in hell. If ye do these things, then shall ye merit to sit with them (*i.e.* the apostles) on their thrones.[1]

" And this also doth he require of you, that ye do not celebrate the Feast of Unleavened Bread, but that ye keep holy the day on which he died. And in place of the Feast of Pentecost, that ye keep the fortieth day after his stoning, on which he went up into heaven. And in place of the Feast of Tabernacles, that ye keep the day of his Nativity, and eight days after that ye shall celebrate his Circumcision."

The Christians promised to do as Cephas commanded them, but they desired him to reside in the midst of them in their great city.

To this he consented. " I will dwell with you," said he, " if ye will promise to permit me to abstain from all food, and to eat only the bread of poverty and drink the water of affliction. Ye must also build me a tower in the midst of the city, wherein I may spend the rest of my days."

This was done. The tower was built and called " Peter," and in this Cephas dwelt till his death six years after. " In truth, he served the God of our fathers, Abraham, Isaac and Jacob, and composed many beautiful hymns, which he dispersed among the Jews, that they might serve as a perpetual memorial of him; and he divided all his hymns among the Rabbis of Israel."

On his death he was buried in the tower.

After his death, a man named Elias assumed the place of messenger of Jeschu, and he declared that Simon

---

[1] Matt. xix. 28.

Cephas had deceived the Christians, and that he, Elias, was an apostle of Jeschu, rather than Cephas, and that the Christians should follow him. The Christians asked for a sign.

Elias said, "What sign do ye ask?" Then a stone fell from the tower Peter, and smote him that he died. "Thus," concludes this first version of the Toledoth Jeschu, "may all Thine enemies perish, O Lord; but may those that love Thee be as the sun when it shineth in its strength!"

Thus ends this wonderful composition, which carries its own condemnation with it.

The two captures and sentences of Jeschu are apparently two forms of Jewish legend concerning Christ's death, which the anonymous writer has clumsily combined.

The scene in Gethsemane is laid on the other side of Jordan. It is manifestly imitated from the Gospels, but not directly, probably from some mediæval sculptured representation of the Agony in the Garden, common outside every large church.[1] In place of an angel appearing to comfort Christ, an evil spirit vexes him. The kiss of Judas is transformed into a genuflexion or prostration before him, and takes place, not in the Garden, but in the Temple. The resistance of the disciples is mentioned. Jeschu is bound to a marble pillar and scourged. Of this the Gospels say nothing; but the pillar is an invariable feature in artistic representations of the scourging. Two of the sayings on the Cross are correctly given. In agreement with the account in the

---

[1] The Oelberg was especially characteristic of German churches, and was erected chiefly in the fifteenth and sixteenth centuries. They remain at Nürnberg, Xanten, Worms, Marburg, Donauwörth, Landshut, Wasserburg, Ratisbon, Klosterneuburg, Wittenberg, Merseburg, Lucerne, Bruges, &c.

Talmud, Jeschu is stoned, and then, to identify the son of Panthera with the son of Mary, is hung on a tree. The tree breaks, and he falls to the ground. The visitor to Ober Ammergau Passion Play will remember the scene of Judas hanging himself, and the tree snapping. The Toledoth Jeschu does not say that Jeschu was crucified, but that he was hung. The suicide of Judas was identified with the death of Jesus. If the author of the anti-evangel saw the scene of the breaking bough in a miracle-play, he would perhaps naturally transfer it to Christ.

The women seated late at night by the sepulchre, or coming early with spices, a feature in miracle-plays of the Passion, are transformed into the disciples weeping above the grave. The angel who addresses them, in the Toledoth Jeschu, becomes Judas.

In miracle-plays, Claudia Procula, the wife of Pilate, assumes a prominence she does not occupy in the Gospels; she may have originated the idea in the mind of the author of Wagenseil's Toledoth, of the Queen Helena. That he confounded the Queen of King Jannæus with the mother of Constantine is not wonderful. The latter was the only historical princess who showed sympathy with the Christians at Jerusalem, and of whose existence the anonymous author was aware, probably through the popular mediæval romance of Helena, " La belle Helène." He therefore fell without a struggle into the gross anachronism of making the Empress Helena the wife of Jannæus, and contemporary with Christ.

In the Toledoth Jeschu of Wagenseil, Simon Peter is represented as a Jew ruling the Christians in favour of the Jews. The Papacy must have been fully organized when this anti-evangel was written, and the Jews must have felt the protection accorded them by the Popes

against their persecutors. St. Gregory the Great wrote
letters, in 591 and 598, in behalf of the Jews who were
maltreated in Italy and Sicily. Alexander II., in 1068,
wrote a letter to the Bishops of Gaul exhorting them to
protect the Jews against the violence of the Crusaders,
who massacred them on their way to the East. He
gave as his reason for their protection the very one put
into Simon Cephas' mouth in the Toledoth Jeschu, that
God had preserved them and scattered them in all
countries as witnesses to the truth of the Gospel. In the
cruel confiscation of their goods, and expulsion from
France by Philip Augustus, and the simultaneous persecution they underwent in England, Innocent III. took
their side, and insisted, in 1199, on their being protected
from violence. Gregory IX. defended them when maltreated in Spain and in France by the Crusaders in 1236,
on their appeal to him for protection. In 1246, the Jews
of Germany appealed to the Pope, Innocent IV., against
the ecclesiastical and secular princes who pillaged them
on false charges. Innocent wrote, in 1247, ordering
those who had wronged them to indemnify them for
their losses.

In 1417, the Jews of Constance came to meet Mar-
tin V., as their protector, on his coronation, with hymns
and torches, and presented him with the Pentateuch,
which he had the discourtesy to refuse, saying that they
might have the Law, but they did not understand it.

The claim made in the Toledoth Jeschu that the
Papacy was a government in the interest of the Jews
against the violence of the Christians, points to the thirteenth century as the date of the composition of this
book, a century when the Jews suffered more from
Christian brutality than at any other period, when
their exasperation against everything Christian was
wrought to its highest pitch, and when they found the

Chair of Peter their only protection against extermination by the disciples of Christ.

Some dim reference may be made to the anti-pope of Jewish blood, Peter Leonis, who took the name of Anacletus II., and who survives in modern Jewish legend as the Pope Elchanan. Anacletus II. (A.D. 1130—1138) maintained his authority in Rome against Innocent II., and from his refuge in the tower of St. Angelo defied the Emperor Lothair, who had marched to Rome to install Innocent. Anacletus was accused of showing favour to the Jews, whose blood he inherited—his father was a Jewish usurer. When Christians shrank from robbing the churches of their silver and golden ornaments, required by Anacletus to pay his mercenaries and bribe the venal Romans, he is said to have entrusted the odious task to the Jews.

Jewish legend has converted the Jewish anti-pope into the son of the Rabbi Simeon Ben Isaac, of Mainz, who died A.D. 1096. According to the story, the child Elchanan was stolen from his father and mother by a Christian nurse, was taken charge of by monks, grew up to be ordained priest, and finally was elected Pope.

As a child he had been wont to play chess with his father, and had learned from him a favourite move whereby to check-mate his adversary.

The Jews of Germany suffered from oppression, and appointed the Rabbi Simeon to bear their complaints to the Pope. The old Jew went to Rome and was introduced to the presence of the Holy Father. Elchanan recognized him at once, and sent forth all his attendants, then proposed a game of chess with the Rabbi. When the Pope played the favourite move of the old Jew, Simeon Ben Isaac sprang up, smote his brow, and cried out, " I thought none knew this move save I and my long-lost child." " I am that child," answered the

Pope, and he flung himself into the arms of the aged Jew.[1]

That the Wagenseil Toledoth Jeschu was written in the eleventh, twelfth or thirteenth century appears probable from the fact stated, that it was in these centuries that the Jews were more subjected to persecution, spoliation and massacre than in any other; and the Toledoth Jeschu is the cry of rage of a tortured people,—a curse hurled at the Founder of that religion which oppressed them.

In the eleventh century the Jews in the great Rhine cities were massacred by the ferocious hosts of Crusaders under Ernico, Count of Leiningen, and the priests Folkmar and Goteschalk. At the voice of their leaders (A.D. 1096), the furious multitude of red-crossed pilgrims spread through the cities of the Rhine and the Moselle, massacring pitilessly all the Jews that they met with in their passage. In their despair, a great number preferred being their own destroyers to awaiting certain death at the hands of their enemies. Several shut themselves up in their houses, and perished amidst flames their own hands had kindled; some attached heavy stones to their garments, and precipitated themselves and their treasures into the Rhine or Moselle. Mothers stifled their children at the breast, saying that they preferred sending them to the bosom of Abraham to seeing them torn away to be nurtured in a religion which bred tigers.

Some of the ecclesiastics behaved with Christian humanity. The Bishops of Worms and Spires ran some risk in saving as many as they could of this defenceless people. The Archbishop of Treves, less generous, gave refuge to such only as would consent to receive baptism, and coldly consigned the rest to the knives and halters

---

[1] Máásè, c. 188. I have told the story more fully in the Christmas Number of "Once a Week," 1868.

of the Christian fanatics. The Archbishop of Mainz was more than suspected of participation in the plunder of his Jewish subjects. The Emperor took on himself the protection and redress of the wrongs endured by the Jews, and it was apparently at this time that the Jews were formally taken under feudal protection by the Emperor. They became his men, owing to him special allegiance, and with full right therefore to his protection.

The Toledoth Jeschu of Wagenseil was composed by a German Jew; that is apparent from its mention of the letter of the synagogue of Worms to the Sanhedrim. Had it been written in the eleventh century, it would not have represented the Pope as the refuge of the persecuted Jews, for it was the Emperor who redressed their wrongs.

But it was in the thirteenth century that the Popes stood forth as the special protectors of the Jews. On May 1, 1291, the Jewish bankers throughout France were seized and imprisoned by order of Philip the Fair, and forced to pay enormous mulcts. Some died under torture, most yielded, and then fled the inhospitable realm. Five years after, in one day, all the Jews in France were taken, their property confiscated to the Crown, the race expelled the realm.

In 1320, the Jews of the South of France, notwithstanding persecution and expulsion, were again in numbers and perilous prosperity. On them burst the fury of the Pastoureaux. Five hundred took refuge in the royal castle of Verdun on the Garonne. The royal officers refused to defend them. The shepherds set fire to the lower stories of a lofty tower; the Jews slew each other, having thrown their children to the mercy of their assailants. Everywhere, even in the great cities, Auch, Toulouse, Castel Sarrazen, the Jews were left to

F

be remorselessly massacred and their property pillaged.
The Pope himself might have seen the smoke of the
fires that consumed them darkening the horizon from
the walls of Avignon. But John XXII., cold, arrogant,
rapacious, stood by unmoved. He launched his excommunication, not against the murderers of the inoffensive
Jews, but against all who presumed to take the Cross
without warrant of the Holy See. Even that same year
he published violent bulls against the poor persecuted
Hebrews, and commanded the Bishops to destroy their
Talmud, the source of their detestable blasphemies ; but
he bade those who should submit to baptism to be protected from pillage and massacre.

The Toledoth Jeschu, therefore, cannot have been
written at the beginning of the fourteenth century,
when the Jews had such experience of the indifference
of a Pope to their wrongs. We are consequently forced
to look to the thirteenth century as its date. And the
thirteenth century will provide us with instances of
persecution of the Jews in Germany, and Popes exerting
themselves to protect them.

In 1236, the Jews were the subject of an outburst of
popular fury throughout Europe, but especially in Spain,
where a fearful carnage took place. In France, the
Crusaders of Guienne, Poitou, Anjou and Brittany killed
them, without sparing the women and children. Women
with child were ripped up. The unfortunate Jews were
thrown down, and trodden under the feet of horses.
Their houses were ransacked, their books burned, their
treasures carried off. Those who refused baptism were
tortured or killed. The unhappy people sent to Rome,
and implored the Pope to extend his protection to them.
Gregory IX. wrote at once to the Archbishop of Bor-
deaux, the Bishops of Saintes, Angoulême and Poictiers,
forbidding constraint to be exercised on the Jews to

force them to receive baptism; and a letter to the King entreating him to exert his authority to repress the fury of the Crusaders against the Jews.

In 1240, the Jews were expelled from Brittany by the Duke John, at the request of the Bishops of Brittany.

In 1246, the persecution reached its height in Germany. Bishops and nobles vied with each other in despoiling and harassing the unfortunate Hebrews. They were charged with killing Christian children and devouring their hearts at their Passover. Whenever a dead body was found, the Jews were accused of the murder. Hosts were dabbled in blood, and thrown down at their doors, and the ignorant mob rose against such profanation of the sacred mysteries. They were stripped of their goods, thrown into prison, starved, racked, condemned to the stake or to the gallows. From the German towns miserable trains of yellow-girdled and capped exiles issued, seeking some more hospitable homes. If they left behind them their wealth, they carried with them their industry.

A deputation of German Rabbis visited the Pope, Innocent IV., at Lyons, and laid the complaints of the Jews before him. Innocent at once took up their cause. He wrote to all the bishops of Germany, on July 5th, 1247, ordering them to favour the Jews, and insist on the redress of the wrongs to which they had been subjected, whether at the hands of ecclesiastics or nobles. A similar letter was then forwarded by him to all the bishops of France.

At this period it was in vain for the Jews to appeal to the Emperor. Frederick II. was excommunicated, and Germany in revolt, fanned by the Pope, against him. A new Emperor had been proposed at a meeting at Budweis to the electors of Austria, Bohemia and Bavaria, but the proposition had been rejected. Henry of Thu-

ringia, however, set up by Innocent, and supported by
the ecclesiastical princes of Germany, had been crowned
at Hochem. A crusade was preached against the Emperor Frederick ; Henry of Thuringia was defeated and
died. The indefatigable Innocent, clinging to the
cherished policy of the Papal See to ruin the unity of
Germany by stirring up intestine strife, found another
candidate in William of Holland. He was crowned at
Aix-la-Chapelle, October 3, 1247. From this time till
his death, four years after, the cause of Frederick de-
clined. Frederick was mostly engaged in wars in Italy,
and had not leisure, if he had the power, to attend to
and right the wrongs of his Jewish vassals.

It was at this period that I think we may conclude
the Toledoth Jeschu of Wagenseil was written.

Another consideration tends to confirm this view.
The Wagenseil Toledoth Jeschu speaks of Elias rising
up after the death of Simon Cephas, and denouncing
him as having led the Christians away.

Was there any Elias at the close of the thirteenth
century who did thus preach against the Pope ? There
was. Elias of Cortona, second General of the Franciscan
Order, the leader of a strong reactionary party opposed
to the Spirituals or Cæsarians, those who maintained the
rule in all its rigour, had been deposed, then carried back
into the Generalship by a recoil of the party wave, then
appealed against to the Pope, deposed once more, and
finally excommunicated. Elias joined the Emperor
Frederick, the deadly foe of Innocent IV., and, sheltered
under his wing, denounced the venality, the avarice, the
extortion of the Papacy. As a close attendant on the
German Emperor, his adviser, as one who encouraged
him in his opposition to a Pope who protected the Jews,
the German Jews must have heard of him. But the
stone of excommunication flung at him struck him

down, and he died in 1253, making a death-bed reconciliation with Rome.

But though it is thus possible to give an historical explanation of the curious circumstance that the Toledoth Jeschu ranges the Pope among the friends of Judaism and the enemies of Christianity, and provide for the identification of Elias with the fallen General of the Minorites,—the story points perhaps to a dim recollection of Simon Peter being at the head of the Judaizing Church at Jerusalem and Rome, which made common cause with the Jews, and of Paul, here designated Elias, in opposition to him.

VII.

THE SECOND TOLEDOTH JESCHU.

WE will now analyze and give extracts from the second anti-evangel of the Jews, the TOLEDOTH JESCHU OF HULDRICH.[1]

It begins thus : "In the reign of King Herod the Proselyte, there lived a man named Papus Ben Jehuda. To him was betrothed Mirjam, daughter of Kalphus; and her brother's name was Simeon. He was a Rabbi, the son of Kalphus. This Mirjam, before her betrothal, was a hair-dresser to women. . . . . She was surpassing beautiful in form. She was of the tribe of Benjamin."

On account of her extraordinary beauty, she was kept locked up in a house; but she escaped through a window, and fled from Jerusalem to Bethlehem with Joseph Pandira, of Nazareth.

As has been already said, Papus Ben Jehuda was a contemporary of Rabbi Akiba, and died about A.D. 140. In the Wagenseil Toledoth Jeschu, Mirjam is betrothed to a Jochanan. In the latter, Mary lives at Bethlehem; in the Toledoth of Huldrich, she resides at Jerusalem.

Many years after, the place of the retreat of Mirjam and Joseph Pandira having been made known to Herod, he sent to Bethlehem orders for their arrest, and for the massacre of the children; but Joseph, who had been forewarned by a kinsman in the court of Herod, fled in time with his wife and children into Egypt.

[1] Joh. Jac. Huldricus : Historia Jeschuæ Nazareni, a Judæis blaspheme corrupta ; Leyden, 1705.

After many years a famine broke out in Egypt, and Joseph and Mirjam, with their son Jeschu and his brethren, returned to Canaan and settled at Nazareth.

"And Jeschu grew up, and went to Jerusalem to acquire knowledge, in the school of Joshua, the son of Perachia (B.C. 90); and he made there great advance, so that he learned the mystery of the chariot and the holy Name.[1]

"One day it fell out that Jeschu was playing ball with the sons of the priests, near the chamber Gasith, on the hill of the Temple. Then by accident the ball fell into the Fish-valley. And Jeschu was very grieved, and in his anger he plucked the hat from off his head, and cast it on the ground and burst into lamentations. Thereupon the boys warned him to put his hat on again, for it was not comely to be with uncovered head. Jeschu answered, Verily, Moses gave you not this law; it is but an addition of the lawyers, and therefore need not be observed.

"Now there sat there, Rabbi Eliezer and Joshua Ben Levi (A.D. 220), and the Rabbi Akiba (A.D. 135) hard by, in the school, and they heard the words that Jeschu had spoken.

"Then said the Rabbi Eliezer, That boy is certainly a Mamser. But Rabbi Joshua, son of Levi, said, He is a Ben-hannidda. And the Rabbi Akiba said also, He is a Ben-hannidda.[2] Therefore the Rabbi Akiba went forth out of the school, and asked Jeschu in what city he was born. Jeschu answered, I am of Nazareth; my father's name is Mezaria,[3] and my mother's name is Karchat.

"Then the Rabbis Akiba, Eliezer and Joshua went into the school of the Rabbi Joshua, son of Perachia, and seized Jeschu by the hair and cut it off in a circle, and washed his

[1] The mystery of the chariot is that of the chariot of God and the cherubic beasts, Ezekiel i. The Jews wrote the name of God without vowels, Jhvh; the vowel points taken from the name Adonai (Lord) were added later.

[2] The story is somewhat different in the Talmudic tract Calla, as already related.

[3] From Mizraim, Egypt.

head with the water Boleth, so that the hair might not grow
again."

Ashamed at this humiliation, according to the Toledoth Jeschu of Huldrich, the boy returned to Nazareth,
where he wounded his mother's breast.

Probably the author of this counter-Gospel saw one
of those common artistic representations of the Mater
Dolorosa with a sword piercing her soul, and invented
the story of Jesus wounding his mother's breast to
account for it.

When Jeschu was grown up, there assembled about
him many disciples, whose names were Simon and
Matthias, Elikus, Mardochai and Thoda, whose names
Jeschu changed.

"He called Simon Peter, after the word Petrus, which in
Hebrew signifies the First. And Matthias he called Matthew;
and Elikus he called Luke, because he sent him forth among
the heathen; and Mardochai he named Mark, because he
said, Vain men come to me; and Thoda he named Pahul
(Paul), because he bore witness of him.

"Another worthless fellow also joined them, named Jochanan, and he changed his name to Jahannus on account of
the miracles Jeschu wrought through him by means of the
incommunicable Name. This Jahannus advised that all the
men who were together should have their heads washed with
the water Boleth, that the hair might not grow on them, and
all the world might know that they were Nazarenes.

"But the affair was known to the elders and to the King.
Then he sent his messengers to take Jeschu and his disciples,
and to bring them to Jerusalem. But out of fear of the people,
they gave timely warning to Jeschu that the King sought to
take and kill him and his companions. Therefore they fled
into the desert of Ai (Capernaum?). And when the servants
of the King came and found them not, with the exception of
Jahannus, they took him and led him before the King. And

the King ordered that Jahannus should be executed with the
sword. The servants of the King therefore went at his command and slew Jahannus, and hung up his head at the gate
of Jerusalem.[1]

"About this time Jeschu assembled the inhabitants of
Jerusalem about him, and wrought many miracles. He laid
a millstone on the sea, and sailed about on it, and cried, I am
God, the Son of God, born of my mother by the power of
the Holy Ghost, and I sprang from her virginal brow.

"And he wrought many miracles, so that all the inhabitants of Ai believed in him, and his miracles he wrought by
means of the incommunicable Name.

"Then Jeschu ordered the law to be done away with, for
it is said in the Psalm, It is time for thee, Lord, to lay too
thine hand, for they have destroyed thy law. Now, said he,
is the right time come to tear up the law, for the thousandth
generation has come since David said, He hath promised to
keep his word to a thousand generations (Ps. cviii. 8).

"Therefore they arose and desecrated the Sabbath.

"When now the elders and wise men heard of what was
done, they came to the King and consulted him and his
council. Then answered Judas, son of Zachar,[2] I am the first
of the King's princes; I will go myself and see if it be true
what is said, that this man blasphemeth.

"Therefore Judas went and put on other clothes like the
men of Ai, and spake to Jeschu and said, I also will learn
your doctrine. Then Jeschu had his head shaved in a ring
and washed with the water Boleth.

"After that they went into the wilderness, for they feared
the King lest he should take them if they tarried at Ai.
And they lost their way; and in the wilderness they lighted
on a shepherd who lay on the ground. Then Jeschu asked

[1] Evidently the author confounds John the Baptist with John the
Apostle.

[2] Judas Iscarioth. In St. John's Gospel he is called the son of Simon
(vi. 71, xiii. 2, 26). Son of Zachar is a corruption of Iscarioth. The
name Iscarioth is probably from Kerioth, his native village, in Judah.

him the right way, and how far it was to shelter. The shepherd answered, The way lies straight before you; and he pointed it out with his foot.

"They went a little further, and they found a shepherd maiden, and Jeschu asked her which way they must go. Then the maiden led them to a stone which served as a signpost. And Peter said to Jeschu, Bless this maiden who has led us hither! And he blessed her, and wished for her that she might become the wife of the shepherd they had met on the road.

"Then said Peter, Wherefore didst thou so bless the maiden? He answered, The man is slow, but she is lively. If he were left without her activity, it would fare ill with him. For I am a God of mercy, and make marriages as is best for man."

This is a German story. There are many such of Jesus and St. Peter to be found in all collections of German household tales. They go together on a journey, and various adventures befal them, and the Lord orders things very differently from what Peter expects. To this follows another story, familiar to English school-boys. The apostles come with their Master to an inn, and ask for food. The innkeeper has a goose, and it is decided that he shall have the goose who dreams the best dream that night. When all are asleep, Judas gets up, plucks, roasts and eats the goose. Next morning they tell their dreams. Judas says, "Mine was the best of all, for I dreamt that in the night I ate the goose; and, lo! the goose is gone this morning. I think the dream must have been a reality." Among English school-boys, the story is told of an Englishman, and Scotchman, and an Irishman. The latter, of course, takes the place of Judas.

Some equally ridiculous stories follow, inserted for the purpose of making our blessed Lord and his apostles contemptible, but not taken, like the two just mentioned, from German folk-lore.

"After that Judas went to Jerusalem, but Jeschu and Peter tarried awaiting him (at Laish), for they trusted him. Now when Judas was come to Jerusalem, he related to the King and the elders the words and deeds of Jeschu, and how, through the power of the incommunicable Name, he had wrought such wonders that the people of Ai believed in him, and how that he had taken to wife the daughter of Karkamus, chief ruler of Ai.

"Then the King and the elders asked counsel of Judas how they might take Jeschu and his disciples. Judas answered, Persuade Jagar Ben Purah, their host, to mix the water of forgetfulness with their wine. We will come to Jerusalem for the Feast of Tabernacles; and then do ye take him and his disciples. For Jager Purah is the brother of the Gerathite Karkamus; but I will persuade Jeschu that Jager Purah is the brother of Karkamus of Ai, and he will believe my words, and they will all come up to the Feast of Tabernacles. Now when they shall have drunk of that wine, then will Jeschu forget the incommunicable Name, and so will be unable to deliver himself out of your hands, so that ye can capture him and hold him fast.

"Then answered the King and the elders, Thy counsel is good; go in peace, and we will appoint a fast. Therefore Judas went his way on the third of the month Tisri (October), and the great assembly in Jerusalem fasted a great fast, and prayed God to deliver Jeschu and his followers into their hands. And they undertook for themselves and for their successors a fast to be held annually on the third of the month Tisri, for ever.

"When Judas had returned to Jeschu, he related to him, I have been attentive to hear what is spoken in Jerusalem, and none so much as wag their tongues against thee. Yea! when the King took Jahannus to slay him, his disciples came in force and rescued him. And Jahannus said to me, Go say

to Jesus, our Lord, that he come with his disciples, and
we will protect him; and see! the host, Jager Purah, is
brother of Karkamus, ruler of Ai, and an uncle of thy betrothed.

" Now when Jeschu heard the words of Judas, he believed
them; for the inhabitants of Jerusalem and their neighbours
fasted incessantly during the six days between the feast of
the New Year and the Day of Atonement,—yea, even on the
Sabbath Day did some of them fast. And when those men
who were not in the secret asked wherefore they fasted at
this unusual time, when it was not customary to fast save on
the Day of Atonement, the elders answered them, This is
done because the King of the Gentiles has sent and threatened us with war.

" But Jeschu and his disciples dressed themselves in the
costume of the men of Ai, that they might not be recognized
in Jerusalem; and in the fast, on the Day of Atonement,
Jeschu came with his disciples to Jerusalem, and entered into
the house of Purah, and said, Of me it is written, Who is
this that cometh from Edom, with dyed garments from
Bozrah? I that speak in righteousness, mighty to save. I
have trodden the wine-press alone, and of the people there
was none with me.[1] For now am I come from Edom to the
house of Purah, and of thee, Purah, was it written, Jegar
Sahadutha![2] For thou shalt be to us a hill of witness and
assured protection. But I have come here to Jerusalem to
abolish the festivals and the holy seasons and the appointed
holy days. And he that believeth in me shall have his
portion in eternal life. I will give forth a new law in Jerusalem, for of me was it written, Out of Zion shall the law
go forth, and the word of the Lord from Jerusalem.[3] And
their sins and unrighteousness will I atone for with my blood.
But after I am dead I will arise to life again; for it is written,

---

[1] Isa. lxiii. 1—3. Singularly enough, this passage is chosen for the
Epistle in the Roman and Anglican Churches for Monday in Holy Week,
with special reference to the Passion.

[2] Gen. xxxi. 47.   [3] Isa. ii. 3.

I kill and make alive; I bring down to hell, and raise up therefrom again.[1]

"But Judas betook himself secretly to the King, and told him how that Jeschu and his disciples were in the house of Purah. Therefore the King sent young priests into the house of Purah, who said unto Jeschu, We are ignorant men, and believe in thee and thy word; but do this, we pray thee, work a miracle before our eyes.

"Then Jeschu wrought before them wonders by means of the incommunicable Name.

"And on the great Day of Atonement he and his disciples ate and drank, and fasted not; and they drank of the wine wherewith was mingled the Water of Forgetfulness, and then betook themselves to rest.

"And when midnight was now come, behold! servants of the King surrounded the house, and to them Purah opened the door. And the servants broke into the room where Jeschu and his disciples were, and they cast them into chains.

"Then Jeschu directed his mind to the incommunicable Name; but he could not recall it, for all had vanished from his recollection.

"And the servants of the King led Jeschu and his disciples to the prison of the blasphemers. And in the morning they told the King that Jeschu and his disciples were taken and cast into prison. Then he ordered that they should be detained till the Feast of Tabernacles.

"And on that feast all the people of the Lord came together to the feast, as Moses had commanded them. Then the King ordered that Jeschu's disciples should be stoned outside the city; and all the Israelites looked on, and heaped stones on the disciples. And all Israel broke forth into hymns of praise to the God of Israel, that these men of Belial had thus fallen into their hands.

"But Jeschu was kept still in prison, for the King would not slay him till the men of Ai had seen that his words were naught, and what sort of a prophet he was proved to be.

[1] 1 Sam. ii. 6.

" Also he wrote letters throughout the land to the councils of the synagogues to learn from them after what manner Jeschu should be put to death, and summoning all to assemble at Jerusalem on the next feast of the Passover to execute Jeschu, as it is written, Whosoever blasphemeth the name of the Lord, he shall surely be put to death, and all the congregation shall certainly stone him.[1]

" But the people of Girmajesa (Germany) and all that country round, what is at this day called Wormajesa (Worms) in the land of the Emperor, and the little council in the town of Wormajesa, answered the King in this wise, Let Jesus go, and slay him not! Let him live till he die and perish.

" But when the feast of the Passover drew nigh, it was heralded through all the land of Judæa, that any one who had aught to say in favour, and for the exculpation, of Jeschu, should declare it before the King. But all the people with one consent declared that Jeschu must die.[2]

" Therefore, on the eve of the Passover, Jeschu was brought out of the prison, and they cried before him, So may all thine enemies perish, O Lord! And they hanged him on a tree outside of Jerusalem, as the King and elders of Jerusalem had commanded.

" And all Israel looked on and praised and glorified God.

" Now when even was come, Judas took down the body of Jeschu from the tree and laid it in his garden in a conduit.

" But when the people of Ai heard that Jeschu had been hung, they became enemies to Israel. And the people of Ai attacked the Israelites, and slew of them two thousand men. And the Israelites could not go to the feasts because of the men of Ai. Therefore the King proclaimed war against Ai; but he could not overcome it, for mightily grew the multitude of those who believed in Jeschu, even under the eyes of the King in Jerusalem.

" And some of these went to Ai, and declared that on the third day after Jeschu had been hung, fire had fallen from

---

[1] Lev. xxiv. 16.   [2] This is taken from Sanhedrim, fol. 43.

heaven, which had surrounded Jeschu, and he had arisen alive, and gone up into heaven.[1]

" And the people of Ai believed what was said, and swore to avenge on the children of Israel the crime they had committed in hanging Jeschu. Now when Judas saw that the people of Ai threatened great things, he wrote a letter unto them, saying, There is no peace to the ungodly, saith the Lord; therefore do the people take counsel together, and the Gentiles imagine a vain thing. Come to Jerusalem and see your false prophet ! For, lo ! he is dead and buried in a conduit.

" Now when they heard this, the men of Ai went to Jerusalem and saw Jeschu lying where had been said. But, nevertheless, when they returned to Ai, they said that all Judas had written was false. For, lo ! said they, when we came to Jerusalem we found that all believed in Jeschu, and had risen and had expelled the King out of the city because he believed not; and many of the elders have they slain. Then the men of Ai believed these words of the messengers, and they proclaimed war against Israel.

" Now when the King and the elders saw that the men of Ai were about to encamp against them, and that the numbers of these worthless men grew—they were the brethren and kinsmen of Jeschu—they took counsel what they should do in such sore straits as they were in.

" And Judas said, Lo ! Jeschu has an uncle Simon, son of Kalpus, who is now alive, and he is an honourable old man. Give him the incommunicable Name, and let him work wonders in Ai, and tell the people that he does them in the name of Jesus. And they will believe Simon, because he is the uncle of Jeschu. But Simon must make them believe that Jeschu committed to him all power to teach them not to ill-treat the Israelites, and he has reserved them for his own vengeance.

" This counsel pleased the King and the elders, and they went to Simon and told him the matter.

[1] It is worth observing how these two false witnesses disagree in almost every particular about our blessed Lord's birth and passion.

" Then went Simon, when he had learned the Name, and drew nigh to Ai, and he raised a cloud and thunder and lightning. And he seated himself on the cloud, and as the thunder rolled he cried, Ye men of Ai, gather yourselves together at the tower of Ai, and there will I give you commandments from Jeschu.

" But when the people of Ai heard this voice, they were sore afraid, and they assembled on all sides about the tower. And lo! Simon was borne thither on the cloud; and he stepped upon the tower. And the men of Ai fell on their faces before him.[1] Then Simon said, I am Simon Ben Kalpus, uncle of Jeschu. Jeschu came and sent me unto you to teach you his law, for Jesus is the Son of God. And lo! I will give you the law of Jesus, which is a new commandment.

" Then he wrought before them signs and wonders, and he said to the people of Ai, Swear to me to obey all that I tell you. And they swore to him. Then said Simon, Go to your own homes. And all the people of Ai returned to their dwellings.

" Now Simon sat on the tower, and wrote the commandments even as the King and elders had decided. And he changed the Alphabet, and gave the letters new names, as secretly to protest that all he taught written in those letters was lies. And this was the Alphabet he wrote: A, Be, Ce, De, E, Ef, Cha, I, Ka, El, Em, En, O, Pe, Ku, Er, Es, Te, U, Ix, Ejed, Zet.

" And this is the interpretation : My father is Esau, who was a huntsman, and was weary ; and lo! his sons believed in Jesus, who lives, as God.

" And Simon composed for the deception of the people of Ai lying books, and he called them 'Avonkelajon' (Evangelium), which, being interpreted, is the End of Ungodliness.

---

[1] This is probably taken from the story of Simon Magus in the Pseudo-Linus. Simon flies from off a high tower. In the Apocryphal Book of the Death of the Virgin, the apostles come to her death-bed riding on clouds. Ai is here Rome, not Capernaum.

But they thought he said, 'Eben gillajon,' which means Father, Son, and Holy Ghost. He also wrote books in the names of the disciples of Jeschu, and especially in that of Johannes, and said that Jeschu·had given him these.

"But with special purpose he composed the Book of Johannes (the Apocalypse), for the men of Ai thought it contained mysteries, whereas it contained pure invention. For instance, he wrote in the Book of Johannes that Johannes saw a beast with seven heads and seven horns and seven crowns, and the name of the beast was blasphemy, and the number of the beast 666. Now the seven heads mean the seven letters which compose in Hebrew the words, 'Jeschu of Nazareth.' And in like manner the number 666 is that which is the sum of the letters composing this name. In like way did Simon compose all the books to deceive the people, as the King and the elders had bidden him.

"And on the sixth day of the third month Simon sat on the cloud, and the people of Ai were gathered together before him to the tower, and he gave them the book Avonkelajon, and said to them, When ye have children born to you, ye must sprinkle them with water, in token that Jeschu was washed with the water Boleth, and ye must observe all the commandments that are written in the book Avonkelajon. And ye must wage no war against the people of Israel, for Jeschu has reserved them to avenge himself on them himself.

"Now when the people of Ai heard these words, they answered that they would keep them. And Simon returned on his cloud to Jerusalem. And all the people thought he had gone up in a cloud to heaven to bring destruction on the Israelites.[1]

"Not long after this, King Herod died, and was succeeded by his son in the kingdom of Israel. But when he had obtained the throne, he heard that the people of Ai had made

[1] The author probably saw representations of the Ascension and of the Last Judgment, with Christ seated with the Books of Life and Death in his hand on a great white cloud, and composed this story out of what he saw, associating the pictures with the floating popular legend of Simon Magus.

images in honour of Jesus and Mary, and he wrote letters to
Ai and ordered their destruction; otherwise he would make
war against them.

"Then the people of Ai sent asking help of the Emperor
against the King of Israel. But the Emperor would not
assist them and war against Israel. Therefore, when the
people of Ai saw that there was no help, they burned the
images and bound themselves before the sons of Israel.

"And about this time Mirjam, the mother of Jeschu, died.
Then the King ordered that she should be buried at the foot
of the tree on which Jeschu had hung; and there he also
had the brothers and sisters of Jeschu hung up. And they
were hung, and a memorial stone was set up on the spot. .

"But the worthless men, their kinsmen, came and destroyed
the memorial stone, and set up another in its stead, on which
they wrote the words, ' Lo! this is a ladder set upon the
earth, whose head reaches to heaven, and the angels of God
ascend and descend upon it, and the mother rejoices here in
her children, Allelujah !'

"Now when the King heard this, he destroyed the memorial they had erected, and killed a hundred of the kindred
of Jeschu.

"Then went Simon, son of Kalpus, to the King and said,
Suffer me, and I will draw away these people from Jerusalem. And the King said, Be it so; go, and the Lord be
with thee! Therefore Simon went secretly to these worthless men, and said to them, Let us go together to Ai, and
there shall ye see wonders which I will work. And some
went to Ai, but others seated themselves beside Simon on
his cloud, and left Jerusalem with him. And on the way
Simon cast down those who sat on the cloud with him upon
the earth, so that they died.[1]

"And when Simon returned to Jerusalem, he told the King

---

[1] In the story of Simon the Sorcerer, it is at the prayer of Simon Peter
that the Sorcerer falls whilst flying and breaks all his bones. Perhaps the
author saw a picture of the Judgment with saints on the cloud with Jesus,
and the lost falling into the flames of hell.

what he had done, and the King rejoiced greatly. And Simon left not the court of the King till his death. And when he died, all the Jews observed the day as a fast, and it was the 9th of the month Teboth (January).

"But those who had gone to Ai at the word of Simon believed that Simon and those with him had gone up together into heaven on the cloud.

"And when men saw what Simon had taught the people of Ai in the name of Jesus, they followed them also, and they took them the daughters of Ai to wife, and sent letters into the furthest islands with the book Avonkelajon, and undertook for themselves, and for their descendants, to hold to all the words of the book Avonkelajon.

"Therefore they abolished the Law, and chose the first day of the week as the Sabbath, for that was the birthday of Jesus, and they ordained many other customs and bad feasts. Therefore have they no part and lot in Israel. They are accursed in this world, and accursed in the world to come. But the Lord bless his people Israel with peace.

"These are the words of the Rabbi Jochanan, son of Saccai, in Jerusalem."

That this second version of the "Life of Jeschu" is later than the first one, I think there can be little doubt. It is more full of absurdities than the first, it adopts German household tales, and exhibits an ignorance of history even more astounding than in the first Life. The preachers of the "Evangelium" marry wives, and there is a burning of images of St. Mary and our Lord. These are *perhaps* indications of its having been composed after the Reformation.

Luther did not know anything of the Life published later by Huldrich. The only Toledoth Jeschu he was acquainted with was that afterwards published by Wagenseil.

PART II.

THE LOST PETRINE GOSPELS.

Under this head are classed all those Gospels whose tendency is Judaizing, which sprang into existence in the Churches of Palestine and Syria.

These may be ranged in two sub-classes—

    a. Those akin to the Gospel of St. Matthew.

    β. Those related to the Gospel of St. Mark.

To the first class belong—

    1. The Gospel of the Twelve, or of the Hebrews.

    2. The Gospel of the Clementines.

To the second class belong, probably—

    1. The Gospel of St. Peter.

    2. The Gospel of the Egyptians.

THE LOST PETRINE GOSPELS.

I.

THE GOSPEL OF THE HEBREWS.

1. *The Fragments extant.*

EUSEBIUS quotes Papias, Irenæus and Origen, as authorities for his statement that St. Matthew wrote his Gospel first in Hebrew.

Papias, a contemporary of Polycarp, who was a disciple of St. John, and who carefully collected all information he could obtain concerning the apostles, declares that " Matthew wrote his Gospel in the Hebrew dialect,[1] and that every one translated it as he was able."[2]

Irenæus, a disciple of Polycarp, and therefore also likely to have trustworthy information on this matter, says, " Matthew among the Hebrews wrote a Gospel in their own language, while Peter and Paul were preaching the gospel at Rome, and founding the Church there."[3]

In a fragment, also, of Irenæus, edited by Dr. Grabe, it is said that " the Gospel according to Matthew was written to the Jews, for they earnestly desired a Messiah

---

[1] 'Εβραΐδι διαλέκτψ.   [2] Euseb. Hist. Eccl. lib. iii. c. 39.

[3] *Ibid.* lib. v. c. 8.

of the posterity of David. Matthew, in order to satisfy
them on this point, began his Gospel with the genealogy
of Jesus.[1]

Origen, in a passage preserved by Eusebius, has this
statement: "I have learned by tradition concerning the
four Gospels, which alone are received without dispute
by the Church of God under heaven, that the first was
written by St. Matthew, once a tax-gatherer, afterwards
an apostle of Jesus Christ, who published it for the
benefit of the Jewish converts, composed in the Hebrew
language."[2]   And again, in his Commentary on St. John,
"We begin with Matthew, who, according to tradition,
wrote first, publishing his Gospel to the believers who
were of the circumcision."

Eusebius, who had collected the foregoing testimonies
on a subject which, in that day, seems to have been un-
disputed, thus records what he believed to be a well-
authenticated historical fact: "Matthew, having first
preached to the Hebrews, delivered to them, when he
was preparing to depart to other countries, his Gospel
composed in their native language."[3]

St. Jerome follows Papias: "Matthew, who is also
Levi, from a publican became an apostle, and he first
composed his Gospel of Christ in Judæa, for those of
the circumcision who believed, and wrote it in Hebrew
words and characters; but who translated it afterwards
into Greek is not very evident. Now this Hebrew Gospel
is preserved to this day in the library at Cæsarea which
Pamphilus the martyr so diligently collected. I also
obtained permission of the Nazarenes of Beræa in Syria,
who use this volume, to make a copy of it. In which
it is to be observed that, throughout, the Evangelist when

---

[1] Spicileg. Patrum, Tom. I.   [2] Euseb. Hist. Eccl. vi. 25.
[3] *Ibid.* iii. 24.

quoting the witness of the Old Testament, either in his own person or in that of the Lord and Saviour, does not follow the authority of the Seventy translators, but the Hebrew Scriptures, from which he quotes these two passages, ' Out of Egypt have I called my Son,' and, ' Since he shall be called a Nazarene.'"[1]   And again: " That Gospel which is called the Gospel of the Hebrews, and which has lately been translated by me into Greek and Latin, and was used frequently by Origen, relates," &c.[2] Again: " That Gospel which the Nazarenes and Ebionites make use of, and which I have lately translated into Greek from the Hebrew, and which by many is called the genuine Gospel of Matthew."[3]   And once more: " The Gospel of the Hebrews, which is written in the Syro-Chaldaic tongue, and in Hebrew characters, which the Nazarenes make use of at this day, is also called the Gospel of the Apostles, or, as many think, is that of Matthew, is in the library of Cæsarea."[4]

St. Epiphanius is even more explicit. He says that the Nazarenes possessed the most complete Gospel of St. Matthew,[5] as it was written at first in Hebrew;[6] and " they have it still in Hebrew characters; but I do not know if they have cut off the genealogies from Abraham to Christ." " We may affirm as a certain fact, that Matthew alone among the writers of the New Testament wrote the history of the preaching of the Gospel in Hebrew, and in Hebrew characters."[7]   This Hebrew Gospel, he adds, was known to Cerinthus and Carpocrates.

The subscriptions of many MSS. and versions bear

---

[1] St. Hieron. De vir. illust., s. v. Matt.

[2] *Ibid.* s. v. Jacobus.   [3] *Ibid.* in Matt. xii. 13.

[4] *Ibid.* Contra. Pelag. iii. 1.

[5] Ἔχουσι δὲ (οἱ Ναζαραῖοι) τὸ κατὰ Μαθαῖον εὐαγγέλιον πληρίστατον ἑβραιστί.—Hær. xxix. 9.

[6] Καθὼς ἐξ ἀρχῆς ἐγράφη.—*Ibid.*   [7] *Ibid.* xxx. 3.

G

the same testimony. Several important Greek codices
of St. Matthew close with the statement that he wrote
in Hebrew; the Syriac and Arabic versions do the same.
The subscription of the Peschito version is, "Finished
is the holy Gospel of the preaching of Matthew, which
he preached in Hebrew in the land of Palestine." That
of the Arabic version reads as follows: "Here ends the
copy of the Gospel of the apostle Matthew. He wrote
it in the land of Palestine, by the inspiration of the Holy
Spirit, in the Hebrew language, eight years after the
bodily ascension of Jesus the Messiah into heaven, and
in the first year of the Roman Emperor, Claudius Cæsar."

The title of Gospel of the Hebrews was only given to
the version known to Jerome and Epiphanius, because
it was in use among the Hebrews. But amongst the
Nazarenes it was called "The Gospel of the Apostles,"[1]
or "The Gospel of the Twelve."[2] St. Jerome expressly
says that "the Gospel used by the Nazarenes is also
called the Gospel of the Apostles."[3] That the same
Gospel should bear two names, one according to its re-
puted authors, the other according to the community
which used it, is not surprising.

Justin Martyr probably alludes to it under a slightly
different name, "The Recollections of the Apostles."[4]
He says that these Recollections were a Gospel.[5] He
adopted the word used by Xenophon for his recollections
of Socrates. What the Memorabilia of Xenophon were

---

[1] Εὐαγγέλιον κατὰ τοὺς ἀποστόλους.

[2] Εὐαγγέλιον κατὰ τοὺς δώδεκα. Origen calls it "The Gospel of the
Twelve Apostles," Homil. i. in Luc. St. Jerome the same, in his Prooem.
in Comment. sup. Matt.

[3] Adv. Pelag. iii. 10.   [4] Ἀπομνημονεύματα τῶν Ἀποστόλων.

[5] "'Εν τοῖς γεγομένοις ὑπ' αὐτῶν ἀπομνημονεύμασιν, ἃ καλεῖται
Εὐαγγέλια." And "ἐν τῷ λεγομένῳ Εὐαγγελίῳ," when speaking of these
Reminiscences, Dialog. cum Tryphon. § 11. Just. Mart. Opera, ed. Cologne,
p. 227.

concerning the martyred philosopher, that the Memorabilia of the Apostles were concerning the martyred Redeemer.

It is probable that this Hebrew Gospel of the Twelve was the only one with which Justin Martyr was acquainted.

Justin Martyr was a native of Samaria, and his acquaintance with Christianity was probably made in the communities of Nazarenes scattered over Syria. By family he was a Greek, and was therefore by blood inclined to sympathize with the Gentile rather than the Jewish Christians. This double tendency is manifest in his writings. He judges the Ebionites, even the narrowest of their sectarian rings, with great tenderness; but he proclaims that Gentiledom had yielded better Christians than Jewdom.[1] Justin distinguishes between the Ebionites. There were those who in their own practice observed the Mosaic Law, believing in Christ as the flower and end of the Law, but without exacting the same observance of believing Gentiles; and there were those who not only observed the Law themselves, but imposed it on their Gentile converts. His sympathies were with the former, whom he regards as the true followers of the apostles, and not with the latter.

Justin's conversion took place circ. A.D. 133. He is a valuable testimony to the divisions among the Nazarenes or Ebionites in the second century, just when Gnostic views were infiltrating among the extreme Judaizing section.

Justin Martyr's Christian training took place in the Nazarene Church, in the orthodox, milder section. He no doubt inherited the traditional prejudice against St. Paul, for he neither mentions him by name, nor quotes any of his writings. That he should have omitted to

[1] 1 Apol. ii.

G 2

quote St. Paul in his Dialogue with Trypho the Jew is
not surprising; but one cannot doubt that had he seen
the Epistles of the Apostle of the Gentiles, he would
have cited them, or shown that they had influenced the
current of his thoughts in his two Apologies addressed
to Gentiles.   He quotes "the book that is called the
Gospel" as if there were but one; but what Gospel was
it?   It has been frequently observed that the quotations
of Justin are closer to the parallel passages in St. Matthew than to those of the other Canonical Gospels.   But
the only Gospel he names is the Gospel of the Twelve.

Did Justin Martyr possess the Gospel of St. Matthew,
or some other?

It is observable that he diverges from the Gospel narrative in several particulars.   It is inconceivable that
this was caused by defect of memory.   Two or three
of those texts in which he differs from our Canonical
Gospels occur several times in his writings, and always
in the same form.[1]   Would it not be strange that his
memory should fail him each time, and on each of these
passages?   But though his memory may have been inaccurate in recording exact words, the differences that
have been noticed between the citations of Justin Martyr
and the Canonical Gospel of St. Matthew are not confined
to words; they extend to particulars, to facts.   Verbal
differences are accountable for by lapse of memory, but
it is not so with facts.   One can understand how in
quoting by memory the mode of expressing the same
facts may vary, but not that the facts themselves should
be different.   If the facts cited are different, we are forced
to conclude that the citations were derived from another
source.   And such is the case with Justin.

[1] Justin Mart. Opp. ed. Cologne; 2 Apol. p. 64; Dialog. cum Tryph.
p. 301; *ibid.* p. 253; 2 Apol. p. 64; Dial, cum Tryph. p. 326; 2 Apol.
pp. 95, 96.

Five or six times does he say that the Magi came from Arabia;[1] St. Matthew says only that they came from the East.[2]

He says that our Lord was born in a cave[3] near Bethlehem; that, when he was baptized, a bright light shone over him; and he gives words which were heard from heaven, which are not recorded by any of the Evangelists.

That our Lord was born in a cave is probable enough, but where did Justin learn it? Certainly not from St. Matthew's Gospel, which gives no particulars of the birth of Christ at Bethlehem. St. Luke says he was born in the stable of an inn. Justin, we are warranted in suspecting, derived the fact of the stable being a cave from the only Gospel with which he was acquainted, that of the Hebrews.

The tradition of the scene of Christ's nativity having been a cave was peculiarly Jewish. It is found in the Apocryphal Gospels of the Nativity and the Protevangelium, both of which unquestionably grew up in Judæa. That Justin should endorse this tradition leads to the conclusion that he found it so stated in his Gospel.

I shall speak of the light and voice at the baptism presently.

St. Epiphanius says that the Ebionite Gospel began with, "In the days of Herod, Caiaphas being the highpriest, there was a man whose name was John," and so on, like the 3rd chap. St. Matthew. But this was the mutilated Gospel of the Hebrews used by the Gnostic Ebionites, who were heretical on the doctrine of the

---

[1] Οἱ ἐξ Ἀραβίας μάγοι, or μάγοι ἀπὸ Ἀραβίας.—Dialog. cum Tryph. pp. 303, 315, 328, 330, 334, &c.

[2] Matt. ii. 1.

[3] Ἐν σπηλαίῳ τινὶ σύνεγγυς τῆς κώμης κατέλυσε.—Dialog. cum Tryph. pp. 303, 304.

nativity of our Lord, and whom Justin Martyr speaks of as rejecting the supernatural birth of Christ.[1]

Among the Nazarenes, orthodox and heretical, but one Gospel was recognized, and that the Hebrew Gospel of the Twelve; but the Gospel in use among the Gnostic Ebionites became more and more corrupt as they diverged further from orthodoxy.

But the primitive Hebrew Gospel was held " in high esteem by those Jews who received the faith."[2] " It is the Gospel," says St. Jerome, " that the Nazarenes use at the present day."[3] " It is the Gospel of the Hebrews that the Nazarenes read," says Origen.[4]

Was this Gospel of the Twelve, or of the Hebrews, the original of St. Matthew's Canonical Greek Gospel, or was it a separate compilation? This is a question to be considered presently.

The statement of the Fathers that the Gospel of St. Matthew was first written in Hebrew, must of course be understood to mean that it was written in Aramaic or Palestinian Syriac.

Now we have extant two versions of the Gospels, St. Matthew's included, in Syriac, the Peschito and the Philoxenian. The latter needs only a passing mention ; it was avowedly made from the Greek, A.D. 508. But the Peschito is much more ancient. The title of " Peschito " is an emphatic Syrian term for that which is "simple," "uncorrupt" and "true;" and, applied from the beginning to this version, it strongly indicates the veneration and confidence with which it has ever been regarded by all the Churches of the East.[5] When this

---

[1] Dial. cum Tryph. p. 291. [2] Euseb. Hist. Eccl. iii. 25.

[3] Adv. Pelag. iii. 1. [4] Comm. in Ezech. xxiv. 7.

[5] " De versione Syriacâ testatur Sionita, quod ut semper in summâ veneratione et auctoritate habita erat apud omnes populos qui Chaldaicâ sive Syriacâ utuntur linguâ, sic publicè in omnibus eorum ecclesiis anti-

version was made cannot be decided by scholars. A copy in the Laurentian Library bears so early a date as A.D. 586; but it existed long before the translation was made by Philoxenus in 508. The first Armenian version from the Greek was made in 431, and the Armenians already, at that date, had a version from the Syriac, made by Isaac, Patriarch of Armenia, some twenty years previously, in 410. Still further back, we find the Peschito version quoted in the writings of St. Ephraem, who lived not later than A.D. 370.[1]

Was this Peschito version founded on the Greek canonical text, or, in the case of St. Matthew, on the "Hebrew" Gospel? I think there can be little question that it was translated from the Greek. There can be no question that the Gospels of St. Mark, St. Luke, St. John, the Acts of the Apostles, the Epistles of St. Paul, and those of the other Epistles contained in this version,[2] are from the Greek, and it is probable that the version of St. Matthew was made at the same time from the received text. The Syrian churches were separated from the Nazarene community in sympathy; their acceptance of St. Paul's Epistles is a proof that they were so; and these Epistles were accepted by them at a very early age, as we gather from internal evidence in the translation.

The Syrian churches would be likely, moreover, when seeking for copies of the Christian Scriptures, to ask for them from churches which were regarded as orthodox, rather than from a dwindling community which was thought to be heretical.

---

quissimis, constitutis in Syriâ, Mesopotamiâ, Chaldæâ, Ægypto, et denique in universis Orientis partibus dispersis ac disseminatis accepta ac lecta fuit."—Walton : London Polyglott, 1657.

[1] In Matt. iii. 17 ; Luke i. 71 ; John i. 3 ; Col. iii. 5.

[2] It omits the 2nd and 3rd Epistles of St. John, the Epistle of Jude, and the Apocalypse.

The Peschito version of St. Matthew follows the canonical Greek text, and not the Gospel of the Hebrews, in such passages as can be compared;[1] not one of the peculiarities of the latter find their echo in the Peschito text.

The Gospel of the Hebrews has not, therefore, been preserved to us in the Peschito St. Matthew. The translations made by St. Jerome in Greek and Latin have also perished. It is not difficult to account for the loss of the book. The work itself was in use only by converted Jews ; it was in the exclusive possession of the descendants of those parties for whose use it had been written. The Greek Gospels, on the other hand, spread as Christianity grew. The Nazarenes themselves passed away, and their cherished Gospel soon ceased to be known among men.

Some exemplars may have been preserved for a time in public libraries, but these would not survive the devastation to which the country was exposed from the Saracens and other invaders, and it is not probable that a solitary copy survives.

But if the entire Gospel of the Hebrews has not been preserved to us, we have got sufficiently numerous fragments, cited by ancient ecclesiastical writers, to permit us, to a certain extent, to judge of the tendencies and character of that Gospel.

It is necessary to observe, as preliminary to our quotations, that the early Fathers cited passages from this Gospel without the smallest prejudice against it either historically or doctrinally. They do not seem to have considered it apocryphal, as open to suspicion, either

---

[1] As in the food of the Baptist, in the narrative of the baptism, in the mention of Zacharias, son of Barachias, in place of Zacharias, son of Jehoiada, the instruction to Peter on fraternal forgiveness, &c. It interprets the name Emmanuel.

because it contained doctrine at variance with the Canonical Greek Gospels, or because it narrated circumstances not found in them. On the contrary, they refer to it as a good, trustworthy authority for the facts of our Lord's life, ànd for the doctrines he taught.

St. Ignatius, in his Epistle to the Smyrnians,[1] has inserted in it a passage relative to the appearance of our Lord to his apostles after his resurrection, not found in the Canonical Gospels, and we should not know whence he had drawn it, had not St. Jerome noticed the fact and recorded it.[2]

St. Clement of Alexandria speaks of the Gospel of the Hebrews in the same terms as he speaks of the writings of St. Paul and the books of the Old Testament.[3] Origen, who makes some quotations from this Gospel, does not, it is true, range it with the Canonical Gospels, but he speaks of it with great respect, as one highly esteemed by many Christians of his time.[4]

In the fourth century, no agreement had been come to as to the value of this Gospel. Eusebius tells us that by some it was reckoned among the Antilegomena, that is, among those books which floated between the Canonical and the Apocryphal Gospels.[5]

The Gospel of St. Matthew and the Gospel of the Hebrews were not identical. It is impossible to doubt this when we examine the passages of the latter quoted by ecclesiastical writers, the majority of which are not to be found in the former, and the rest differ from the Canonical Gospel, either in details or in the construction of the passages which correspond.

Did the difference extend further? This is a ques-

[1] Ignat. Ad. Smyrn. c. 3.　　[2] Catal. Script. Eccl. 15.
[3] Clem. Alex. Strom. ii. 9.　　[4] Hom. xv. in Jerem.
[5] Hist. Eccl. iii. 25. Some of those books of the New Testament now regarded as Canonical were also then reckoned among the Antilegomena.

tion it is impossible to answer positively in one way or the other, since we only know those passages of the Gospel of the Nazarenes which have been quoted by the early Fathers.

But it is probable that the two Gospels did not differ from each other except in these passages; for if the divergence was greater, one cannot understand how St. Jerome, who had both under his eyes, could have supposed one to have been the Hebrew original of the other. And if both resembled each other closely, it is easy to suppose that the ecclesiastical writers who quoted from the Nazarene Gospel, quoted only those passages which were peculiar to it.

Let us now examine the principal fragments of this Gospel that have been preserved.

There are some twenty in all, and of these only two are in opposition to the general tone of the first Canonical Gospel.

With one of these I shall begin the series of extracts.

"*And straitway,*" said Jesus, "*the Holy Spirit [my mother] took me, and bore me away to the great mountain called Thabor.*" [1]

Origen twice quotes this passage, once in a fuller form. "(She) *bore me by one of my hairs to the great mountain called Thabor.*" The passage is also quoted by St. Jerome.[2] Origen and Jerome take pains to give this passage an orthodox and unexceptionable meaning. Instead of rejecting the passage as apocryphal, they labour to explain it away—a proof of the high estimation in which the Gospel of the Twelve was held. The

---

[1] Ἄρτι ἔλαβε μέ ἡ μήτηρ μοῦ τὸ ἅγιον πνεῦμα, ἐν μιᾷ τῶν τριχῶν μοῦ, καὶ ἀνήνεγκε μὲ εἰς τὸ ὄρος τὸ μέγα Θαβώρ.—Origen : Hom. xv. in Jerem., and in Johan.

[2] "Modo tulit me mater mea Spiritus Sanctus in uno capillorum meorum."—Hieron. in Mich. vii. 6.

words, "my mother," are, it can scarcely be doubted, a
Gnostic interpolation, as probably are also the words,
"by one of my hairs;" for on one of the occasions on
which Origen quotes the passage, these words are omitted.
Probably they did not exist in all the copies of the
Gospel.

Our Lord was "led by the Spirit into the wilderness"
after his baptism.[1] Philip was caught away by the
Spirit of the Lord from the road between Jerusalem and
Gaza, and was found at Azotus.[2] The notion of trans-
portation by the Spirit was therefore not foreign to the
authors of the Gospels.

The Holy Spirit was represented by the Elkesaites as
a female principle.[3] The Elkesaites were certainly one
with the Ebionites in their hostility to St. Paul, whose
Epistles, as Origen tells us, they rejected.[4] And that
they were a Jewish sect which had relations with Ebionitism appears from a story told by St. Epiphanius, that
their supposed founder, Elxai, went over to the Ebionites in the time of Trajan.[5] They issued from the same
fruitful field of converts, the Essenes.

The term by which the Holy Spirit is designated in
Hebrew is feminine, and lent itself to a theory of the
Holy Spirit being a female principle, and this rapidly
slid into identification of the Spirit with Mary.

The Clementines insist on the universe being compounded of the male and the female elements. There
are two sorts of prophecy, the male which speaks of the
world to come, the female which deals with the world
that is; the female principle rules this world, the body,

---

[1] Matt. iv. 1.   [2] Acts viii. 39.

[3] Τὴν δε θήλειαν καλεῖσθαι ἅγιον πνεῦμα.—Hippolyt. Refut. ix. 13,
ed. Dunker, p. 462. So also St. Epiphanius, εἶναι δὲ καὶ τὸ πνεῦμα
θηλεῖαν.—Hæres. xix. 4, liii. 1.

[4] Ap. Euseb. Hist. Eccles. vi. 38.   [5] Hæres. xix. 1, xxx. 17.

all that is visible and material. Beside this female principle stands Christ, the male principle, ruling the spirits of men, and all that is invisible and immaterial.[1] The Holy Spirit, brooding over the deep and calling the world into being, became therefore the female principle in the Elkesaite Trinity.

In Gnosticism, this deification of the female principle, which was represented as Prounikos or Sophia among the Valentinians, led to the incarnation of the principle in women who accompanied the heresiarchs Simon and Apelles. Thus the Eternal Wisdom was incarnate in Helena, who accompanied Dositheus and afterwards Simon Magus,[2] and in the fair Philoumena who associated with Apelles.

The same influence seems imperceptibly to have been at work in the Church of the Middle Ages, and in the pictures and sculptures of the coronation of the Virgin. Mary seems in Catholic art to have assumed a position as one of the Trinity.

In the original Gospel of the Hebrews, the passage probably stood thus: "And straightway the Holy Spirit took me, and bore me to the great mountain Thabor;" and Origen and Jerome quoted from a text corrupted by the Gnostic Ebionites. The words "bore me by one of my hairs" were added to assimilate the translation to that of Habbacuc by the angel, in the apocryphal addition to the Book of Daniel.

We next come to a passage found in the Stromata of Clement of Alexandria, who compares it with a sentence

---

[1] Homilies, iii. 20—27.

[2] In the "Refutation of Heresies" attributed by the Chevalier Bunsen and others to St. Hippolytus, Helena is said in Simonian Gnosticism to have been the "lost sheep" of the Gospels, the incarnation of the world principle—found, recovered, redeemed, by Simon, the incarnation of the divine male principle.

from the Theætetus of Plato: "*He who wondereth shall reign, and he who reigneth shall rest.*"[1]

This, like the preceding quotation, has a Gnostic hue ; but it is impossible to determine its sense in the absence of the context. Nor does the passage in the Theætetus throw any light upon it. The whole of the passage in St. Clement is this : " The beginning of (or search after) truth is admiration," says Plato. " And Matthias, in saying to us in his Traditions, Wonder at what is before you, proves that admiration is the first step leading upwards to knowledge. Therefore also it is written in the Gospel of the Hebrews, He who shall wonder shall reign, and he who reigns shall rest."

What were these Traditions of Matthias ? In another place St. Clement of Alexandria mentions them, and quotes a passage from them, an instruction of St. Matthias : " If he who is neighbour to one of the elect sins, the elect sins with him ; for if he (the elect) had conducted himself as the Word requires, then his neighbour would have looked to his ways, and not have sinned."[2] And, again, he says that the followers of Carpocrates appealed to the authority of St. Matthias—probably, therefore, to this book, his Traditions—as an excuse for giving rein to their lusts.

These Traditions of St. Matthias evidently contained another version of the same passage, or perhaps a portion of the same discourse attributed to our Lord, which ran somehow thus : " *Wonder at what is before your eyes*

---

[1] Ὁ θαυμάσας βασιλεύσει, γεγράπται, καὶ ὁ βασιλεύσας ἀναπαύσεται. Clem. Alex. Stromata, i. 9.

[2] Strom. lib. vii. This was exaggerated in the doctrine of the Albigenses in the twelfth and thirteenth centuries. The "Perfects," the ministers of the sect, "reconciled" the converted. But if one of the Perfect sinned (*i.e.* ate meat or married), all whom he had reconciled fell with him from grace, even those who were dead and in heaven.

(*i.e.* the mighty works that I do); *for he that wondereth shall reign, and he that reigneth shall rest.*"

It is not impossible that this may be a genuine reminiscence of part of our Lord's teaching.

Justin Martyr, in his Dialogue with Trypho the Jew, says that Jesus exercised the trade of a carpenter, and that he made carts, yokes, and like articles.[1]

Where did he learn this? Not from St. Matthew's Gospel; probably from the lost Gospel which he quotes.

St. Jerome quotes as a saying of our Lord, "*Be ye proved money-changers.*"[2] He has no hesitation in calling it a saying of the Saviour. It occurs again in the Clementine Homilies[3] and in the Recognitions.[4] It is cited much more fully by St. Clement of Alexandria in his Stromata: "*Be ye proved money-changers; retain that which is good metal, reject that which is bad.*"[5] Neither St. Jerome, St. Clement of Alexandria, nor the author of the Clementines, give their authority for the statement they make, that this is a saying of the Lord; but we may, I think, fairly conclude that St. Jerome drew it from the Hebrew Gospel he knew so well, having translated it into Greek and Latin, and which he looked upon as an unexceptionable authority.

Whence the passage came may be guessed by the use made of it by those who quote it. It probably followed our Lord's saying, "I am not come to destroy the Law, but to fulfil it." "Nevertheless, be ye proved exchangers; retain that which is good metal, reject that which is bad."

---

[1] Dial. cum Tryph. § 88.

[2] "Sicut illud apostoli libenter audire : Omnia probate ; quod bonum est tenete ; et Salvatoris verba dicentis : Esto probati nummularii."—Epist. ad Minervium et Alexandrum.

[3] Homil. ii. 51, iii. 50, xviii. 20. Γίνεσθε τραπεζίται δόκιμοι.

[4] Recog. ii. 51.   [5] Stromat. i. 28.

Another passage is not given to us verbatim by St. Jerome; he merely alludes to it in one of his Commentaries, saying that Jesus had declared him guilty of a grievous crime who saddened the spirit of his brother.[1] It probably occurred in the portion of the Gospel of the Hebrews corresponding with the 18th chapter of St. Matthew, and may be restored somewhat as follows : " Woe unto the world because of offences ! for it must needs be that offences come ; *but woe to that man by whom the offence cometh, and the soul of his brother be made sore.* Wherefore if thy hand or thy foot offend thee," &c.

Another passage is in perfect harmony with the teaching of our Lord, and, like that given last, may very possibly have formed part of his teaching. It is also given by St. Jerome, and therefore in Latin : *" Be never glad unless ye are in charity with your brother."*[2]

St. Jerome, in his treatise against Pelagius, quotes from the Gospel of the Hebrews the following passage : *" If thy brother has sinned in word against thee, and has made satisfaction, forgive him unto seven times a day. Simon, his disciple, said unto him, Until seven times! The Lord answered, saying, Verily I say unto thee, until seventy times seven ;"* and then probably, *" for I say unto thee, Be never glad till thou art in charity with thy brother."*[3]

The Gospel of the Nazarenes supplied details not found in that of St. Matthew. It related of the man with the withered hand, healed by our Lord,[4] that he

---

[1] " Inter maxima ponitur crimina qui fratris sui spiritum contristaverit." St. Hieron. Comm. in Ezech. xvi. 7.

[2] " Nunquam læti sitis nisi cum fratrem vestrum videritis in charitate."

[3] " Si peccaverit frater tuus in verbo, et satis tibi fecerit, septies in die suscipe eum. Dixit illi Simon discipulus ejus : Septies in die ! Respondit Dominus et dixit ei : Etiam ego dico tibi, usque septuagies septies."—Adv. Pelag. i. 3.

[4] Matt. xxvii. 16.

was a mason,[1] and gave the words of the appeal made to
Jesus by the man invoking his compassion: "*I was a
mason, working for my bread with my hands. I pray
thee, Jesus, restore me to soundness, that I eat not my bread
in disgrace.*"[2]

It relates, what is found in St. Mark and St. Luke,
but not in St. Matthew, that Barabbas was cast into
prison for sedition and murder;[3] and it gives the interpretation of the name, "Son of a Rabbi."[4]   These particulars may be correct; there is no reason to doubt them.
The interpretation of the name may be only a gloss which
found its way into the text.

Eusebius says that Papias "gives a history of a woman
who had been accused of many sins before the Lord,
which is also contained in the Gospel according to the
Hebrews."[5]   Of this we know nothing further, for the
text is not quoted by any ancient writers; but probably
it was the same story as that of the woman taken in
adultery related in St. John's Gospel.[6]   But then, why
did not Eusebius say that Papias gave "the history of
the woman accused of adultery, which is also related in
the Gospel of St. John"?   Why does he speak of that
story as being found in a Gospel written in the Syro-
Chaldæan tongue, with which he himself was unacquainted,[7] when the same story was in the well-known
Canonical Greek Gospel of St. John?   The conclusion
one must arrive at is, either that the stories were suffi-

---

[1] "Homo iste qui aridam habet manum in Evangelio quo utuntur
Nazaræi cæmentarius scribitur."—Hieron. Comm. in Matt. xii. 13.

[2] "Homo iste . . . scribitur istius modi auxilium precans, Cæmentarius
eram, manibus victum quæritans; precor te, Jesu, ut mihi restituas sani-
tatem, ne turpiter manducem cibos."—*Ibid.*

[3] *Ibid.* xxvii. 16.

[4] "Filius Magistri eorum interpretatus."—*Ibid.*

[5] Hist. Eccl. iii. 39.   [6] viii. 3—11.

[7] He probably knew it through a translation.

ciently differently related for him not to recognize them
as the same, or that the incident in St. John's Gospel is
an excerpt from the Gospel of the Hebrews, or rather
from a translation of it, grafted into the text of the
Canonical Gospel. The latter opinion is favoured by
some critics, who think that the story of the woman
taken in adultery did not belong to the original text,
but was inserted in it in the fourth or fifth century.

Those passages of the Gospel of the Nazarenes which
most resemble passages in the Gospel of St. Matthew
are not, however, identical with them ; some differ only
in the wording, but others by the form in which they
are given.

And the remarkable peculiarity about them is, that
the lessons in the Gospel of the Hebrews seem preferable
to those in the Canonical Gospel. This was apparently
the opinion of St. Jerome.

In chap. vi. ver. 11 of St. Matthew's Gospel, we have
the article of the Lord's Prayer, "Give us this day our
daily bread." The words used in the Greek of St. Matthew are, τὸν ἄρτον ἡμῶν τὸν ἐπιούσιον. The word ἐπιούσιος
is one met with nowhere else, and is peculiar. The
word οὐσία means originally that which is essential, and
belongs to the true nature or property of things. In
Stoic philosophy it had the same significance as ὕλη,
matter ; ἐπιούσιον ἄρτον would therefore seem most justly
to be rendered by *supersubstantial*, the word employed
by St. Jerome.

"Give us this day our supernatural bread." But in
the Gospel of the Nazarenes, according to St. Jerome,
the Syro-Chaldaic word for ἐπιούσιον was מחר, which
signifies "to-morrow's," that is, our "future," or "daily"
bread. "*Give us this day the bread for the morrow*,"[1] certainly was synonymous with, "Give us this day our

[1] Comm. in Matt. i. 6.

daily bread." It is curious that the Protestant Reformers, shrinking from translating the word ἐπιούσιον according to its apparently legitimate rendering, lest they should give colour to the Catholic idea of the daily bread of the Christian soul being the Eucharist, should have adopted a rendering more in accordance with an Apocryphal than with a Canonical Gospel.

In St. Matthew, xxiii. 35, Jesus reproaches the Jews for their treatment of the prophets, and declares them responsible for all the blood shed upon the earth, "from the blood of righteous Abel unto the blood of Zacharias, son of Barachias, whom ye slew between the Temple and the altar."

Now the Zacharias to whom our Lord referred was Zechariah, son of Jehoiada, and not of Barachias, who was stoned "in the court of the house of the Lord" by order of Joash.[1] Zacharias, son of Barachias, was not killed till long after the death of our Lord. He was massacred by the zealots inside the Temple, shortly before the siege, *i.e.* about A.D. 69.

Either, then, the Greek Gospel of St. Matthew was not written till after the siege of Jerusalem, and so this anachronism passed into it, or the error is due to a copyist, who, having heard of the murder of Zacharias, son of Barachias, but who knew nothing of the Zacharias mentioned in Chronicles, corrected the Jehoiada of the original into Barachias, thinking that thereby he was rectifying a mistake.

Now in the Gospel of the Nazarenes the name stood correctly, and the passage read, "*from the blood of righteous Abel unto the blood of Zacharias, the son of Jehoiada.*"[2]

---

[1] 2 Chron. xxiv. 20.

[2] "In Evangelis quo utuntur Nazareni, pro filio Barachiæ, filium Jojadæ reperimus scriptum."—Hieron. in Matt. xxiii. 35.

In both these last quoted passages, the preference is to be given to the Nazarene Gospel, and probably also in that relating to forgiveness of a brother. The lost Gospel in that passage requires the brother to make satisfaction. It is no doubt the higher course to forgive a brother, whether he repent or not, seventy times seven times in the day; but it may almost certainly be concluded that our Lord meant that the forgiveness should be conditional on his repentance, for in St. Luke's Gospel the repentance of the trespassing brother is distinctly required. " If thy brother trespass against thee, rebuke him; and if he repent, forgive him. And if he trespass against thee seven times a day, and seven times in a day turn again to thee, saying, I repent; thou shalt forgive him." [1] In St. Luke this is addressed to all the disciples; in St. Matthew, to Peter alone; but there can be little doubt that both passages refer to the same instruction, and that the fuller accounts in St. Luke and the Gospel of the Hebrews are the more correct. There may be less elevation in the precept, subject to the two restrictions, first, that the offence should be a verbal one, and secondly, that it should be apologized for; but it brings it more within compass of being practised.

We come next to a much longer fragment, which shall be placed parallel with the passage with which it corresponds in St. Matthew.

THE GOSPEL OF THE HEBREWS.	ST. MATTHEW xix. 16—24.
" *Another rich man said unto him: Master, what good thing shall I do that I may live? He said unto him: O man, fulfil the Laws and the Prophets. And he answered*	" And, behold, one came and said unto him, Good Master, what good thing shall I do, that I may have eternal life? " And he said unto him,

---

[1] Luke xvii. 3, 4.

him, I have done so. Then said he unto him, Go, sell all that thou hast, and give to the poor, and come, follow me.

" *Then the rich man began to smite his head, and it pleased him not. And the Lord said unto him, How sayest thou, I have fulfilled the Law and the Prophets, when it is written in the Law, Thou shalt love thy neighbour as thyself; and lo! many of thy brethren, sons of Abraham, are covered with filth, and dying of hunger, and thy house is full of many good things, and nothing therefrom goeth forth at any time unto them.*

" *And turning himself about, he said unto Simon, his disciple, sitting near him, Simon, son of Jonas, it is easier for a camel to go through the eye of a needle, than for a rich man to enter into the kingdom of heaven.*" [1]

Why callest thou me good? there is none good but one, that is, God : but if thou wilt enter into life, keep the commandments.

"He saith unto him, Which? Jesus said, Thou shalt do no murder, Thou shalt not commit adultery, Thou shalt not steal, Thou shalt not bear false witness,

" Honour thy father and thy mother : and, Thou shalt love thy neighbour as thyself.

" The young man saith unto him, All these things have I kept from my youth up : what lack I yet?

" Jesus said unto him, If thou wilt be perfect, go and sell that thou hast, and give to the poor, and thou shalt have treasure in heaven : and come and follow me.

" But when the young man heard that saying, he went away sorrowful : for he had great possessions.

---

[1] " Dixit ad eum alter divitum : Magister, quid bonum faciens vivam ? Dixit ei : Homo, leges et prophetas fac. Respondit ad eum : Feci. Dixit ei : Vade, vende omnia quæ possides et divide pauperibus, et veni, sequere me. Cæpit autem dives scalpere caput suum et non placuit ei. Et dixit ad eum Dominus : Quomodo dicis : Legem feci et prophetas, quoniam scriptum est in lege : Dilige proximum tuum sicut teipsum, et ecce multi fratres tui filii Abrahæ amicti sunt stercore, morientes præ fame, et domus tua plena est multis bonis et non egreditur omnino aliquid ex ea ad eos. Et conversus dixit Simoni discipulo suo sedenti apud se : Simon fili Joannæ, facilius est camelum intrare per foramen acus quam divitem

> " Then said Jesus unto his
> disciples, Verily I say unto
> you, That a rich man shall
> hardly enter into the kingdom
> of heaven.
>
> " And again I say unto
> you, It is easier for a camel
> to go through the eye of a
> needle, than for a rich man
> to enter into the kingdom of
> God."

The comparison of these two accounts is not favourable to that in the Canonical Gospel. It is difficult to understand how a Jew could have asked, as did the rich young man, what commandments he ought to keep in order that he might enter into life. The Decalogue was known by heart by every Jew. Moreover, the narrative in the lost Gospel is more connected than in the Canonical Gospel. The reproach made by our Lord is admirably calculated to bring home to the rich man's conscience the truth, that, though professing to observe the letter of the Law, he was far from practising its spirit; and this leads up quite naturally to the declaration of the difficulty of a rich man obtaining salvation, or rather to our Lord's repeating a proverb probably common at the time in the East.[1]

And lastly, in the proverb addressed aside to Peter, instead of to the rich young man, that air of harshness which our Lord's words bear in the Canonical Gospel, as spoken to the young man in his sorrow, entirely dis-

---

in regnum cœlorum."—Origen, Tract. viii. in Matt. xix. 19. The Greek text has been lost.

[1] It is found in the Talmud, Beracoth, fol. 55, *b*; Baba Metsia, fol. 38, *b*; and it occurs in the Koran, Sura vii. 38.

appears. The proverb is uttered, not in stern rebuke,
but as the expression of sad disappointment, when the
rich man has retired.

Another fragment from the Gospel of the Hebrews
relates to the baptism of our Lord.

The Gospel of St. Matthew gives no explanation of
the occasion, the motive, of Jesus coming to Jordan to
the baptism of John. It says simply, "Then cometh
Jesus from Galilee to Jordan unto John, to be baptized
of him."[1] But the Nazarene Gospel is more explicit.

"*Behold, his mother and his brethren said unto him,
John the Baptist baptizeth for the remission of sins; let
us go and be baptized of him. But he said unto them,
What sin have I committed, that I should be baptized of
him, unless it be that in saying this I am in ignorance?*"[2]

This is a very singular passage. We do not know
the context, but we may presume that our Lord yields
to the persuasion of his mother. Such is the tradition
preserved in another apocryphal work, the "Preaching
of St. Paul," issuing from an entirely different source,
from a school hostile to the Nazarenes.[3]

Another fragment continues the account after a gap.

"*And when the Lord went up out of the water, the whole
fountain of the Holy Spirit descended and rested upon
him, and said unto him, My Son, I looked for thee in all
the prophets, that thou mightest come, and that I might*

---

[1] Matt. iii. 13.

[2] "In Evangelio juxta Hebræos . . . . narrat historia : Ecce, mater
Domini et fratres ejus dicebant ei, Joannes Baptista baptizat in remis-
sionem peccatorum, eamus et baptizemur ab eo. Dixit autem eis ; quid
peccavi, ut vadam et baptizer ab eo ? Nisi forte hoc ipsum, quod dixi,
ignorantia est."—Cont. Pelag. iii. 2.

[3] "Ad accipiendum Joannis baptisma pæne invitum a Matre sua Maria
esse compulsum."—In a treatise on the re-baptism of heretics, published
by Rigault at the end of his edition of St. Cyprian.

rest upon thee. For thou art my rest, thou art my first-
begotten Son, who shalt reign throughout eternity."[1]

But this is not the only version we have of the narrative in the Gospel of the Hebrews. St. Epiphanius
gives us another, which shall be placed parallel with
the corresponding account in St. Matthew.

GOSPEL OF THE HEBREWS.   ST. MATTHEW iii. 13—17.

" *The people having been*   " Then cometh Jesus from
baptized, Jesus came also, and   Galilee to Jordan unto John,
was baptized by John. And   to be baptized of him.
as he came out of the water,   " But John forbad him,
the heavens opened, and he   saying, I have need to be
saw the Holy Spirit of God   baptized of thee, and cometh
descending under the form of   thou to me?
a dove, and entering into him.   " And Jesus answering,
And a voice was heard from   said unto him, Suffer it to be
heaven, Thou art my beloved   so now : for thus it becometh
Son, and in thee am I well   us to fulfil all righteousness.
pleased. And again, This   Then he suffered him.
day have I begotten thee. And   " And Jesus, when he was
suddenly there shone a great   baptized, went up straightway
light in that place. And John   out of the water ; and, lo, the
seeing it, said, Who art thou,   heavens were opened unto
Lord? Then a voice was   him, and he saw the Spirit of
heard from heaven, This is   God descending like a dove,
my beloved Son, in whom I   and lighting upon him :
am well pleased. Thereat   " And lo a voice from
John fell at his feet and said,   heaven, saying, This is my
I pray thee, Lord, baptize me.   beloved Son, in whom I am
But he would not, saying,   well pleased."

---

[1] " Factum est autem cum ascendisset Dominus de aqua, descendit fons
omnis Spiritus Sancti, et requievit super eum et dixit illi, Fili mi, in
omnibus prophetis expectabam te, ut venires et requiescerem in te. Tu
es enim requies mea, tu es filius meus primogenitus, qui regnas in sem-
piternum."—In Mich. vii. 6.

*Suffer it, for so it behoveth
that all should be accomplished.*"[1]

That the Gospel stood as in this latter passage quoted
in the second century among the orthodox Christians
of Palestine is probable, because with it agrees the brief
citation of Justin Martyr, who says that when our Lord
was baptized, there shone a great light around, and a
voice was heard from heaven, saying, "Thou art my
Son, this day have I begotten thee." Both occur in the
Ebionite Gospel; neither in the Canonical Gospel.[2]

This Gospel was certainly known to the writer of the
Canonical Epistle to the Hebrews, for he twice takes
this statement as authoritative. "For unto which of
the angels said he at any time, Thou art my Son, this
day have I begotten thee?" and more remarkably,
"Christ glorified not himself to be made an high-priest;
but he that said unto him, Thou art my Son, to-day
have I begotten thee."[3]　In the latter passage the

---

[1] St. Epiph. Hæres. xxx. § 13.　Τοῦ λαοῦ βαπτισθέντος, ἦλθε καὶ
'Ιησοῦς καὶ ἐβαπτίσθη ὑπὸ τοῦ 'Ιωάννου.　Καὶ ὡς ἀνῆλθεν ἀπὸ τοῦ
ὕδατος, ἠνοίχησαν οἱ οὐρανοὶ, καὶ εἶδε τὸ πνεῦμα τοῦ Θεοῦ τὸ ἅγιον
εἶδει ἐν περιστερᾶς κατελθούσης καὶ εἰσελθούσης εἰς αὐτόν.　Καὶ φωνὴ
ἐγένετο ἐκ τοῦ οὐρανοῦ, λέγουσα· Σύ μου εἶ ὁ ἀγαπητός, ἐν σοὶ
ηὐδόκησα.　Καὶ πάλιν· 'Εγὼ σήμερον γεγέννηκα σε.　Καὶ εὐθὺς περιέλαμψε τὸν τόπον φῶς μέγα.　Ὁ ἰδὼν ὁ 'Ιωάννης λέγει αὐτῷ· Σύ τίς εἶ,
κύριε; Καὶ πάλιν φωνὴ ἐξ οὐρανοῦ πρὸς αὐτόν· Οὗτός ἐστιν ὁ υἱός μου
ὁ ἀγαπητός, ἐφ' ὃν ηὐδόκησα.　Καὶ τότε ὁ 'Ιωάννης προσπεσὼν αὐτῷ
ἔλεγε· Δέομαι σου, κύριε, σύ με βάπτισον.　Ὁ δὲ ἐκώλυεν αὐτῷ, λέγων·
Ἄφες, ὅτι οὕτως ἐστὶ πρέπον πληρωθῆναι πάντα.

[2] I put them in apposition:

　　Justin. Καὶ πῦρ ἀνήφθη ἐν τῷ 'Ιορδάνη.—Dial. cum Tryph. § 88.
　　Epiphan. Καὶ εὐθὺς περιέλαμψε τὸν τόπον φῶς μέγα.—Hæres.
　　xxx. § 13.

　　Justin. Υἱός μου εἶ σύ· ἐγὼ σήμερον γεγέννηκα σε.—Dial. cum
　　Tryph. § 88 and 103.

　　Epiphan. 'Εγὼ σήμερον γεγέννηκα σε.—Hæres. xxx. § 13.

[3] Heb. i. 5, v. 5.

author is speaking of the calling of priests being miraculous and manifest; and then he cites this call of
Christ to the priesthood as answering these requirements.

The order of events is not the same in the Gospel of
the Twelve and in that of St. Matthew: verses 14 and
15 of the latter, modified in an important point, come
in the Ebionite Gospel after verses 16 and 17.

There is a serious discrepancy between the account of
the baptism of our Lord in St. Matthew and in St. John.
In the former Canonical Gospel, the Baptist forbids
Christ to be baptized by him, saying, " I have need to
be baptized of thee, and comest thou to me?" But
Jesus bids him: " Suffer it to be so now, for thus it
becometh us to fulfil all righteousness." Then Jesus is
baptized, and the heavens are opened. But in St. John's
Gospel, the Baptist says, " I knew him not: but he that
sent me to baptize with water, the same said unto me,
Upon whom thou shalt see the Spirit descending, and
remaining upon him, the same is he which baptizeth
with the Holy Ghost. And I saw, and bare record, that
this is the Son of God."[1]

Now the account in the Gospel of the Twelve removes
this discrepancy. John does not know Jesus till after
the light and the descent of the dove and the voice, and
then he asks to be baptized by Jesus.

It is apparent that the passage in the lost Gospel is
more correct than that in the Canonical one. In the
latter there has been an inversion of verses destroying
the succession of events, and thus producing discrepancy
with the account in St. John's Gospel.

With these passages from the Gospel of the Twelve
may be compared a curious one from the Testament of
the Twelve Patriarchs. It occurs in the Testament of

[1] John i. 29—34.

H

Levi, and is a prophecy of the Messiah. " The heavens shall open for thee, and from above the temple of glory the voice of the Father shall dispense sanctification upon him, as has been promised unto Abraham, the father of Isaac."

The passage quoted by St. Epiphanius is wholly unobjectionable doctrinally. It is not so with that quoted by St. Jerome; it is of a very different character. It exhibits strongly the Gnostic ideas which infected the stricter sect of the Ebionites.

It was precisely on the baptism of the Lord that they laid the greatest stress; and it is in the account of that event that we should expect to find the greatest divergence between the texts employed by the orthodox and the heretical Nazarenes. Before his baptism he was nothing. It was then only that the "full fount of the Holy Ghost" descended on him, his election to the Messiahship was revealed, and divine power was communicated to him to execute the mission entrusted to him. A marked distinction was drawn between two portions in the life of Jesus—before and after his baptism. In the first they acknowledged nothing but the mere human nature, to the entire exclusion of everything supernatural; while the sudden accruing of supernatural aid at the baptism marked the moment when he became the Messiah. Thus the baptism was the beginning of their Gospel.

Before that, he is liable to sin, he suggests that his believing himself to be free from sin may have precipitated him into sin, the sin of ignorance. And " *even in the prophets, after they had received the unction of the Holy Ghost, there was found sinful speech.*"[1] This quotation follows, in St. Jerome, immediately after the say-

---

[1] "Etiam in prophetis quoque, postquam uncti sunt Spiritu sancto, inventus est sermo peccati."—Contr Pel ii. 8.

ing cited above enjoining forgiveness, but it in no way dovetails into it; the passage concerning the recommendation by St. Mary and the brethren that they should go up to be baptized of John for the remission of sins, comes in the same chapter, and there can be little doubt that this reference to the prophets as sinful formed part of the answer of the Virgin to Jesus when he spoke of his being sinless.

St. Jerome obtained his copy of the Gospel of the Hebrews from Beræa in Syria, and not therefore from the purest source. Had he copied and translated the codex he found in the library of Pamphilus at Cæsarea, instead of that he procured from Beræa, it is probable that he would have found it not to contain the passages of Gnostic tendency.

These interpolations were made in the second century, when Gnostic ideas had begun to affect the Ebionites, and break them up into more or less heretical sects.

Their copies of the Gospel of the Hebrews differed, for the Gnostic Ebionites curtailed it in some places, and amplified it in others.

In reconstructing the primitive lost Gospel of the Nazarenes, it is very necessary to note these Gnostic passages, and to withdraw them from the text. We shall come to some more of their additions and alterations presently. It is sufficient for us to note here that the heretical Gospel in use among the Gnostic Ebionites was based on the orthodox Gospel of the Hebrews. The existence of these two versions explains the very different treatment their Gospel meets with at the hands of the Fathers of the Church. Some, and these the earliest, speak of this Gospel with reverence, and place it almost on a line with the Canonical Gospels; others speak of it with horror, as an heretical corruption of the Gospel of St. Matthew. The former saw the primitive text, the latter the curtailed and amplified version in use among the heretical Ebionites.

St. Paul, in his first Epistle to the Corinthians, alludes to one of the appearances of our Lord after his resurrection, of which no mention is made in the Canonical Gospels: "After that, he was seen of James." [1] But according to his account, this appearance took place after several other manifestations, viz. after that to Cephas, that to the Twelve, and that to five hundred brethren at once. But it preceded another appearance to "all the apostles." If we take the first and second to have occurred on Easter-day, and the last to have been the appearance to them again "after eight days," when St. Thomas was present, then the appearance to St. James must have taken place between the "even" of Easter-day and Low Sunday.

Now the Gospel of the Hebrews gives a particular account of this visit to James, which however, according to this account, took place early on Easter-day, certainly before Christ stood in the midst of the apostles in the upper room on Easter-evening.

St. Jerome says, "The Gospel according to the Hebrews relates that after the resurrection of the Saviour, *'The Lord, after he had given the napkin to the servant of the priest, went to James, and appeared to him. Now James had sworn with an oath that he would not eat bread from that hour when he drank the cup of the Lord, till he should behold him rising from amidst them that sleep.'* And again, a little after, *'The Lord said, Bring a table and bread.'* And then, *'He took bread and blessed and brake, and gave it to James the Just, and said unto*

---

[1] 1 Cor. xv. 7.

him, My brother, eat thy bread, for the Son of Man is risen from among them that sleep.'[1]

This touching incident is quite in keeping with what we know about St. James, the Lord's brother.

James the Just, according to Hegesippus, "neither drank wine nor fermented liquors, and abstained from animal food;"[2] and though the account of Hegesippus is manifestly fabulous in some of its details, still there is no reason to doubt that James belonged to the ascetic school among the Jews, as did the Baptist before him, and as did the orthodox Ebionites after him. The oath to abstain from food till a certain event was accomplished was not unusual.[3]

What is meant by "the Saviour giving the napkin to the servant of the priest," it is impossible to conjecture without the context. The napkin was probably that which had covered his face in the tomb, but whether the context linked this on to the cycle of sacred sindones impressed with the portrait of the Saviour's suffering face, cannot be told. The designation of "the Just" as applied to James is for the purpose of distinguishing him from James the brother of John. He does not bear ·that name in the Canonical Gospels, but the title may have been introduced by St. Jerome to avoid confusion, or it may have been a marginal gloss to the text.

The story of this appearance found its way into the

---

[1] "Evangelium . . . secundum Hebræos . . . post resurrectionem Salvatoris refert :—Dominus autem, cum dedisset sindonem servo sacerdotis, ivit ad Jacobum et apparuit ei. Juraverat enim Jacobus, se non comesturum panem ab illa hora, qua biberat calicem Domini, donec videret eum resurgentem a dormientibus.—Rursusque post paululum : Afferte, ait Dominus, mensam et panem. Statimque additur :—Tulit panem et benedixit, ac fregit, et dedit Jacobo justo, et dixit ei : Frater mi, comede panem tuum, quia resurrexit Filius hominis a dormientibus."—Hieron. De viris illustribus, c. 2.

[2] Euseb. H. E. lib. ii. c. 23.   [3] Acts xxiii. 14.

writings of St. Gregory of Tours,[1] who no doubt drew it from St. Jerome; and thence it passed into the Legenda Aurea of Jacques de Voragine.

If the Lord did appear to St. James on Easter-day, as related in this lost Gospel, then it may have been in the morning, and not after his appearance to the Twelve, or on his appearance in the evening he may have singled out and addressed James before all the others, as on that day week he addressed St. Thomas. In either case, St. Paul's version would be inaccurate as to the order of manifestations. The pseudo-Abdias, not in any way trustworthy, thus relates the circumstance:

"James the Less among the disciples was an object of special attachment to the Saviour, and he was inflamed with such zeal for his Master that he would take no meat when his Lord was crucified, and would only eat again when he should see Christ arisen from the dead; for he remembered that when Christ was alive he had given this precept to him and to his brethren. That is why he, with Mary Magdalene and Peter, was the first of all to whom Jesus Christ appeared, in order to confirm his disciples in the faith; and that he might not suffer him to fast any longer, a piece of an honeycomb having been offered him, he invited James to eat thereof."[2]

Another fragment of the lost Gospel of the Hebrews also relates to the resurrection:

---

[1] Hist. Eccl. Francorum, i. 21.

[2] The "History of the Apostles" purports to have been written by Abdias B. of Babylon, disciple of the apostles, in Hebrew. It was translated into Greek, and thence, it was pretended, into Latin by Julius Africanus. That it was rendered from Greek has been questioned by critics. As we have it, it belongs to the ninth century; but the publication of Syriac versions of the legends on which the book of Abdias was founded, Syriac versions of the fourth century, which were really translated from the Greek, show that some Greek originals must have existed at an early age which are now lost.

"*And when he had come to [Peter and] those that were with Peter, he said unto them, Take, touch me, and see that I am not a bodiless spirit. And straightway they touched him and believed.*"[1]

St. Ignatius, who cites these words, excepting only those within brackets, does not say whence he drew them; but St. Jerome informs us that they were taken from the Gospel of the Hebrews. At the same time he gives the passage with greater fulness than St. Ignatius.

The account in St. Matthew contains nothing at all like this; but St. Luke mentions these circumstances, though with considerable differences. The Lord having appeared in the midst of his disciples, they imagine that they see a spirit. Then he says, " Why are ye troubled? and why do thoughts arise in your hearts ? Behold my hands and my feet, that it is I myself: handle me, and see; for a spirit hath not flesh and bones, as ye see me have." [2]

The narrative in St. Luke's Gospel is fuller than that in the Gospel of the Hebrews, and is not derived from it. In the Nazarene Gospel, as soon as the apostles see and touch, they believe. But in the Canonical Gospel of St. Luke, they are not convinced till they see Christ eat.

Justin Martyr cites a passage now found in the Canonical Gospel of St. John, but not exactly as there, evidently therefore obtaining it from an independent source, and that source was the Gospel of the Twelve,

---

[1] Καὶ ὅτε πρὸς τοὺς περὶ Πέτρον ἦλθεν ἔφη αὐτοῖς· λάβετε, ψηλαφήσατε με, καὶ ἴδετε, ὅτι οὐκ εἰμὶ δαιμόνιον ἀσώματον. Καὶ εὐθὺς αὐτοῦ ἥψαντο καὶ ἐπίστευσαν.—Ignat. Ep. ad Smyrn. c. 3. St. Jerome also : " Et quando venit ad Petrum et ad eos qui cum Petro erant, dixit eis : Ecce palpate me et videte quia non sum dæmonium incorporale. Et statim tetigerunt eum et crediderunt."—De Script. Eccl. 16. Eusebius quotes the passage after Ignatius. Hist. Eccl. iii. 37.

[2] Luke xxiv. 37—39.

the only one with which he was acquainted, the only one then acknowledged as Canonical in the Nazarene Church.

The passage is, " *Christ has said, Except ye be regenerate, ye cannot enter into the kingdom of heaven.*"[1]

In St. John's Gospel the parallel passage is couched in the third person: " Except a man be born again, he cannot see the kingdom of God."[2] The difference stands out more clearly in the Greek than in English.

We may conjecture that the primitive Gospel of the Hebrews contained an account of the interview of Nicodemus with our Lord. When we come to consider the Gospel used by the author of the Clementine Homilies and Recognitions, we shall find that the instruction on new birth made to Nicodemus was familiar to him, but not exactly in the form in which it is recorded by St. John.

St. Jerome informs us that the lost Gospel we are considering did not relate that the veil of the Temple was rent in twain when Jesus gave up the ghost, but that the lintel stone, a huge stone, fell down.[3]

That this tradition may be true is not unlikely. The rocks were rent, and the earth quaked, and it is probable enough that the Temple was so shaken that the great lintel stone fell.

St. Epiphanius gives us another fragment:

" *I am come to abolish the sacrifices: if ye cease not from sacrificing, the wrath of God will not cease from weighing upon you.*"[4]

---

[1] Καὶ γὰρ ὁ Χριστὸς εἶπεν· ἂν μὴ ἀναγεννηθῆτε, οὐ μὴ εἰσελθῆτε εἰς τὴν βασιλείαν τῶν οὐρανῶν.—1 Apolog. § 61. Oper. p. 94.

[2] Ἐὰν μήτις γεννηθῇ ἄνωθεν, οὐ δύναται ἰδεῖν τὴν βασιλείαν τοῦ Θεοῦ.—John iii. 3.

[3] "In Evangelio . . . legimus non velum templi scissum, sed superliminare templi miræ magnitudinis corruisse."—Epist. 120, Ad Helibiam.

[4] Ἐλθὸν καταλῦσαι τὰς θυσίας, καὶ ἐὰν μὴ παύσασθε τοῦ θύειν, οὐ παύσεται ἀφ' ὑμῶν ἡ ὀργή.—Epiphan. Hæres. xxx. § 16.

In the Clementine Recognitions, a work issuing from the Ebionite anti-Gnostic school, we find that the abolition of the sacrifices was strongly insisted on. The abomination of idolatry is first exposed, and the strong hold that Egyptian idolatry had upon the Israelites is pointed out; then we are told Moses received the Law, and, in consideration of the prejudices of the people, tolerated sacrifice:

"When Moses perceived that the vice of sacrificing to idols had been deeply ingrained into the people from their association with the Egyptians, and that the root of this evil could not be extracted from them, he allowed them to sacrifice indeed, but permitted it to be done only to God, that by any means he might cut off one half of the deeply ingrained evil, leaving the other half to be corrected by another, and at a future time; by him, namely, concerning whom he said himself, A prophet shall. the Lord your God raise unto you, whom ye shall hear, even as myself, according to all things which he shall say to you. Whosoever shall not hear that prophet, his soul shall be cut off from his people." [1]

In another place the Jewish sacrifices are spoken of as sin.[2]

This hostility to the Jewish sacrificial system by Ebionites who observed all the other Mosaic institutions was due to their having sprung out of the old sect of the Essenes, who held the sacrifices in the same abhorrence.[3]

That our Lord may have spoken against the sacrifices is possible enough. The passage may have stood thus: "Think not that I am come to destroy the Law and the Prophets; I am not come to destroy, but to fulfil; nevertheless, I tell you the truth, I am come to destroy the

---

[1] Recog. i. 36.   [2] Recog. i. 54.

[3] Joseph. Antiq. xviii. 1, 5; Philo Judæus. Περὶ τοῦ πάντα σπουδαῖον εἶναι ἐλεύθερον. See what has been said on this subject already, p. 16.

sacrifices. But be ye approved money-changers, choose
that which is good metal, reject that which is bad."

It is probable that in the original Hebrew Gospel
there was some such passage, for St. Paul, or whoever
was the author of the Epistle to the Hebrews, apparently
alludes to it twice. He says, "When he cometh into
the world he saith, Sacrifice and offering thou wouldst
not, but a body hast thou prepared me."[1] The plain
meaning of which is, not that David had used those
words centuries before, in prophecy, but that Jesus had
used them himself when he came into the world. If
the writer of the Epistle did quote a passage from the
Hebrew Gospel, it will have been the second from the
same source.

In the Ebionite Gospel, "by a criminal fraud," says
St. Epiphanius, a protestation has been placed in the
mouth of the Lord against the Paschal Sacrifice of the
Lamb, by changing a positive phrase into a negative
one.

When the disciples ask Jesus where they shall prepare the Passover, he is made to reply, not, as in St. Luke,
that with desire he had desired to eat this Passover, but,
"*Have I then any desire to eat the flesh of the Paschal
Lamb with you ?*"[2]

The purpose of this interpolation of two words is
clear. The Samaritan Ebionites, like the Essenes, did
not touch meat, regarding all animal food with the
greatest repugnance.[3] By the addition of two words
they were able to convert the saying of our Lord into a
sanction of their superstition. But this saying of Jesus

[1] Heb. x. 5.

[2] (Μὴ) ἐπιθυμίᾳ ἐπεθύμησα (κρέας) τοῦτο τό πάσχα φαγεῖν μεθ' ὑμῶν·
Epiph. Heræs. xxx. 22. The words added to those in St. Luke are placed
in brackets ; cf. Luke xxii. 15.

[3] Epiphan. Hæres. xxx. 15.

is now found only in St. Luke's Gospel. It must have stood originally without the Μὴ and the κρέας in the Gospel of the Twelve.

Another of their alterations of the Gospel was to the same intent. Instead of making St. John the Baptist eat locusts and wild honey, they gave him for his nourishment wild honey only, ἐγχρίδας, instead of ἀχρίδας and μελί ἄγριον.

The passage in which this curious change was made is remarkable. It served as the introduction to the Gospel in use among the Gnostic Ebionites.

"*A certain man, named Jesus, being about thirty years of age, hath chosen us ; and having come to Capernaum, he entered into the house of Simon, whose surname was Peter, and he said unto him, As I passed by the Sea of Tiberias, I chose John and James, the sons of Zebedee, Simon and Andrew, Thaddæus, Simon Zelotes and Judas Iscariot ; and thee, Matthew, when thou wast sitting at thy tax-gatherer's table, then I called thee, and thou didst follow me.   And you do I choose to be my twelve apostles to bear witness unto Israel.*

"*John baptized ; and the Pharisees came to him, and they were baptized of him, and all Jerusalem also.   He had a garment of camels' hair, and a leathern girdle about his loins, and his meat was wild honey, and the taste thereof was as manna, and as a cake of oil.*"

Apparently after this announcement of his choice of the apostles there followed something analogous to the preface in St. Luke's Gospel, to the effect that these apostles, having assembled together, had taken in hand to write down those things that they remembered concerning Christ and his teaching.   And it was on this account that the Gospel obtained the name of the "Recollections of the Apostles," or the "Gospel of the Twelve."

The special notice taken of St. Matthew, who is singled out from the others in this address, is significant of the relation supposed to exist between the Gospel and the converted publican. If we had the complete introduction, we should probably find that in it he was said to have been the scribe who wrote down the apostolic recollections.

2. *Doubtful Fragments.*

THERE are a few fragments preserved by early ecclesiastical writers which we cannot say for certain belonged to the Gospel of the Hebrews, but which there is good reason to believe formed a part of it.

Origen, in his Commentary on St. Matthew, quotes a saying of our Lord which is not to be found in the Canonical Gospels. Origen, we know, was acquainted with, and quoted respectfully, the Gospel of the Hebrews. It is therefore probable that this quotation is taken from it : "*Jesus said, For the sake of the weak I became weak, for the sake of the hungry I hungered, for the sake of the thirsty I thirsted.*" [1]

That this passage, full of beauty, occurred after the words, "This kind goeth not out but by prayer and fasting," in commenting on which Origen quotes it, is probable. It is noteworthy that it is quoted in comment on St. Matthew's Gospel, the one to which the lost Gospel bore the closest resemblance, and one which Origen would probably consult whilst compiling his Commentary on St. Matthew.[2]

---

[1] Καὶ Ἰησοῦς γοῦν φησὶ, Διὰ τοὺς ἀσθενοῦντας ἠσθένουν, καὶ διὰ τοὺς πεινῶντας ἐπείνων, καὶ διὰ τοὺς διψῶντας ἐδίψων. In Matt. xvii. 21.

[2] Perhaps this passage was in the mind of St. Paul when he wrote of himself, "To the weak became I as weak, that I might gain the weak." 1 Cor. ix. 22.

The saying is so beautiful, and so truly describes the love of our Lord, that we must wish to believe it comes to us on such high authority as the Gospel of the Twelve.

Another saying of Christ is quoted both by Clement of Alexandria and by Origen, without saying whence they drew it, but by both as undoubted sayings of the Saviour. It ran:

"*Seek those things that are great, and little things will be added to you.*" "*And seek ye heavenly things, and the things of this world will be added to you.*"[1]

It will be seen, the form as given by St. Clement is better and simpler than that given by Origen. It is probable, however, that they both formed members of the same saying, following the usual Hebrew arrangement of repeating a maxim, giving it a slightly different turn or a wider expansion. In two passages in other places Origen makes allusion to this saying without quoting it directly.[2]

In the Acts of the Apostles, St. Luke puts into the mouth of St. Paul a saying of Christ, which is not given by any evangelist, in these words : " Remember the words of the Lord Jesus, how he said, *It is more blessed to give than to receive.*"[3] It is curious that this saying should not have been inserted by St. Luke in his Gospel. Whether this saying found its way into the Hebrew Gospel it is impossible to tell.

In the Epistle of St. Barnabas another utterance of Christ is given. This Epistle is so distinctly of a Judaizing character, so manifestly belongs to the Naza-

---

[1] Αἰτεῖσθε γάρ, φησί, τὰ μεγάλα, καὶ τὰ μικρὰ ὑμῖν προστεθήσαται. Clemens Alex. Stromatæ, i. Καὶ αἰτεῖτε τὰ ἐπουράνια, καὶ τὰ ἐπίγεια ὑμῖν προστεθήσεται.—Origen, De Orat. 2 and 43.

[2] Cont. Cels. vii. and De Orat. 53.

[3] Acts xx. 35. It is also quoted as a saying of our Lord in the Apostolic Constitutions, iv. 3.

rene school, that such a reference in it makes it more
than probable that it was taken from the Gospel received as Canonical among the Nazarenes. The saying
of St. Barnabas is, " All the time of our life and of our
faith will not profit us, if we have not in abhorrence
the evil one and future temptation, even as the Son of
God said, *Resist all iniquity and hold it in abhorrence.*"[1]
Another saying in the Epistle of St. Barnabas is, " *They
who would see me, and attain to my kingdom, must possess
me through afflictions and sufferings.*"[2]

In the second Epistle of St. Clement of Rome to the
Corinthians occurs a very striking passage : " Wherefore
to us doing such things the Lord said, *If ye were with
me, gathered together in my bosom, and did not keep my
commandments, I would cast you out, and say unto you,
Depart from me, I know not whence ye are, ye workers of
iniquity.*"[3]

We can well understand this occurring in an anti-
Pauline Gospel.

Again. " The Lord said, *Be ye as lambs in the midst
of wolves. Peter answered and said unto him, But what
if the wolves shall rend the lambs ? Jesus said unto Peter,
The lambs fear not the wolves after their death ; and ye
also, do not ye fear them that kill you, and after that
have nothing that they can do to you, but fear rather him
who, after ye are dead, has power to cast your soul and
body into hell fire.*"[4]

---

[1] Ep. 4.

[2] Οὗτοι, φησὶν, οἱ θέλοντές με ἰδεῖν, καὶ ἅψασθαί μου τῆς βασιλείας, ὀ-
φείλουσι θλιβέντες καὶ παθόντες λαβεῖν με.—Ep. 7.

[3] Διὰ τοῦτο ταῦτα ἡμῶν πρασσόντων, εἶπεν ὁ κύριος, 'Εὰν ἦτε μετ'
ἐμοῦ συνηγμένοι ἐν τῷ κόλπῳ μου, καὶ μὴ ποιεῖτε τὰς ἐντολάς μου, ἀπο-
βαλῶ ὑμᾶς καὶ ἐρῶ ὑμῖν, ὑπάγετε ἀπ' ἐμοῦ, οὐκ οἶδα ὑμᾶς, ἐργάται ἀνομίας.
2 Ep. ad Corinth. 4.

[4] Λέγει γὰρ ὁ κύριος, ἔσεσθε ὡς ἀρνία ἐν μέσῳ λύκων. 'Αποκριθεὶς δὲ
ὁ Πέτρος αὐτῷ λέγει, 'Εὰν οὖν διασπαράξωσιν οἱ λύκοι τα ἀρνία ; Εἰπεν

This is clearly another version of the passage, Matt. x. 16—26. In one particular it is fuller than in the Canonical Gospel; it introduces St. Peter as speaking and drawing forth the exhortation not to fear those who kill the body only. But it is without the long exhortation contained in the 17—27th verses of St. Matthew.

Another saying from the same source is, " This, therefore, the Lord said, *Keep the flesh chaste and the seal undefiled, and ye shall receive eternal life.*" [1] The seal is the unction of confirmation completing baptism, and in the primitive Church united with it. It is the σφραγίς so often spoken of in the Epistles of St. Paul.[2]

Justin Martyr contributes another saying. We have already seen that in all likelihood he quoted from the Gospel of the Hebrews, or the Recollections of the Twelve, as he called it. He says, " On this account also our Lord Jesus Christ said, *In those things in which I shall overtake you, in those things will I judge you.*" [3] Clement of Alexandria makes the same quotation, slightly varying the words. Justin and Clement apparently both translated from the original Hebrew, but did not give exactly the same rendering of words, though they gave the same sense.

Clement gives us another saying, but does not say

ὁ Ἰησοῦς τῷ Πέτρῳ. Μὴ φοβείσθωσαν τὰ ἀρνία τοὺς λύκους μετὰ τὸ ἀποθανεῖν αὐτά. Καὶ ὑμεῖς μὴ φοβεῖσθε τοὺς ἀποκτείνοντας ὑμᾶς, καὶ μηδὲν ὑμῖν δυναμένους ποιεῖν, ἀλλὰ φοβεῖσθε τὸν μετὰ τὸ ἀποθανεῖν ὑμας ἔχοντα ἐξουσίαν ψυχῆς καὶ σώματος τοῦ βαλεῖν εἰς γέενναν πυρὸς. *Ibid.* 5.

[1] Ἄρα οὖν τοῦτο λέγει: Τηρήσατε τὴν σάρκα ἀγνὴν καί τὴν σφραγίδα ἄσπιλον, ἵνα τὴν αἰώνιον ζωὴν ἀπολάβητε.—*Ibid.* 8.

[2] Rom. iv. 11; 2 Cor. i. 22; Eph. i. 13, iv. 30; 2 Tim. ii. 19.

[3] Ἐν οἷς ἀν ὑμᾶς καταλάβω, ἐν τούτοις καὶ κρινῶ.—Just. Mart. in Dialog. c. Trypho. Ἐφ' οἷς γὰρ εὕρω ἡμᾶς, φησὶν, ἐπι τούτοις καὶ κρινῶ. Clem. Alex. Quis dives salv. 40.

from what Gospel he drew it. "The Lord commanded in a certain Gospel, *My secret is for me and for the children of my house.*" [1]

---

3. *The Origin of the Gospel of the Hebrews.*

WE come now to a question delicate, and difficult to answer—the Origin of the Gospel of the Hebrews; delicate, because it involves another, the origin of the Gospels of St. Matthew and St. Mark; difficult, because of the nature of the evidence on which we shall have to form our opinion.

Because the Gospel of the Hebrews is not preserved, is not in the Canon, it does not follow that its value was slight, its accuracy doubtful. Its disappearance is due partly to the fact of its having been written in Aramaic, but chiefly to that of its having been in use by an Aramaic-speaking community which assumed first a schismatical, then a heretical position, so that the disfavour which fell on the Nazarene body enveloped and doomed its Gospel as well.

The four Canonical Gospels owe their preservation to their having been in use among those Christian communities which coalesced under the moulding hands of St. John. Those parties which were reluctant to abandon their peculiar features were looked upon with coldness, then aversion, lastly abhorrence. They became more and more isolated, eccentric, prejudiced, impracticable. Whilst the Church asserted her catholicity, organized her constitution, established her canon, formulated her creed, adapted herself to the flux of ideas, these narrow

---

[1] Μυστήριον ἐμὸν ἐμοὶ καὶ τοῖς υἱοῖς τοῦ οἴκου μου.—Clem. Alex. Strom. v.

sects spent their petty lives in accentuating their peculiarities till they grew into monstrosities; and when
they fell and disappeared, there fell and disappeared
with them those precious records of the Saviour's words
and works which they had preserved.

The Hebrew Gospel was closely related to the Gospel
of St. Matthew; that we know from the testimony of
St. Jerome, who saw, copied and translated it. That
it was not identical with the Canonical first Gospel is
also certain. Sufficient fragments have been preserved
to show that in many points it was fuller, in some less
complete, than the Greek Gospel of St. Matthew. The
two Gospels were twin sisters speaking different tongues.
Was the Greek of the first Gospel acquired, or was it
original? This is a point deserving of investigation
before we fix the origin and determine the construction
of the Hebrew Gospel.

According to a fragment of a lost work by Papias,
written about the middle of the second century, under
the title of "Commentary on the Sayings of the Lord,"[1]
the apostle Matthew was the author of a collection of
the "sayings," λόγια, of our blessed Lord. The passage
has been already given, but it is necessary to quote it
again here: "Matthew wrote in the Hebrew dialect the
sayings, and every one interpreted them as best he was
able."[2] These "logia" could only be, according to the
signification of the word (Rom. iii. 2; Heb. v. 12;
Pet. iv. 11; Acts vii. 38), a collection of the sayings of
the Saviour that were regarded as oracular, as "the
words of God." That they were the words of Jesus,
follows from the title given by Papias to his commentary, Λόγια κυριακὰ.

---

[1] Λογίων κυριακῶν ἐξηγήσεις.

[2] Ματθαῖος μὲν οὖν ἑβραΐδι διαλέκτῳ τὰ λόγια συνεγράψατο, ἡρμήνευσε
δὲ αὐτὰ ὡς ἦν δυνατὸς ἕκαστος.

This brief notice is sufficient to show that Matthew's collection was not the Gospel as it now stands. It was no collection of the acts, no biography, of the Saviour; it was solely a collection of his discourses.

This is made clearer by what Papias says in the same work on St. Mark. He relates that the latter wrote not only what Jesus had *said*, but also what he *did*;[1] whereas St. Matthew wrote only what had been *said*.[2]

The work of Matthew, therefore, contained no doings, πραχθέντα, but only sayings, λεχθέντα, which were, according to Papias, written in Hebrew, *i.e.* the vernacular Aramaic, and which were translated into Greek by every one as best he was able.

This notice of Papias is very ancient. The Bishop of Hierapolis is called by Irenæus "a very old man,"[3] and by the same writer is said to have been "a friend of Polycarp," and "one who had heard John."[4] That this John was the apostle is not certain. It was questioned by Eusebius in his mention of the Procemium of Papias. John the priest and John the apostle were both at Ephesus, and both lived there at the close of the first century. Some have thought the Apocalypse to have been the work of the priest John, and not of the apostle. Others have supposed that there was only one John. However this may be, it is certain that Papias lived at a time when it was possible to obtain correct information relating to the origin of the sacred books in use among the Christians.

According to the Procemium of Papias, which Eusebius has preserved, the Bishop of Hierapolis had obtained his knowledge, not directly from the apostles, nor from

---

[1] τὰ ὑπὸ τοῦ Χριστοῦ ἢ λεχθέντα ἢ πραχθέντα; and οὐ ποιούμενος σύνταξιν τῶν κυριακῶν λογίων.

[2] συνεγράψατο τὰ λόγια.　　　[3] ἀρχαῖος ἀνήρ.

[4] Iren. c. Hæres. v. 33.

the apostle John, but from the mouths of men who had companied with old priests and disciples of the apostles, and who had related to him what Andrew, Peter, Philip, Thomas, James, John and other disciples of the Lord had said (εἶπεν). Besides the testimony of these priests, Papias appealed further to the evidence of Aristion and the priest John, disciples of the Lord,[1] still alive and bearing testimony when he wrote. "And," says Papias, "I do not think that I derived so much benefit from books as from the living voice of those that are still surviving." [2]

Papias, therefore, had his information about the apostles second-hand, from those "who followed them about." Nevertheless, his evidence is quite trustworthy. He takes pains to inform us that he used great precaution to obtain the truth about every particular he stated, and the means of obtaining the truth were at his disposal. That Papias was a man "of a limited comprehension"[3] does not affect the trustworthiness of his statement. Eusebius thus designates him because he believed in the Millennium ; but so did most of the Christians of the first age, as well as in the immediate second coming of Christ, till undeceived by events.

The statement of Papias does not justify us in supposing that Matthew wrote the Gospel in Hebrew, but only a collection of the logia, the sayings of Jesus. Eusebius did not mistake the Sayings for the Gospel, for he speaks separately of the Hebrew Gospel,[4] without connecting it in any way with the testimony of Papias.

According to Eusebius, Papias wrote his Commentary in five books.[5] It is not improbable, therefore, that the

---

[1] Scarcely actual disciples and eye-witnesses.

[2] Euseb. Hist. Eccl. iii. 39.   [3] σφόδρα σμικρὸς τὸν νοῦν.

[4] καθ᾽ Ἑβραιοὺς εὐαγγέλιον.   H. E. iii. 25, 27, 39 ; iv. 22.

[5] συγγράμματα πέντε.

"Logia" were broken into five parts or grouped in five discourses, and that he wrote an explanation of each discourse in a separate book or chapter.

The statement of Papias, if it does not refer to the Gospel of St. Matthew as it now stands, does refer to one of the constituent parts of that Gospel, and does explain much that would be otherwise inexplicable.

1. St. Matthew's Gospel differs from St. Mark's in that it contains long discourses, sayings and parables, which are wanting or only given in a brief form in the second Canonical Gospel. It is therefore probable that in its composition were used the "Logia of the Lord," written by Matthew.

2. If the collection of "Sayings of the Lord" consisted, as has been suggested, of five parts, then we find traces in the Canonical Matthew of five groups of discourses, concluded by the same formulary: "And it came to pass when Jesus had ended these sayings" (τοὺς λόγους τούτους), or "parables," vii. 28, xi. 1, xiii. 53, xix. 1, xxvi. 1. It is not, however, possible to restore all the "logia" to their primitive positions, for they have been dispersed through the Canonical Gospel, and arranged in connection with the events which called them forth. In the "Sayings of the Lord" of Matthew, these events were not narrated; but all the sayings were placed together, like the proverbs in the book of Solomon.

3. The "Logia" of the Lord were written by Matthew in Hebrew, i.e. in the vernacular Aramaic. If they have formed the groundwork, or a composite part of the Canonical Gospel, we are likely to detect in the Greek some traces of their origin. And this, in fact, we are able to do.

a. In the first place, we have the introduction of

Aramaic words, as Raka (v. 22),[1] Mammon (vi. 22),[2] Gehenna (v. 22),[3] Amen (v. 18).[4] Many others might be cited, but these will suffice.

β. Next, we have the use of illustrations which are only comprehensible by Hebrews, as " One jot and one tittle shall in no wise fall." The Ἰῶτα of the Greek text is the Aramaic Jod (v. 18); but the " one tittle" is more remarkable. In the Greek it is " one horn," or " stroke."[5] The idea is taken from the Aramaic orthography. A stroke distinguishes one consonant from another, as ה and ח from ד. With this the Greeks had nothing that corresponded.

γ. We find Hebraisms in great number in the discourses of our Lord given by St. Matthew.[6]

δ. We find mistranslations. The Greek Canonical text gives a wrong meaning, or no meaning at all, through misunderstanding of the Aramaic. By restoration of the Aramaic text we can rectify the translation. Thus:

Matt. vii. 6, " Give not that which is holy to dogs, neither cast ye your pearls before swine." The word " holy," τὸ ἅγιον, is a misinterpretation of the Aramaic קְרָשָׁא, a gold jewel for the ear, head or neck.[7] The translator mistook the word for קוּרשָׁא, or קורשׁא without ו, " the holy." The sentence in the original therefore

---

[1] Aram. רֵיקָא.   [2] Aram. מָמוֹנָא

[3] Aram. גֵּיהִנָּם   [4] Aram. אָמֵן

[5] μιά κεραία, Aram. קוֹץ or עֲוָחָן.

[6] vi. 7, βαττολογεῖν ; v. 5, κληρονομεῖν τὴν γῆν ; v. 2, ἀγνοίγειν τὸ στόμα ; v. 3, πτωχοί ; v. 9, υἱοὶ τοῦ θεοῦ; v. 12, μισθὸς πολύς; v. 39, τῷ πονηρῷ ; vi. 25 ; x. 28, 39, ψυχή, for life ; vi. 22, 23, ἁπλοῦς and πονηρὸς, sound and sick ; vi. 11, ἄρτος, for general food ; the " birds of heaven," in vi. 25, &c. &c.

[7] Targum, Gen. xxiv. 22, 47 ; Job xlii. 11 ; Exod. xxxii. 2 ; Judges viii. 24 ; Prov. xi. 22, xxv. 12 ; Hos. ii. 13.

ran, "Give not a gold jewel to dogs, neither cast pearls before swine."

Matt. v. 37, "Let your conversation be Yea, yea, Nay, nay." This is meaningless. But if we restore the construction in Aramaic we have יִחְוָא לְכָם חֵן חֵן לָאו לָאו, and the meaning is, "In your conversation let your yea be yea, and your nay be nay." The yea, yea, and nay, nay, in the Hebrew come together, and this misled the translator. St. James quotes the saying rightly (v. 12), "Let your yea be yea, and your nay, nay; lest ye fall into condemnation." It is a form of a Rabbinic maxim, "The yea of the righteous is yea, and their nay is nay." It is an injunction to speak the truth.

We have therefore good grounds for our conjecture that St. Matthew's genuine "Sayings of the Lord" form a part of the Canonical Gospel.

We have next to consider, Whence came the rest of the material, the record of the "doings of the Lord," which the compiler interwove with the "Sayings"?

We have tolerably convincing evidence that the compiler placed under contribution both Aramaic and Greek collections.

For the citations from the Old Testament are not taken exclusively from the Hebrew Scriptures, nor from the Greek translation of the Seventy; but some are taken from the Greek translation, and some are taken from the Hebrew, or from a Syro-Chaldæan Targum or Paraphrase, probably in use at the time.

Matt. i. 23, "A virgin shall be with child, and shall bring forth a son." This is quoted as a prophecy of the miraculous conception. But it is only a prophecy in the version of the LXX., which renders the Hebrew word παρθένος, "virgin." The Hebrew word does not mean virgin exclusively, but "a young woman." We may therefore conclude that verses 22, 23, were additions by the Greek compiler of the Gospel, unacquainted with the original Hebrew text.

Matt. ii. 15, " Out of Egypt have I called my son." This is quoted literally from the Hebrew text. That of the LXX. has, " Out of Egypt have I called my children," τὰ τέκνα. This made the saying of Hosea no prophecy of our Lord; consequently he who inserted this reference can have known only the Hebrew text, and not the Greek version. But in ii. 18, the compiler follows the LXX. And again, ii. 23, " He shall be called a Nazarene," Ναζωραῖος. The Hebrew is נֵצֶר, of which Ναζωραῖος is no translation. The LXX. have Ναζιραῖος. The compiler was caught by the similarity of sounds.

Matt. iii. 3. Here the construction of the LXX. is followed, which unites " in the wilderness " with " the voice of one crying." The Hebrew was therefore not known by the compiler.

Matt. iv. 15. Here the LXX. is not followed, for the word γῆ is used in place of χώρα. The quotation is not, moreover, taken exactly from Isaiah, but apparently from a Targum.

Matt. viii. 17. This quotation is nearer the original Hebrew than the rendering of the LXX.

Matt. xii. 18—21. In this citation we have an incorrect rendering of the Hebrew לְהוֹרָתוֹ, " at his teaching," made by the LXX. " in his name," adopted without hesitation by the compiler. He also accepts the erroneous rendering of " islands," made " nation," " Gentiles," by the LXX.

But, on the other hand, " till he send forth judgment unto victory," is taken from neither the original Hebrew nor from the LXX., and is probably derived from a Targum.

Thus in this passage we have apparently a combination of two somewhat similar accounts—the one in Greek, the other in Aramaic.

Matt. xiii. 35. This also is a compound text. The first half is from the LXX., but the second member is from a Hebrew Targum.

Matt. xxvii. 3. In the Hebrew, the field is not a "potter's," nor is it in the LXX., who use χωνευτήριον, "the smelting-furnace." The word in the Hebrew signifies "treasury." The composer of the Gospel therefore must have quoted from a Targum, and been ignorant both of the genuine Hebrew Scriptures and of the Greek translation of the Seventy.

These instances are enough to show that the material used for the compilation of the first Canonical Gospel was very various; that the author had at his disposal matter in both Aramaic and Greek.

We shall find, on looking further, that he inserted two narratives of the same event in his Gospel in different places, if they differed slightly from one another, when coming to him from different sources.

The following are parallel passages :

iv. 23 And Jesus went about all Galilee, teaching in their synagogues, and preaching the gospel of the kingdom, and healing all manner of sickness and all manner of disease among the people.

ix. 35 And Jesus went about all the cities and villages, teaching in their synagogues, and preaching the gospel of the kingdom, and healing every sickness and every disease among the people.

v. 29 And if thy right eye offend thee, pluck it out, and cast it from thee : for it is profitable for thee that one of thy members should perish,

xviii. 9 And if thine eye offend thee, pluck it out, and cast it from thee: it is better for thee to enter into life with one eye, rather than having

and not that thy whole body should be cast into hell.

30 And if thy right hand offend thee, cut it off, and cast it from thee : for it is profitable for thee that one of thy members should perish, and not that thy whole body should be cast into hell.

32 But I say unto you, That whosoever shall put away his wife, saving for the cause of fornication, causeth her to commit adultery: and whosoever shall marry her that is divorced committeth adultery.

vi. 14 For if ye forgive men their trespasses, your heavenly Father will also forgive you:

15 But if ye forgive not men their trespasses, neither will your Father forgive your trespasses.

vii. 16 Ye shall know them by their fruits. Do men gather grapes of thorns, or figs of thistles?

17 Even so every good tree bringeth forth good fruit; but a corrupt tree bringeth forth evil fruit.

18 A good tree cannot bring forth evil fruit, neither can a corrupt tree bring forth good fruit.

two eyes to be cast into hell fire.

8 Wherefore if thy hand or thy foot offend thee, cut them off, and cast them from thee: it is better for thee to enter into life halt or maimed, rather than having two hands or two feet to be cast into everlasting fire.

xix. 9 And I say unto you, Whosoever shall put away his wife, except it be for fornication, and shall marry another, committeth adultery: and whoso marrieth her which is put away doth commit adultery.

xviii. 35 So likewise shall my heavenly Father do also unto you, if ye from your hearts forgive not every one his brother their trespasses.

xii. 33 Either make the tree good, and his fruit good; or else make the tree corrupt, and his fruit corrupt: for the tree is known by his fruit.

ix. 13 But go ye and learn what that meaneth, I will have mercy, and not sacrifice.

ix. 34 But the Pharisees said, He casteth out devils through the prince of the devils.

x. 15 Verily I say unto you, It shall be more tolerable for the land of Sodom and Gomorrha in the day of judgment, than for that city.

17 But beware of men: for they will deliver you up to the councils, and they will scourge you in their synagogues;

22 And ye shall be hated of all men for my name's sake.

xii. 39 But he answered and said unto them, An evil and adulterous generation seeketh after a sign; and there shall no sign be given to it, but the sign of the prophet Jonas.

xiii. 12 For whosoever hath, to him shall be given, and he shall have more abundance: but whosoever hath not, from him shall be taken away even that he hath.

xiv. 5 And when he would have put him to death, he feared the multitude, because they counted him as a prophet.

xii. 7 But if ye had known what this meaneth, I will have mercy, and not sacrifice.

xii. 24 But when the Pharisees heard it, they said, This fellow doth not cast out devils, but by Beelzebub the prince of the devils.

xi. 24. But I say unto you, That it shall be more tolerable for the land of Sodom in the day of judgment, than for thee.

xxiv. 9 Then shall they deliver you up to be afflicted, and shall kill you: and ye shall be hated of all nations for my name's sake.

xvi. 4 A wicked and adulterous generation seeketh after a sign; and there shall no sign be given unto it, but the sign of the prophet Jonas.

xxv. 29 For unto every one that hath shall be given, and he shall have abundance: but from him that hath not shall be taken away even that which he hath.

xxi. 26 But if we shall say, Of men; we fear the people; for all hold John as a prophet.

xvi. 19 And I will give unto thee the keys of the kingdom of heaven: and whatsoever thou shalt bind on earth shall be bound in heaven: and whatsoever thou shalt loose on earth shall be loosed in heaven.

xviii. 18 Verily I say unto you, Whatsoever ye shall bind on earth shall be bound in heaven: and whatsoever ye shall loose on earth shall be loosed in heaven.

xvii. 20 And Jesus said unto them, Because of your unbelief: for verily I say unto you, If ye have faith as a grain of mustard seed, ye shall say unto this mountain, Remove hence to yonder place; and it shall remove; and nothing shall be impossible unto you.

xxi. 21 Jesus answered and said unto them, Verily I say unto you, If ye have faith, and doubt not, ye shall not only do this which is done to the fig tree, but also if ye shall say unto this mountain, Be thou removed, and be thou cast into the sea; it shall be done.

xxiv. 11 And many false prophets shall rise, and shall deceive many.

xxiv. 24 For there shall arise false Christs, and false prophets, and shall shew great signs and wonders: insomuch that, if it were possible, they shall deceive the very elect.

xxiv. 23 Then if any man shall say unto you, Lo, here is Christ, or there; believe it not.

xxiv. 26 Wherefore if they shall say unto you, Behold, he is in the desert; go not forth: behold, he is in the secret chambers; believe it not.

The existence in the first Canonical Gospel of these duplicate passages proves that the editor of it in its present form made use of materials from different sources, which he worked together into a complete whole. And these duplicate passages are the more remarkable, because, where his memory does not fail him, he takes pains to avoid repetition.

It would seem therefore plain that the compiler of St. Matthew's Gospel made use of, first, a Collection of the Sayings of the Lord, of undoubted genuineness, drawn up by St. Matthew; second, of two or more Collections of the Sayings and Doings of the Lord, also, no doubt, genuine, but not necessarily by St. Matthew.

One of these sources was made use of also by St. Mark in the composition of his Gospel.

According to the testimony of Papias:

" John the Priest said this : Mark being the interpreter of Peter, whatsoever he recorded he wrote with great accuracy, but not, however, in the order in which it was spoken or done by our Lord, for he neither heard nor followed our Lord, but, as before said, he was in company with Peter, who gave him such instruction as occasion called forth, but did not study to give a history of our Lord's discourses ; wherefore Mark has not erred in anything, by writing this and that as he has remembered them ; for he was carefully attentive to one thing, not to pass by anything that he heard, nor to state anything falsely in these accounts." [1]

It has been often asked and disputed, whether this statement applies to the Gospel of St. Mark received by the Church into her sacred canon.

It can hardly be denied that the Canonical Gospel of Mark does answer in every particular to the description of its composition by John the Priest. John gives five characteristics to the work of Mark :

1. A striving after accuracy.[2]

2. Want of chronological succession in his narrative, which had rather the character of a string of anecdotes and sayings than of a biography.[3]

---

[1] Euseb. Hist. Eccl. iii. 39.

[2] ἀκριβῶς ἔγραψεν, and ἐποιήσατο πρόνοιαν τοῦ μηδὲν παραλιπεῖν ἢ ψεύδασθαι.

[3] Οὐ μέντοι τάξει, and ἔνια γράψας, ὡς ἀπεμνημόνευσεν.

3. It was composed of records of both the *sayings* and the *doings* of Jesus.[1]

4. It was no syntax of sayings (σύνταξις λογίων), like the work of Matthew.[2]

5. It was the composition of a companion of Peter.[3]

These characteristic features of the work of Mark agree with the Mark Gospel, some of the special features of which are:

1. Want of order: it is made up of a string of episodes and anecdotes, and of sayings manifestly unconnected.

2. The order of events is wholly different from that in Matthew, Luke and John.

3. Both the sayings and the doings of Jesus are related in it.

4. It contains no long discourses, like the Gospel of St. Matthew, arranged in systematic order.

5. It contains many incidents which point to St. Peter as the authority for them, and recall his preaching.

To this belong—the manner in which the Gospel opens with the baptism of John, just as St. Peter's address (Acts x. 37—41) begins with that event also; the many little incidents mentioned which give token of having been related by an eye-witness, and in which the narrative of St. Matthew is deficient.[4] St. Mark's

---

[1] λεχθέντα καὶ πραχθέντα.

[2] Ματθαῖος τὰ λόγια συνετάξατο—. Μάρκος . . . οὐκ ὥσπερ σύνταξιν τῶν κυριακῶν λογίων ποιούμενος.

[3] Μάρκος ἑρμηνευτὴς Πέτρου γενόμενος ἔγραφεν.

[4] Mark i. 20, "they left their father Zebedee in the ship *with the day-labourers;*" i. 31, "*he took her by the hand;*" ii. 3, "a paralytic *borne of four;*" 4, "they broke up the roof and let down the bed;" iii. 10, "they pressed upon him to touch him;" iii. 20, "they could not so much as eat bread;" iii. 32, "the multitude sat about him;" iv. 36, "they took him *even as he was,*" without his going home first to get what was necessary; iv. 38, "*on a pillow;*" v. 3—5, v. 25—34, vi. 40, the

Gospel is also rich in indications of the feelings of the people toward Jesus, such as an eye-witness must have observed,[1] and of notices of movements of the body—small significant acts, which could not escape one present who described what he had seen.[2]

That the composer of St. Matthew's Gospel made use of the material out of which St. Mark compiled his, that is, of the memorabilia of St. Peter, is evident. Whole passages of St. Mark's Gospel occur word for word, or nearly so, in the Gospel of St. Matthew.[3]

Moreover, it is apparent that sometimes the author of St. Matthew's Gospel misunderstood the text. A few instances must suffice here.

Mark ii. 18: "And the disciples of John and of the Pharisees were fasting. And they came to him and said to him, Why do the disciples of John, and the disciples of the Pharisees, fast, and thy disciples fast not?" It is clear that it was then a fasting season, which the disciples of Jesus were not observing. The "they" who came to him does not mean "the disciples

---

ranks, the hundreds, the green grass; vi. 53—56, x. 17, there came one running, and kneeled to him; x. 50, "casting away his robe;" xi. 4, "a colt tied by the door without in a place where two ways met;" xi. 12—14, xi. 16, xiii. 1, the disciples notice the *great stones* of which the temple was built; xiv. 3, 5, 8, xiv. 31, "he spoke yet more vehemently;" xiv. 51, 52, 66, "he warmed himself at the fire;" xv. 21, "coming out of the country;" xv. 40, 41, Salome named.

[1] Mark i. 33, 45, ii. 2, 13, iii. 9, 20, 32, iv. 10, v. 21, 24, 31, vi. 31, 55, viii. 34, xi. 18.

[2] Mark i. 7, "he bowed himself;" iii. 5, "he looked round with anger;" ix. 38, "he sat down;" x. 16, "he took them up in his arms, and laid his hands on them;" x. 23, "Jesus looked round about;" xiv. 3, "she broke the box;" xiv. 4, "they murmured;" xiv. 40, "they knew not what to answer him;" xiv. 67, &c.

[3] Compare

Mark iv. 4 sq.; viii. 1 sq.; x. 42 sq.; xiii. 28 sq.; xiv. 43 sq. &c.
Matt. xiii 4 sq.; xv. 32 sq.; xx. 28 sq.; xxiv. 32 sq.; xxvi. 47 sq. &c.

of John and of the Pharisees," but certain other persons. Καὶ ἔρχονται is so used in St. Mark's Gospel in several places, like the French " on venait."

But the compiler of St. Matthew's Gospel did not understand this use of the verb without a subject expressed, and he made "the disciples of John" ask the question.

Mark vi. 10: Ὅπου ἂν εἰσέλθητε εἰς οἰκίαν, ἐκεῖ μένετε ἕως ἂν ἐξέλθητε ἐκεῖθεν. That is, "Wherever (i.e. in whatsoever town or village) ye enter into a house, therein remain (i.e. in that house) till ye go away thence (i.e. from that city or village)." By leaving out the word *house*, Matthew loses the sense of the command (x. 11), " Into whatsoever town or village ye enter—remain in it till ye go out of it."

Mark vii. 27, 28. The Lord answers the Syro-Phœnician woman, " Let the children first be filled: for it is not meet to take the children's bread, and to cast it unto the dogs." The woman answers, " Yes, Lord; yet the dogs under the table eat of the children's crumbs." The meaning is, God gives His grace and mercy first to the Jews (the children); and this must not be taken from the Jews to be given to the heathen (the dogs). True, answers the woman; but the heathen do partake of the blessings that overflow from the portion of the Jews.

But the so-called Matthew did not catch the signification, and the point is lost in his version (xv. 27). He makes the woman answer, " The dogs eat of the crumbs which fall from *their masters'* table."

Mark x. 13. According to St. Mark, parents brought their children to Christ, probably with some superstitious idea, to be touched. This offended the disciples. " They rebuked those that brought them." But Jesus was displeased, and said to the disciples, " Suffer the little

children to come unto me." And instead of fulfilling
the superstitious wishes of the parents, he took the
children in his arms and blessed them. But the text
used by St. Matthew's compilator was probably defective
at the end of verse 13, and ended, "and his disciples
rebuked . . . ." The compiler therefore completed it
with αὐτοῖς instead of τοῖς προσφέρουσιν, and then misunderstood verse 14, and applied the ἄφετε differently:
"Let go the children, and do not hinder them from
coming to me." In St. Mark, the disciples rebuke the
parents; in St. Matthew, they rebuke the children, and
intercept them on their way to Christ.

Mark xii. 8: "They slew him and cast him out," *i.e.*
cast out the dead body. The compiler of St. Matthew's
Gospel did not see this. He could not understand how
that the son was killed and then cast out of the vineyard; so he altered the order into, "They cast him out
and slew him" (xxi. 38).[1]

Examples might be multiplied, but these must suffice.
If I am not mistaken, they go far to prove that the
author of St. Matthew's Gospel used the material, or
some of the material, out of which St. Mark's Gospel
was composed.

But there are also other proofs. The text of St. Mark
has been taken into that of St. Matthew's Gospel, but
not without some changes, corrections which the compiler made, thinking the words of the text in his
hands were redundant, vulgar, or not sufficiently explicit.

Thus Mark i. 5: "The whole Jewish land and all
they of Jerusalem," he changed into, "Jerusalem and all
Judæa."

---

[1] For more examples, see Scholten, Das älteste Evangelium, Elberfeld,
1869, pp. 66—78.

Mark i. 12: "The Spirit driveth," ἐκβάλλει, he softened into "led," ἀνήχθη.

Mark iii. 4: "He saith, Is it lawful to do good on the Sabbath-days, or to do evil ?" In St. Matthew's Gospel, before performing a miracle, Christ argues the necessity of showing mercy on the Sabbath-day, and supplies what is wanting in St. Mark—the conclusion, "Wherefore it is lawful to do well on the Sabbath-days" (xii. 12).

Mark iv. 12: "That seeing they might not see, and hearing they might not hear." This seemed harsh to the compiler of St. Matthew. It was as if unbelief and blindness were fatally imposed by God on men. He therefore alters the tenor of the passage, and attributes the blindness of the people, and their incapability of understanding, to their own grossness of heart (xiii. 14, 15).

Mark v. 37: "The ship was freighted," in St. Matthew, is altered into, "the ship was covered" with the waves (viii. 34).

Mark vi. 9: "Money in the girdle," changed into, "money in the girdles" (x. 9).

Mark ix. 42: "A millstone were put on his neck," changed to, "were hung about his neck" (xviii. 6).

Mark x. 17: "Sell all thou hast;" Matt. xix. 21, "all thy possessions."

Mark xii. 30: "He took a woman;" Matt. xxii. 25, "he married."

But if it be evident that the author of St. Matthew's Gospel laid under contribution the material used by St. Mark, it is also clear that he did not use St. Mark's Gospel as it stands. He had the fragmentary memorabilia of which it was made up, or a large number of them, but unarranged. He sorted them and wove them

I 3

in with the "Logia" written by St. Matthew, and *afterwards*, independently, without knowledge, probably, of what had been done by the compiler of the first Gospel, St. Mark compiled his. Thus St. Matthew's is the first Gospel in order of composition, though much of the material of St. Mark's Gospel was written and in circulation first.

This will appear when we see how independently of one another the compiler of St. Matthew and St. Mark arrange their "memorabilia."

It is unnecessary to do more to illustrate this than to take the contents of Matt. iv.—xiii.

According to St. Matthew, after the Sermon on the Mount, Christ heals the leper, then enters Capernaum, where he receives the prayer of the centurion, and forthwith enters into Peter's house, where he cures the mother-in-law, and the same night crosses the sea.

But according to St. Mark, Christ cast out the unclean spirit in the synagogue at Capernaum, then healed Peter's wife's mother, and, not the same night but long after, crossed the sea. On his return he went through the villages preaching, and then healed the leper.

The accounts are the same, but the order is altogether different. The deutero-Matthew must have had the material used by Mark under his eye, for he adopts it into his narrative; but he cannot have had St. Mark's Gospel, or he would not have so violently disturbed the order of events.

The compiler has been guilty of an inaccuracy in the use of "Gergesenes" instead of Gadarenes. St. Mark is right. Gadara was situated near the river Hieromax, east of the Sea of Galilee, over against Scythopolis and Tiberias, and capital of Peræa. This agrees exactly with what is said in the Gospels of the miracle performed

in the "country of the Gadarenes." The swine rushed
violently down a steep place and perished in the lake.
Jesus had come from the N.W. shore of the Sea to
Gadara in the S.E. But the country of the Gergesenes
can hardly be the same as that of the Gadarenes. Ge-
rasa, the capital, was on the Jabbok, some days' journey
distant from the lake. The deutero-Matthew was therefore ignorant of the topography of the neighbourhood
whence Levi, that is Matthew, was called.

St. Mark says that Christ healed one demoniac in the
synagogue of Capernaum, then crossed the lake, and
healed the second in Gadara. But St. Matthew, or
rather the Greek compiler of St. Matthew's Gospel, has
fused these two events into one, and makes Christ heal
both possessed men in the country of the Gergesenes.
In like manner we have twice the healing of two blind
men (ix. 27 and xx. 30), whereas the other evangelists
know of only single blind men being healed on both
occasions. How comes this ? The compiler had two
accounts of each miracle of healing the blind, slightly
varying. He thought they referred to the same occasion, but to different persons, and therefore made Christ
heal two men, whereas he had given sight to but one.

In the former case the compiler had not such a cir-
cumstantial account of the restoration to sound mind of
the demoniac in the synagogue as St. Mark had received
from St. Peter. He knew only that on the occasion of
Christ's visit to the Sea of Tiberias he had recovered
two men who were possessed, and so he made the healing of both take place simultaneously at the same spot.

An equally remarkable instance of the fact that St.
Matthew's Gospel was made up of fragmentary "recollections" by various eye-witnesses, is that of the dumb
man possessed with a devil, in ix. 32. At Capernaum,

after having restored Jairus' daughter to life and healed the two blind men, the same day the dumb man 'is brought to him. The devil is cast out, the dumb speaks, and the Pharisees say, " He casteth out devils through the prince of the devils."

This is exactly the same account which has been used by St. Luke (xi. 14). But in xii. 22 we have the same incident over again. There is brought unto Christ one possessed with a devil, blind and dumb; him Christ heals; whereupon the Pharisees say, " This fellow doth not cast out devils but by Beelzebub the prince of the devils." Then follows the solemn warning against blasphemy.

It is clear that the Greek compiler of St. Matthew's Gospel must have had two independent accounts of this miracle, one with the warning against blasphemy appended to it, the other without. He gives both accounts, one as occurring at Capernaum, the other much later, after Jesus had gone about Galilee preaching, and the Pharisees had conspired against him.

St. Matthew says that after the healing of Peter's wife's mother, Jesus, that same evening, cured many sick, and in the night crossed to the country of the Gergesenes. But St. Mark says that he remained that night at Capernaum, and rose early next morning before day, and went into a solitary place. According to him, this crossing over the sea did not occur till long after.

The following table will show how remarkably discordant is the arrangement of events in the two evangels. The order of succession differs, but not the events and teaching recorded; surely a proof that both writers composed these Gospels out of similar but fragmentary accounts available to both. The following table will show this disagreement at a glance.

ST. MATTHEW.	ST. MARK.

St. Matthew.

(At Capernaum), iv. 13.

1. Goes about preaching in the villages of Galilee (23), 1.

2. { Sermon on the Mount (v.—vii.).

·3. Leper cleansed (viii. 2—4).

4. Centurion's servant healed (5—13).

5. Peter's wife's mother healed (14, 15).

6. At even cures the sick (16).

7. Same night crosses the sea (18—27).

(In the country of Gergesenes).

8. Heals two demoniacs (28—39).

(Returns to Capernaum), ix. 1.

9. { Sick of the palsy healed (2—8).

10. Calls Matthew (9).

11. Hemorrhitess cured (20—22).

12. Jairus' daughter restored (18—26).

13. Two blind men healed (27—30).

14. Dumb man healed (32, 33).

15. Warning against blasphemy (34).

(Goes about Galilee), 35 and xi. 1.

16. Sends out the Twelve (x).

(Probably at Capernaum).

17. John's disciples come to him (xi. 2—6).

18. Denunciation of cities of Galilee (20—24).

19. Plucks the ears of corn (xii. 1—9).

20. Heals the withered hand (10—13).

21. Consultation against Jesus (14). (Leaves Capernaum), 15.

22. Heals deaf and dumb man (22).

23. Denunciation of blasphemy (24—32).

St. Mark.

(At Capernaum), i. 21.

— { Heals man with unclean spirit (23—28).

5. Peter's mother-in-law healed (30, 31).

6. At even heals the sick (32—34).

— Next day rises early and goes into a solitary place (35—37). (Leaves Capernaum).

1. Goes about the villages of Galilee (38, 39).

3. Heals the leper (40, 41).

(Outside the town of Capernaum), 45.

(Returns to Capernaum), ii. 1.

9. { Sick of the palsy healed (2—13).

10. Levi called (14).

19. Plucks the ears of corn (23—28).

20. Heals the withered hand (iii. 1—5).

21. Consultation against Jesus (6). (Leaves Capernaum), 7.

6. Heals many sick (10—12).

— Goes into a mountain and chooses the Twelve (13—19).

15, 23. The Pharisees blaspheme; warning against blasphemy (22—30).

24. Mother and brethren seek him (31—35).

25. { Teaches from the ship; parable of the sower (iv. 1—20).

7. Crosses the lake in a storm (35—41).

(In the country of Gadarenes).

8. Heals the demoniac (v. 1—20).

(Returns to Capernaum), 21.

11. { Hemorrhitess healed (25—34).

12. Jairus' daughter restored (22—43).

The order in St. Luke is again different. Jesus calls
Levi, chooses the Twelve, preaches the sermon on the
plain, heals the Centurion's servant, goes then from place
to place preaching. Then occurs the storm on the lake,
and after having healed the demoniac Jesus returns to
Capernaum, cures the woman with the bloody flux, raises
Jairus' daughter and sends out the Twelve.

In the Gospel of St. Mark, the parable of the sower is
spoken on "the same day" on which, in the evening,
Jesus crosses the lake in a storm.

In the Gospel of St. Matthew, this parable is spoken
long after, on "the same day" as his mother and brethren seek him, and this is after he has been in the
country of the Gadarenes, has returned to Capernaum,
gone about Galilee preaching, come back again to Capernaum, but has been driven away again by the conspiracy
of the Pharisees.

It would appear from an examination of the two Gospels that articles 23, 24 and 25 composed one document,
for both St. Matthew and St. Mark used it as it is, in a
block, only they differ as to where to build it in.

19, 20 and 21 formed another block of Apostolic
Memorabilia, and was built in by the deutero-Matthew
in one place and by St. Mark in another. 5 and 6, and
again 9 and 10, were smaller compound recollections
which the compiler of St. Matthew's Gospel and St.
Mark obtained in their concrete forms. On the other
hand, 3 and 16 formed recollections consisting of but
one member, and are thrust into the narrative where the
two compilers severally thought most suitable. We are

therefore led by the comparison of the order in which events in our Lord's life are related by St. Matthew and St. Mark, to the conclusion, that the author of the first Gospel as it stands had not St. Mark's Gospel in its complete form before him when he composed his record.

We have yet another proof that this was so.

St. Matthew's Gospel is not so full in its account of some incidents in our Lord's life as is the Gospel of St. Mark.

The compiler of the first Gospel has shown throughout his work the greatest anxiety to insert every particular he could gather relating to the doings and sayings of Jesus. This has led him into introducing the same event or saying over a second time if he found more than one version of it. Had he all the material collected in St. Mark's Gospel at his disposal, he would not have omitted any of it.

But we do not find in St. Matthew's Gospel the following passages:

Mark iv. 26—29, the parable of the seed springing up, a type of the growth of the Gospel without further labour to the minister than that of spreading it abroad. The meaning of this parable is different from that in Matt. xii. 24—30, and therefore the two parables are not to be regarded as identical.

Mark viii. 22—26. By omitting the narrative of what took place at Bethsaida, an apparent gap occurs in the account of St. Matthew after xvi. 4—12. The journey across the sea leads one to expect that Christ and his disciples will land somewhere on the coast. But Matthew, without any mention of a landing at Bethsaida, translates Jesus and the apostolic band to Cæsarea Philippi. But in Mark, Jesus and his disciples land at Bethsaida, and after having performed a miracle of healing there on a blind man—a miracle, the particulars of which are very full and interesting—they go on foot to Cæsarea Philippi (viii. 27). That the compiler of the first Gospel should have left this incident out deliberately is not credible.

Mark ix. 38, 39. In St. Matthew's collection of the Logia of our Lord there existed probably the saying of Christ, "He that is not with me is against me" (Matt. xii. 30). St. Mark narrates the circumstances which called forth this remark. But the deutero-Matthew evidently did not know of these circumstances; he therefore leaves the saying in his record without explanation.[1]

Mark xii. 41—44. The beautiful story of the poor widow throwing her two mites into the treasury, and our blessed Lord's commendation of her charity, is not to be found in St. Matthew's Gospel. Is it possible that he could have omitted such an exquisite anecdote had he possessed it?

Mark xiv. 51, 52. The account of the young man following, having the linen cloth cast about his naked body, who, when caught, left the linen cloth in the hands of his captors and ran off naked—an account which so unmistakably exhibits the narrative to have been the record of some eye-witness of the scene, is omitted in St. Matthew. On this no stress, however, can be laid. The deutero-Matthew may have thought the incident too unimportant to be mentioned.

---

[1] Mark ix. 37—50 is another instance of difference of order of sayings between him and St. Matthew.

With Mark ix. 37 corresponds Matt. x. 40.

„	„ 40	„	„	xii. 30.
„	„ 41	„	„	x. 42.
„	„ 42	„	„	xviii. 6.
„	„ 43	„	„	v. 29 and xviii. 8.
„	„ 47	„	„	xvii. 9.
„	„ 50	„	„	v. 13.

Enough has been said to show conclusively that the deutero-Matthew, if we may so term the compiler of the first Canonical Gospel, had not St. Mark's Gospel before him when he wrote his own, that he did not cut up the Gospel of Mark, and work the shreds into his own web.

Both Gospels are mosaics, composed in the same way. But the Gospel of St. Mark was composed only of the "recollections" of St. Peter, whereas that of St. Matthew was more composite. Some of the pieces which were used by Mark were used also by the deutero-Matthew. This is patent: how it was so needs explanation.

It is probable that when the apostles founded churches, their instructions on the sayings and doings of Jesus were taken down, and in the absence of the apostles were read by the president of the congregation. The Epistles which they sent were, we know, so read,[1] and were handed on from one church to another.[2] But what was far more precious to the early believers than any letters of the apostles about the regulation of controversies, were their recollections of the Lord, their Memorabilia, as Justin calls them. The earliest records show us the Gospels read at the celebration of the Eucharist.[3] The ancient Gospels were not divided into chapters, but into the portions read on Sundays and festivals, like our "Church Services." Thus the Peschito version in use in the Syrian churches was divided in this manner: "Fifth day of the week of the Candidates" (Matt. ix. 5—17), "For the commemoration of the Dead" (18—26), "Friday in the fifth week in the Fast" (27—38), "For the commemoration of the Holy Apostles" (36—38, x. 1—15), "For the commemoration of Martyrs" (16—33), "Lesson for the Dead" (34—42), "Oblation for the beheading of

---

[1] Col. iv. 16; 1 Thess. v. 27. [2] Col. iv. 16.

[3] Apost. Const. viii. 5.

John" (xi. 1—15), "Second day in the third week of the Fast" (16—24).

To these fragmentary records St. Luke alludes when he says that "many had taken in hand to arrange in a consecutive account (ἀνατάξασθαι διήγησιν) those things which were most fully believed" amongst the faithful. These he "traced up from the beginning accurately one after another" (παρηκολουθηκότι ἄνωθεν πᾶσιν ἀκριβῶς καθεξῆς). Here we have clearly the existence of records disconnected originally, which many strung together in consecutive order, and St. Luke takes pains, as he tells us, to make this order chronological.

Some Churches had certain Memorabilia, others had a different set. That of Antioch had the recollections of St. Peter, that of Jerusalem the recollections of St. James, St. Simeon and St. Jude. St. Luke indicates the source whence he drew his account of the nativity and early years of the Lord,—the recollections of St. Mary, the Virgin Mother, communicated to him orally. He speaks of the Blessed Virgin as keeping the things that happened in her heart and pondering on them.[1] Another time it is contemporaries, Mary certainly included.[2] On both occasions it is in reference to events connected with our Lord's infancy. Why did he thus insist on her having taken pains to remember these things? Surely to show whence he drew his information. He narrates these events on the testimony of her word; and her word is to be relied on; for these things, he assures us, were deeply impressed on her memory.

The "Memorabilia" in use in the different Churches founded by the apostles would probably be strung together in such order as they were generally read. How early the Church began to have a regulated order of seasons, an ecclesiastical year, cannot be ascertained

[1] Luke ii. 19, 51.　　　[2] Luke i. 66.

with certainty; but every consideration leads us to suspect that it grew up simultaneously with the constitution
of the Church. With the Church of the Hebrews this
was unquestionably the case. The Jews who believed
had grown up under a system of fasts and festivals
in regular series, and, as we know, they observed these
even after they were believers in Christ. Paul, who
broke with the Law in so many points, did not venture
to dispense with its sacred cycle of festivals. He hasted
to Jerusalem to attend the feast of Pentecost.[1] At
Ephesus, even, he observed it.[2] St. Jerome assures us
that Lent was instituted by the apostles.[3] The Apostolic
Constitutions order the observance of the Sabbath, the
Lord's-day, Pentecost, Christmas, Epiphany, the days of
the Apostles, that of St. Stephen, and the anniversaries
of the Martyrs.[4] Indeed, the observance of the Lord's-
day, instituted probably by St. Paul, involves the principle which would include all other sacred commemo-
rations; for if one day was to be set apart as a memorial
of the resurrection, it is probable that others would be
observed in memory of the nativity, the passion, the
ascension, &c.

As early as there was any sort of ecclesiastical year
observed, so early would the "Memorabilia" of the
apostles be arranged as appropriate to these seasons.
But such an arrangement would not be chronological;
therefore many took in hand, as St. Luke tells us, to
correct this, and he took special care to give the succession of events as they occurred, not as they were read,
by obtaining information from the best sources available.

It is probable that the "Recollections" of St. Peter,
written in disjointed notes by St. Mark, were in circulation through many Churches before St. Mark composed .

[1] Acts xx. 16.   [2] 1 Cor. xvi. 8.

[3] Epist. xxvii. ad Marcellam.   [4] Apost. Const. viii. 33.

his Gospel out of them. From Antioch to Rome they were read at the celebration of the divine mysteries; and some of them, found in the Churches of Asia Minor, have been taken by St. Luke into his Gospel. Others circulating in Palestine were in the hands of the deutero-Matthew, and grafted into his compilation. But as St. Luke, St. Mark, and the composer of the first Gospel, acted independently, their chronological sequences differ. Their Gospels are three kaleidoscopic groups of the same pieces.[1]

Had St. Matthew any other part in the composition of the first Canonical Gospel than contributing to it his "Syntax of the Lord's Sayings"? Of that we can say nothing for certain. It is possible enough that many of the "doings" of Jesus contained in the Gospel may be memorabilia of St. Matthew, circulating in *anecdota*.

A critical examination of St. Matthew's Gospel reveals *four* sources whence it was drawn, three threads of different texture woven into one. These are:

1. The "Memorabilia" of St. Peter, used afterwards by St. Mark. These the compiler of the first Gospel attached mechanically to the rest of his material by such formularies as "in those days," "at that time," "then," "after that," "when he had said these things."

2. The "Logia of the Lord," composed by St. Matthew.

3. Another series of sayings and doings, from which the following passages were derived: iii. 7—10, 12, iv. 3—11, viii. 19—22, ix. 27, 32—34, xi. 2—19. Some of these were afterwards used by St. Luke.[2] Were these by St. Matthew? It is possible.

---

[1] St. Luke, however, has much that was not available to the deutero-Matthew, and St. Mark rigidly confined himself to the use of St. Peter's recollections only.

[2] St. Luke's Gospel contains Hebraisms, yet he was not a Jew (Col. iv. 11, 14). This can only be accounted for by his using Aramaic texts which he translated. From these the Acts of the Apostles are free.

4. To the fourth category belong chapters i. and ii., iii. 3, xiv. 15, the redaction of iv. 12, 13, 14, 15, v. 1, 2, 19, vii. 22, 23, viii. 12, 17, x. 5, 6, xi. 2, xii. 17—21, xiii. 35—43, 49, 50, the redaction of xiv. 13a, xiv. 28—31, xv. 24, xvii. 24b—27, xix. 17a, 19b, 28, xx. 16, xxi. 2, 7, xxi. 4, 5, xxiii. 10, 13, 15, 23, 25, 27, 29, 35, the redaction of xxiv. 3, 20, 51b, xxv. 30b, xxvi. 2, 15, 25, xxvii. 51—53, xxvii. 62—66, xxviii. 1a, 2—4, 8, 9, 11—15.

Was this taken from a collection of the recollections of St. Matthew, and the series 3 from another set of Apostolic Memorabilia? That it is not possible to decide.

Into the reasons which have led to this separation of the component parts 3, 4, the peculiarities of diction which serve to distinguish them, we cannot enter here; it would draw us too far from the main object of our inquiry.[1]

The theory that the Synoptical Gospels were composed of various disconnected materials, variously united into consecutive biographies, was accepted by Bishop Marsh, and it is the only theory which relieves the theologian from the unsatisfactory obligation of making "harmonies" of the Gospels. If we adopt the received popular conception of the composition of the Synoptical Gospels, we are driven to desperate shifts to fit them together, to reconcile their discrepancies.

The difficulty, the impossibility, of effecting such a harmony of the statements of the evangelists was felt

[1] Cf. Scholten: Das älteste Evangelium; Elberfeld, 1869. See also on St. Matthew's and St. Mark's Gospels, Saunier: Ueber der Quellen des Evang. Marc., Berlin, 1825; De Wette: Lehrb. d. Hist. Krit. Einleit. in d. N.T., Berl. 1848; Baur: Der Ursprung der Synop. Evang., Stuttg. 1843; Köstlin: Das Markus Evang., Leipz. 1850; Wilke: Der Urevang., Dresd. 1838; Réville: Etudes sur l'Evang. selon St. Matt., Leiden, 1862, &c.

by the early Christian writers. Origen says that the
attempt to reconcile them made him giddy. Among
the writings of Tatian was a Diatessaron, or harmony of
the Gospels. Eusebius adventured on an explanation
"of the discords of the Evangelists." St. Ambrose
exercised his pen on a concordance of St. Matthew with
St. Luke; St. Augustine wrote "De consensu Evange-
listarum," and in his effort to force them into agreement was driven to strange suppositions—as that when
our Lord went through Jericho there was a blind man
by the road-side leading into the city, and another by
the road-side leading out of it, and that both were healed
under very similar circumstances.

Apollinaris, in the famous controversy about Easter,
declared that it was irreconcilable with the Law that
Christ should have suffered on the great feast-day, as
related by St. Matthew, but that the Gospels disagreed
among themselves on the day upon which he suffered.[1]
The great Gerson sought to remove the difficulties in a
"Concordance of the Evangelists," or "Monotessaron."

Such an admission as that the Synoptical Gospels
were composed in the manner I have pointed out, in no
way affects their incomparable value. They exhibit to
us as in a mirror what the apostles taught and what
their disciples believed. Faith does not depend on the
chronological sequence of events, but on the verity of
those events. "See!" exclaimed St. Chrysostom, "how
through the contradictions in the evangelical history
in minor particulars, the truth of the main facts transpires, and the trustworthiness of the authors is made
manifest!"

In everything, both human and divine, there is an

---

[1] Chron. Paschale, p. 6, ed. Ducange. Τῇδε μεγάλη ἡμέρᾳ τῶν ἀζύμων
αὐτος ἔπαθεν, καὶ διηγοῦνται Ματθαῖον οὕτω λέγειν· ὅθεν ἀσύμφωνος,
τῷ νόμῳ ἡ νόησις αὐτῶν, καὶ στασιάζειν δοκαῖν κατ᾽ αὐτοὺς τὰ εὐαγγελία.

union of infallibility in that which is of supreme importance, and of fallibility in that which concerns not salvation. The lenses through which the light of the world
shone to remote ages were human scribes liable to error.
Θεῖα πάντα καὶ ἀνθρώπινα πάντα, was the motto Tholuck
inscribed on his copy of the Sacred Oracles.

Having established the origin of the Gospel of St.
Matthew, we are able now to see our way to establish-
ing that of the Gospel of the Twelve, or Gospel of the
Hebrews.

No doubt it also was a mosaic made out of the
same materials as the Gospel of St. Matthew. There
subsisted side by side in Palestine a Greek-speaking
and an Aramaic-speaking community of Christians, the
one composed of proselytes from among the Gentiles,
the other of converts from among the Jews. This
Gentile Church in Palestine was scarcely influenced by
St. Paul; it was under the rule of St. Peter, and therefore was more united to the Church at Jerusalem in
habits of thought, in religious customs, in reverence
for the Law, than the Churches of "Asia" and Greece.
There was no antagonism between them. There was,
on the contrary, close intercourse and mutual sympathy.

Each community, probably, had its own copies of
Apostolic Memorabilia, not identical, but similar. Some
of the "recollections" were perhaps written only in
Aramaic, or only in Greek, so that the collection of one
community may have been more complete in some particulars than the collection of the other. The necessity
to consolidate these Memorabilia into a consecutive narrative became obvious to both communities, and each
composed "in order" the scraps of record of our Lord's
sayings and doings they possessed and read in their sacred
mysteries. St. Matthew's "Logia of the Lord" was used
in the compilation of the Hebrew Gospel; one of the

translations of it, which, according to Papias, were numerous, formed the basis also of the Greek Gospel.

The material used by both communities, the motive actuating both communities, were the same; the results were consequently similar. That they were not absolutely identical was the consequence of their having been compiled independently.

Thus the resemblance was sufficient to make St. Jerome suppose the Hebrew Gospel to be the same as the Greek first Gospel; nevertheless, the differences were as great as has been pointed out in the preceding pages.

THE CLEMENTINE GOSPEL.

WE have now considered all the fragments of the Gospel of the Hebrews that have been preserved to us in the writings of Justin Martyr, Origen, Jerome and Epiphanius.

But there is another storehouse of texts and references to a Gospel regarded as canonical at a very early date by the Nazarene or Ebionite Church. This storehouse is that curious collection of the sayings and doings of St. Peter, the Clementine Recognitions and Homilies.

That the Gospel used by the author or authors of the Clementines was that of the Hebrews cannot be shown; but it is probable that it was so.

The Clementines were a production of the Judaizing party in the Primitive Church, and it was this party which, we know, used the Gospel of the Twelve, or of the Hebrews.

The doctrine in the Clementine Recognitions and Homilies bears close relations to that of the Jewish Essenes. The sacrificial system of the Jewish Church is rejected. It was not part of the revelation to Moses, but a tradition of the elders.[1]

Distinction in meats is an essential element of religion. Through unclean meats devils enter into men, and produce disease. To eat of unclean meats places men in the power of evil spirits, who lead them to

---

[1] Homil. iii. 45.

idolatry and all kinds of wickedness. So long as men abstain from these, so long are the devils powerless against them.[1]

The observance of times is also insisted on—times at which the procreation of children is lawful or unlawful; and disease and death result from neglect of this distinction. "In the beginning of the world men lived long, and had no diseases. But when through carelessness they neglected the observance of the proper times . . . . they placed their children under innumerable afflictions."[2] It is this doctrine that is apparently combated by St. Paul.[3] He relaxes the restraints which Nazarene tradition imposed on marital intercourse.

The rejection of sacrifices obliged the Nazarene Church to discriminate between what is true and false in the Scriptures; and, with the Essenes, they professed liberty to judge the Scriptures and reject what opposed their ideas. Thus they refused to acknowledge that "Adam was a transgressor, Noah drunken, Abraham guilty of having three wives, Jacob of cohabiting with two sisters, Moses was a murderer," &c.[4]

The moral teaching of the Clementines is of the most exalted nature. Chastity is commended in a glowing, eloquent address of St. Peter.[5] Poverty is elevated into an essential element of virtue. Property is, in itself, an evil. "To all of us possessions are sins. The deprivation of these is the removal of sins." "To be saved, no one should possess anything; but since many have possessions, or, in other words, sins, God sends, in love, afflictions . . . . that those with possessions, but yet having some measure of love to God, may, by temporary inflictions, be saved from eternal punishments."[6]

---

[1] Homil. ix. 9—12.
[2] Homil. xix. 22.
[3] Gal. iv. 10.
[4] Homil. ii. 38, 50, 52.
[5] Homil. xiii. 13—21.
[6] Homil. xv. 9; see also 7.

"Those who have chosen the blessings of the future kingdom have no right to regard the things here as their own, since they belong to a foreign king (*i.e.* the prince of this world), with the exception only of water and bread, and those things procured by the sweat of the brow, necessary for the maintenance of life, and also one garment."[1]

Thus St. Peter is represented as living on water, bread and olives, and having but one cloak and tunic.[2] And Hegesippus, as quoted by Eusebius, describes St. James, first bishop of Jerusalem, as "drinking neither wine nor fermented liquors, and abstaining from animal food. A razor never came upon his head, he never anointed himself with oil, and never used a bath. He never wore woollen, but linen garments."[3]

The Ebionites looked upon Christ as the Messiah rather than as God incarnate. They gave him the title of Son of God, and claimed for him the highest honour, but hesitated to term him God. In their earnest maintenance of the Unity of the Godhead against Gnosticism, they shrank from appearing to divide the Godhead. Thus, in the Clementines, St. Peter says, "Our Lord neither asserted that there were gods except the Creator of all, nor did he proclaim himself to be God, but he pronounced him blessed who called him the Son of that God who ordered the universe."[4]

The Ebionitism of the Clementines is controversial. It was placed face to face with Gnosticism. Simon Magus, the representative of Gnosticism, as St. Peter is the representative of orthodoxy, in the Recognitions and Homilies, contends that the God of the Jews, the Demiurge, the Creator of the world, is evil. He attempts to prove this by showing that the world is full of pain

[1] Homil. xv. 7.   [2] Homil. xii. 6.
[3] Hist. Eccl. ii. 23.   [4] Homil. xvi. 15.

K 2

and misery. The imperfections of the world are tokens of imperfection in the Creator. He takes the Old Testament. He shows from texts that the God of the Jews is represented as angry, jealous, repentant; that those whom He favours are incestuous, adulterers, murderers.

This doctrine St. Peter combats by showing that present evils are educative, curative, disguised blessings; and by calling all those passages in Scripture which attribute to God human passions, corruptions of the sacred text in one of its many re-editions. " God who created the world has not in reality such a character as the Scriptures assign Him," says St. Peter; "for such a character is contrary to the nature of God, and therefore manifestly is falsely attributed to Him."[1]

From this brief sketch of the doctrines of the Ebionite Church from which the Clementines emanated, it will be seen that its Gospel must have resembled that of the Hebrews, or have been founded on it. The " Recollections of the Twelve" probably existed in several forms, some more complete than others, some purposely corrupted. The Gospel of the Hebrews was in use in the orthodox Nazarene Church. The Gospel used by the author of the Clementines was in use in the same community. It is therefore natural to conclude their substantial identity.

But though substantially the same, and both closely related to the Canonical Gospel of St. Matthew, they were not completely identical; for the Clementine Gospel diverged from the received text of St. Matthew more widely than we are justified in concluding did that of the Gospel of the Hebrews.

That it was in Greek and not in Hebrew is also probable. The converts to Christianity mentioned in the Recognitions and Homilies are all made from Heathen-

[1] Homil. xviii. 22.

ism, and speak Greek. It is at Cæsarea, Tripolis, Laodicæa, that the churches are established which are spoken of in these books,—churches filled, not with Jews, but with Gentile converts, and therefore requiring a Gospel in Greek.

The Clementine Gospel was therefore probably a sister compilation to that of the Hebrews and of St. Matthew. The Memorabilia of the Apostles had circulated in Hebrew in the communities of pure Jews, in Greek in those of Gentile proselytes. These Memorabilia were collected into one book by the Hebrew Church, by the Nazarene proselytes, and by the compiler of the Canonical Gospel of St. Matthew. This will explain their similarity and their differences.

From what has been said of the Clementines, it will be seen that their value is hardly to be over-estimated as a source of information on the religious position of the Petrine Church. Hilgenfeld says: "There is scarcely any single writing which is of such importance for the history of the earliest stage of Christianity, and which has yielded such brilliant disclosures at the hands of the most careful critics, with regard to the earliest history of the Christian Church, as the writings ascribed to the Roman Clement, the Recognitions and the Homilies."[1]

No conclusion has been reached in regard to the author of the Clementines. It is uncertain whether the Homilies and the Recognitions are from the same hand. Unfortunately, the Greek of the Recognitions is lost. We have only a Latin translation by Rufinus of Aquileia (d. 410), who took liberties with his text, as he informs Bishop Gaudentius, to whom he addressed his

---

[1] Hilgenfeld: Die Clementinischen Recognitionen und Homilien ; Jena, 1848.   Compare also Uhlhorn: Die Homilien und Recognitionen ; Göttingen, 1854 ; and Schliemann: Die Clementinen ; Hamburg, 1844.

preface. He found that the copies of the book he had
differed from one another in some particulars. Portions
which he could not understand he omitted. There is
reason to suspect that he altered such quotations as he
found in it from the Gospel used by the author, and
brought them, perhaps unconsciously, into closer con-
formity to the received text. In examining the Gospel
employed by the author of the Clementines, we must
therefore trust chiefly to those texts quoted in the
Homilies.

Various opinions exist as to the date of the Clementines. They have been attributed to the first, second,
third and fourth centuries. If we were to base our
arguments on the work as it stands, the date to be
assigned to it is the first half of the third century. A
passage from the Recognitions is quoted by Origen in
his Commentary on Genesis, written in A.D. 231; and
mention is made in the work of the extension of the
Roman franchise to all nations under the dominion of
Rome, an event which took place in the reign of Cara-
calla (A.D. 211). The Recognitions also contain an
extract from the work *De Fato*, ascribed to Bardesanes,
but which was really written by one of his scholars.
But it has been thought, not without great probability,
that this passage did not originally belong to the Recognitions, but was thrust into the text about the middle of
the third century.[1]

I have already pointed out the fact that the Church
in the Clementines is never called "Christian;" that the
word is never employed. It belonged to the community
established by Paul, and with it the Church of Peter had

---

[1] Merx, Bardesanes von Edessa, Halle, 1863, p. 113. That the "Recognitions" have undergone interpolation at different times is clear from
Book iii., where chapters 2—12 are found in some copies, but not in the
best MSS.

no sympathy. To believe in the mission of Christ is, in the Clementine Homilies, to become a Jew. The convert from Gentiledom by passing into the Church passes under the Law, becomes, as we are told, a Jew. But the convert is made subject not to the Law as corrupted by the traditions of the elders, but to the original Law as re-proclaimed by Christ.

The author of the Recognitions twice makes St. Peter say that the only difference existing between him and the Jews is in the manner in which they view Christ. To the apostles he is the Messiah come in humility, to come again in glory. But the Jews deny that the Messiah was to have two manifestations, and therefore reject Christ.[1]

Although we cannot rely on the exact words of the quotations from the Gospel in the "Recognitions," there are references to the history of our Lord which give indications of narratives contained in the Gospel used by the pseudo-Clement, therefore by the Ebionite Christians whose views he represents. We will go through all such passages in the order in which they occur in the "Recognitions."

The first allusion to a text parallel to one in the Canonical Gospels is this: "Not only did they not believe, but they added blasphemy to unbelief, saying he was a gluttonous man and slave of his belly, and that he was influenced by a demon."[2] The parallel passage is in St. Matthew xi. 18, 19. It is curious to notice that in the Recognitions the order is inverted. In St. Matthew, "they say, He hath a devil. . . . . They say, Behold a man gluttonous, and a wine-bibber;" and that the term "wine-bibber" is changed into "slave of his belly." Probably therefore in this instance the author of the

---

[1] Recog. i. 43, 50.   [2] *Ibid.* i. 40.

Clementines borrowed from a different text from St. Matthew.

In the very next chapter the Recognitions approaches St. Matthew closer than the lost Gospel. For in the account of the crucifixion it is said that "the veil of the Temple was rent," whereas the Gospel of the Hebrews stated that the lintel of the Temple had fallen. But here I suspect we have the hand of Rufinus the translator. We can understand how, finding in the text an inaccuracy of quotation, as he supposed, he altered it.

The next passage relates to the resurrection. "For some of them, watching the place with all care, when they could not prevent his rising again, *said that he was a magician;* others pretended that he was stolen away."[1] The Canonical Gospels say nothing about this difference of opinion among the Jews, but St. Matthew states that it was commonly reported among them that his disciples had stolen his body away. Not a word about any suspicion that he had exercised witchcraft, a charge which we know from Celsus was brought against Christ later.

The next passage is especially curious. It relates to the unction of Christ. "He was the Son of God, and the beginning of all things; he became man; *him God anointed with oil that was taken from the wood of the Tree of Life;* and from this anointing he is called Christ."[2] Then St. Peter goes on to argue: "In the present life, Aaron, the first high-priest, was anointed with a composition of chrism, which was made after the pattern of that spiritual ointment of which we have spoken before . . . . But if any one else was anointed with the same ointment, as deriving virtue from it, he became either king, or prophet, or priest. If, then, this temporal grace, compounded by men, had such efficacy, *consider*

---

[1] Recog. i. 42.   [2] *Ibid.* 45.

how potent was that ointment extracted by God from a branch of the Tree of Life, when that which was made by men could confer so excellent dignities among men."

Here we have trace of an apparent myth relating to the unction of Jesus at his baptism. Was there any passage to this effect in the Hebrew Gospel translated by St. Jerome ? It is hard to believe it. Had there been, we might have expected him to allude to it.

But that there was some unction of Christ mentioned in the early Gospels, I think is probable. If there were not, how did Jesus, so early, obtain the name of Christ, the Anointed One ? That name was given to him before his divinity was wholly believed in, and when he was regarded only as the Messiah—nay, even before the apostles and disciples had begun to see in him anything higher than a teacher sent from God, a Rabbi founding a new school. It is more natural to suppose that the sur-name of the Anointed One was given to him because of some event in his life with which they were acquainted, than because they applied to him prophecies at a time when certainly they had no idea that such prophecies were spoken of him.

If some anointing did really accompany the baptism, then one can understand the importance attached to the baptism by the Elkesaites and other Gnostic sects ; and how they had some ground for their doctrine that Jesus became the Christ only on his baptism. It is remark-able that, according to St. John's Gospel, it is directly after the baptism that Andrew tells his brother Simon, "We have found the Messias, which is . . the Anointed."[1] Twice in the Acts is Jesus spoken of as the Anointed : "Thy holy child Jesus, whom Thou hast anointed."[2] The second occasion is remarkable, for it again appa-rently associates the anointing with the baptism.

[1] John i. 41.   [2] Acts iv. 27.

St. Peter "opened his mouth and said . . . . The word
which God sent unto the children of Israel . . . . that
word ye know, which was published throughout all
Judæa, and began from Galilee after the baptism which
John preached; how God anointed Jesus of Nazareth
with the Holy Ghost and with power." [1] I do not say
that such an anointing did take place, but that it is probable it did.   When Gnosticism fixed on this anointing
as the communication to Christ of his divine mission
and Messiahship, then mention of it was cut out of the
Gospels in possession of the Church, and consequently
the Canonical Gospels are without it to this day.   But
the Christian ceremonial of baptism, which was founded
on what took place at the baptism of the Lord, maintained this unction as part of the sacrament, in the
Eastern Church never to be dissociated from the actual
baptism, but in the Western Church to be separated
from it and elevated into a separate sacrament—Confirmation.

But if in the original Hebrew Gospel there was mention of the anointing of Jesus at or after his baptism, as
I contend is probable, this mention did not include an
account of the oil being expressed from the branch of
the Tree of Life ; that is a later addition, in full agreement with the fantastic ideas which were gradually per-
meating and colouring Judaic Christianity.

After the baptism, " *Jesus put out*, by the grace of
baptism, *that fire which the priest kindled for sins;* for,
from the time when he appeared, the chrism has ceased,
by which the priesthood or the prophetic or the kingly
office was conferred." [2] The Homilies are more explicit : " He put out the fire on the altars." [3] There was
therefore in the Gospel used by the author of the

---

[1] Acts x. 34—38.   [2] Recog. i. c. 48.

[3] Πῦρ βώμων ἐσβέννυσέν, Homil. iii. 26.

Clementines an account of our Lord, after his anointing, entering into the Temple and extinguishing the altar fires.

In St. John's Gospel, on which we may rely for the chronological sequence of events with more confidence than we can on the Synoptical Gospels, the casting of the money-changers out of the Temple took place not long after the baptism. In St. Matthew's account it took place at the close of the ministry, in the week of the Passion. That this exhibition of his authority marked the opening of his three years' ministry rather than the close is most probable, and then it was, no doubt, that he extinguished the fires on the altar, according to the Gospel used by the author of the Clementines. Whether this incident occurred in the Gospel of the Hebrews it is not possible to say.

We are told that "James and John, the sons of Zebedee, had a command . . . . not to enter into their cities (*i.e.* the cities of the Samaritans), nor to bring the word of preaching to them."[1] "And when our Master sent us forth to preach, he commanded us, But into whatsoever city or house we should enter, we should say, Peace be to this house. And if, said he, a son of peace be there, your peace shall come upon him; but if there be not, your peace shall return unto you. Also, that going from house to city, we should shake off upon them the very dust which adhered to our feet. But it shall be more tolerable for the land of Sodom and Gomorrha in the day of judgment than for that city or house."[2] The Gospel of the Clementines, it is plain, contained an account of the sending forth of the apostles almost identical with that in St. Matthew, x.

" And . . . . Jesus himself declared that John was

---

[1] Recog. i. c. 57.   [2] *Ibid.* ii. 30, also ii. 3.

greater than all men and all the prophets."[1] The corresponding passage is in St. Matthew.[2]

The Beatitudes, or some of them, were in it. "He said, *Blessed are the poor;* and promised earthly rewards; and promised that those who maintain righteousness shall be satisfied with meat and drink."[3] "Our Master, inviting his disciples to patience, impressed on them the blessing of peace, which was to be preserved with the labour of patience. . . . . He charges (the believers) to have peace among themselves, and says to them, *Blessed are the peacemakers, for they shall be called the very sons of God.*"[4] "The Father, whom only those can see who are pure in heart."[5] Again strong similarity with slight difference. "He said, *I am not come to send peace on earth, but a sword; and henceforth you shall see father separated from son, son from father, husband from wife, and wife from husband, mother from daughter, and daughter from mother, brother from brother, father-in-law from daughter-in-law, friend from friend.*"[6] This is fuller than the corresponding passage in St. Matthew.[7]

"*It is enough for the disciple to be as his master.*"[8] "He mourned over those who lived in riches and luxury, and bestowed nothing upon the poor; showing that they must render an account, because they did not pity their neighbours, even when they were in poverty, whom they ought to love as themselves."[9] "In like manner he charged the Scribes and Pharisees during the last period of his teaching . . . . with hiding the key of knowledge which they had handed down to them from Moses, by which the gate of the heavenly kingdom might be

---

[1] Recog. i. c. 60.
[2] Matt. xi. 9, 11.
[3] Recog. i. c. 61, ii. c. 28.
[4] *Ibid.* ii. 27, 29.
[5] *Ibid.* ii. 22, 28.
[6] *Ibid.* ii. 28, 32.
[7] Matt. x. 34—36.
[8] Recog. ii. 27; Matt. x. 25.
[9] *Ibid.* 29.

opened."[1] The key of knowledge occurs only in St.
Luke's Gospel. Had the author of the Clementines any
knowledge of that Gospel? I do not think so, or we
should find other quotations from St. Luke. St. Matthew
says, "Woe unto you, Scribes and Pharisees, hypocrites!
for ye shut up (κλείετε) the kingdom of heaven."[2] St.
Luke says, "Ye have taken away the key (τὴν κλεῖδα) of
knowledge."[3] The author of the Clementines says, "Ye
have hidden the key," not "taken away." I do not
think, when the expression in St. Matthew suggests the
"key," that we need suppose that the author of the
Recognitions quoted from St. Luke; rather, I presume,
from his own Gospel, which in this passage resembled
the words in St. Luke rather than those in St. Matthew,
without, however, being exactly the same.[4]

"*Every kingdom divided against itself shall not stand.*"[5]
"*Seek ye first the kingdom of God and his righteousness,
and all these things shall be added to you.*"[6] The writer
knew, in the same terms as St. Matthew, our Lord's
sayings: "*Give not that which is holy to dogs, neither
cast your pearls before swine.*"[7] "*Whosoever shall look
upon a woman to lust after her, hath committed adultery
with her in his heart. . . . . If thy right eye offend thee,
pluck it out, and cast it from thee; for it is profitable for
thee that one of thy members perish, rather than thy whole
body be cast into hell-fire.*"[8]

---

[1] Recog. ii. 30.   [2] Matt. xxiii. 13.

[3] Luke xi. 52.

[4] Recog. ii. c. 46 : "They must seek his kingdom and righteousness
which the Scribes and Pharisees, having received the key of knowledge,
have not shut in but shut out." The same Syro-Chaldaic expression has
been variously rendered in Greek by St. Matthew and St. Luke. See
Lightfoot : Horæ Hebraicæ in Luc. xi. 52.

[5] Recog. ii. 31, 35.   [6] *Ibid.* iii. 41, 37, 20.

[7] *Ibid.* iii. i.   [8] *Ibid.* vii. 37.

The woes denounced on the Scribes and Pharisees,[1] and the saying that the Queen of the South should "rise in judgment against this generation,"[2] are given in the Recognitions as in St. Matthew; as also that "the harvest is plenteous,"[3] "that no man can serve two masters,"[4] and the saying on the power of faith to move mountains.[5]

We have the parables of the goodly pearl,[6] of the marriage supper,[7] and of the tares,[8] but also that of the sower,[9] which does not occur in St. Matthew, but in St. Luke. This therefore was found in the Gospel used by the author of the Recognitions. There are two other apparent quotations from St. Luke: "*I have come to send fire on the earth, and how I wish that it were kindled;*"[10] and the story of the rich fool.[11] The first, however, is differently expressed from St. Luke. There are just two more equally questionable quotations: "*Be ye merciful, as also your heavenly Father is merciful, who makes his sun to rise upon the good and the evil, and rains upon the just and the unjust.*"[12] We have the Greek in one of the Homilies.[13] In St. Luke it runs, "Be ye therefore merciful, as your Father also is merciful."[14] In St. Matthew, "Love your enemies, bless them that curse you, do good to them that hate you, and pray for them that despitefully use you, and persecute you; that ye may be the children of your Father which is in heaven: for he maketh his sun to rise on the evil and on the good, and

---

[1] Recog. vi. 11.
[2] *Ibid.* vi. 14.
[3] *Ibid.* iv. 4.
[4] *Ibid.* v. 9.
[5] *Ibid.* v. 2.
[6] *Ibid.* iii. 62.
[7] *Ibid.* iv. 35.
[8] *Ibid.* iii. 38.
[9] *Ibid.* iii. 14.
[10] *Ibid.* vi. 4.
[11] *Ibid.* x. 45.
[12] *Ibid.* v. 13, iii. 38.
[13] Hom. iii. 57.
[14] Luke vi. 36.

sendeth rain on the just and on the unjust." [1] Is it not clear that either the pseudo-Clement condensed the direction, "Love your enemies, bless them that curse you, do good to them that hate you, and pray for them that despitefully use you, and persecute you," into the brief maxim, "Be ye good and merciful,"—or that, and this is more probable, there were concurrent traditional accounts of our Lord's saying, and that St. Matthew, St. Luke, and the writer of the Gospel used by the pseudo-Clement, made use of independent texts in their compilations?

The next passage is a saying of our Lord on the cross, which is given in the Recognitions: "*Father, forgive them their sin, for they know not what they do.*" [2] In the Homilies we have the original Greek: "Father, forgive them their sins, for they know not what they do." [3] Rufinus has unconsciously altered the text in translating it by making "sins" singular instead of plural.

It is not necessary to note the insignificant difference of the word ἅ in the Homily and the word τί in the Gospel. But who cannot see that the addition of the words, "their sins," completely changes the thought of the Saviour? Jesus prays God to forgive the Jews the crime they commit in crucifying him, and not to pardon all the sins of their lives that they have committed. The addition of these two words not merely modify the thought; they represent another of an inferior order. They would not have been introduced into the text if the author of the Gospel used by the pseudo-Clement had had the Gospel of St. Luke before him. These words were certainly not derived from St. Luke; they are due

---

[1] Matt. v. 44—46.　　　　　[2] Recog. vi. 5.

[3] Πάτερ ἄφες αὐτοῖς τὰς ἁμαρτίας αὐτῶν οὐγὰρ οἴδασιν ἅ ποιούσιν. Hom. xi. 20. In St. Luke it runs, Πάτερ ἄφες αὐτοῖς· οὐ γὰρ οἴδασι τί ποιοῦσι.—Luke xxiii. 34.

to a separate recollection or tradition of the sayings of
the Saviour on the cross. Those sayings we may well
believe were cherished in the memory of the early disciples. Tradition always modifies, weakens, renders
commonplace the noblest thoughts and most striking
sayings, and colours the most original with a tint of
triviality.[1]

We find in both the Recollections and Homilies a
passage which has been thought to be a quotation from
St. John: " *Verily I say unto you, That unless a man is
born again of water, he shall not enter into the kingdom
of heaven.*"[2] Here, again, the hand of Rufinus is to be
traced. The same quotation is made in the Homilies,
and it stands there thus : " *Verily I say unto you, Unless
ye be born again of the water of life* (or *the living water*)
*in the name of the Father, and of the Son, and of the
Holy Ghost, ye cannot enter into the kingdom of heaven.*"[3]

That the narrative of the interview with Nicodemus
was in the Gospel of the Hebrews, we learned from
Justin Martyr quoting it. We will place the parallel
passages opposite each other :

GOSPEL OF THE HEBREWS.	GOSPEL OF ST. JOHN,
Justin Martyr, 1 Apol. 61.	c. iii. 3, 5.
" *Christ said, Except ye be born again, ye cannot enter into the kingdom of heaven.*"	" 3. Jesus answered and said unto him, Verily, verily, I say unto thee, Except a man be born again, he cannot see the kingdom of God."

*　　*　　*　　　　*　　*　　*

---

[1] M. Nicolas : Etudes sur les Evangiles Apocryphes, pp. 72, 73.

[2] Recog. vi. 9.

[3] Ἀμὴν λέγω ὑμῖν, ἐαν μὴ ἀναγεννηθῆτε ὕδατι ζωῆς (in another place ὕδατι ζῶντι), εἰς ὄνομα πατρὸς, υἱοῦ καὶ ἁγίου πνεύματος, οὐ μὴ εἰσελθῆτε εἰς τὴν βασιλείαν τῶν οὐρανῶν.—Homil. xi. 26.

PSEUDO-CLEMENT, Hom. xi. 26.

"*And Christ said (with an oath),*[1] *Verily I say unto you, Unless ye are born again of the water of life (in the name of the Father, and of the Son, and of the Holy Ghost), ye cannot enter into the kingdom of heaven.*"

" 5. Jesus answered, Verily, verily, I say unto thee, Except a man be born of water and spirit, he cannot enter into the kingdom of God."

The fragment in the Homilies clearly belongs to the same narrative as the fragment in Justin's Apology. Both are addressed in the second person plural, " Except ye be born again ;" in the Gospel of St. John the first is, " Except a man be born again ;" the second, " Except a man be born of water and spirit ;" both in the third person singular. The form of the first answer in Justin differs from that in St. John: " he cannot enter the kingdom," " he cannot see the kingdom."

That these are independent accounts I can hardly doubt. The words, " in the name of the Father, and of the Son, and of the Holy Ghost," are an obvious interpolation, perhaps a late one, in the text of the Homilies ; for Rufinus would hardly have omitted to translate this, though he did allow himself to make short verbal alterations.

There is another apparent quotation from St. John in the fifth book of the Recognitions: " *Every one is made the servant of him to whom he yields subjection.*"[2] But here again the quotation is very questionable. St. John's version of our Lord's saying is, " Whosoever committeth sin is the servant of sin." St. Paul is much nearer:

---

[1] Recognitions vi. 9: " For thus hath the true prophet testified to us with an oath : Verily I say unto you," &c. The oath is, of course, the 'Aμὴν, ἀμὴν.

[2] Recog. v. 13 ; John viii. 34.

"Know ye not, that to whom ye yield yourselves servants to obey, his servants ye are to whom ye obey; whether of sin unto death, or of obedience unto righteousness?"[1]

The quotation in the Recognitions is not from St. Paul, for the author expressly declares it is a saying of our Lord. St. Paul could not have had St. John's Gospel under his eye when he wrote, for that Gospel was not composed till long after he wrote the Epistle to the Romans. He gives no hint that he is quoting a saying of our Lord traditionally known to the Roman Christians. He apparently makes appeal to their experience when he says, "Know ye not." Yet this fragment of an ancient lost Gospel in the Clementine Recognitions gives another colour to his words; they may be paraphrased, "Know ye not that saying of Christ, To whom ye yield yourselves servants to obey, his servants ye are?" It appears, therefore, that this is an earlier recorded reminiscence of our Lord's saying than that of St. John.

There is one, and only one, apparent quotation from St. Paul in the Recognitions: "In God's estimation, he is not a Jew who is a Jew among men, nor is he a Gentile that is called a Gentile, but he who, believing in God, fulfils his law and does his will, though he be not circumcised."[2] St. Paul's words are: "He is not a Jew which is one outwardly; neither is that circumcision which is outward in the flesh; but he is a Jew which is one inwardly; and circumcision is that of the heart, in the spirit, and not in the letter."

There is no doubt a resemblance between these passages. But it is probable that the resemblance is due solely to community of thought in the minds of both

---

[1] Rom. vi. 16. [2] Recog. v. 34; Rom. ii. 28.

writers. It would be extraordinary if this were a quotation, for the author of the Recognitions nowhere quotes from any Epistle, not even from those of St. Peter; and that he, an Ebionite, should quote St. Paul, whose Epistles the Ebionites rejected, is scarcely credible.

The Recognitions mention the temptation: " The prince of wickedness . . . . presumed that he should be worshipped by him by whom he knew that he was to be destroyed. Therefore our Lord, confirming the worship of one God, answered him, It is written, Thou shalt worship the Lord thy God, and Him only shalt thou serve. And he, terrified by this answer, and fearing lest the true religion of the one and true God should be restored, hastened straightway to send forth into this world false prophets and false apostles and false teachers, who should speak, indeed, in the name of Christ, but should accomplish the will of the demon."[1] Here we have Christ indicated as the one who was to restore that true worship of God which Moses had instituted, but which the Ebionites, with their Essene ancestors, asserted had been defaced and corrupted by false traditions. And in opposition to this, the devil sends out false apostles, false teachers, to undo this work, calling themselves, however, apostles of Christ. There can be little doubt who is meant. The reference is to St. Paul, Silas, and those who accepted his views, in opposition to those of St. James and St. Peter.

In Homily xii. is a citation which seems to indicate the use of the third Canonical Gospel. At first sight it appears to be a combination of a passage of St. Matthew and a parallel passage of St. Luke. It is preceded in the Homily by a phrase not found in the Canonical Gospels, but which is given, together with what follows,

---

[1] Recog. iv. 34. The same in the Homilies, xi. 35.

as a declaration of the Saviour. The three passages are
placed side by side for comparison :

HOMILY xii. 19.	MATT. xviii. 7.	LUKE xvii. 1.
"*It must be that good things come, and happy is he by whom they come. In like manner it must be that evil things come, but woe to him by whom they come.*"[1]	"It must needs be that offences come; but woe to that man by whom the offence cometh."	"It is impossible but that offences will come; but woe to him through whom they come."

The passage in the Homily is more complete than
those in St. Matthew and St. Luke. The two Canonical
Evangelists made use of imperfect fragments destitute
of one member of the sentence. One cannot but wish
to believe that our Lord pronounced a benediction on
those who did good in their generation.

"There is amongst us," says St. Peter in his second
Homily, " one Justa, a Syro-Phœnician, a Canaanite by
race, whose daughter was oppressed with a grievous
disease. And she came to our Lord, crying out and
entreating that he would heal her daughter. But he,
being asked by us also, said, '*It is not lawful to heal the
Gentiles, who are like unto dogs on account of their using
various meats and practices, while the table in the kingdom
has been given to the sons of Israel.*' But she, hearing
this, and begging to partake as a dog of the crumbs that
fall from this table, having changed what she was (*i.e.*
having given up the use of forbidden food), by living
like the sons of the kingdom, obtained healing for her

---

[1] Τὰ ἀγαθὰ ἐλθεῖν δεῖ, μακάριος δὲ δι' οὗ ἔρχεται· ὁμοίως καὶ τὰ κακὰ
ἀνάγκη ἐλθεῖν, οὐαὶ δὲ δι' οὗ ἔρχεται.

daughter as she asked. For she being a Gentile, and remaining in the same course of life, he would not have healed her had she persisted to live as do the Gentiles, on account of its not being lawful to heal a Gentile."[1]

That the Ebionites perverted the words of our Lord to make them support their tenets on distinction of meats is obvious.

In the Clementine Homilies we have thrice repeated a saying of our Lord which we know of from St. Jerome and St. Clement of Alexandria, who speak of it as undoubtedly a genuine saying of Christ, "*Be ye good money-changers.*"[2]

This text is used by the author of the Clementines to prove the necessity of distinguishing between the gold and the dross in Holy Scripture. And to this he adds the quotation, "*Ye do therefore err, not knowing the true things of the Scriptures; and for this reason ye are ignorant also of the power of God.*"[3]

The following are some more fragments from the Clementine Homilies:

"*He said, I am he of whom Moses prophesied, saying, A prophet shall the Lord your God raise unto you of your brethren, like unto me: him hear ye in all things; and whosoever will not hear the prophet shall die.*"[4] This saying of Moses is quoted by both St. Peter and St. Stephen in their addresses, as recorded in the Acts. It is probable, therefore, that our Lord had claimed this prophecy to have been spoken of him. But St. Luke had never heard that he had done so, as he makes no allusion to it in his Gospel or in the speeches he puts in the mouths of Peter and Stephen in the Acts.

---

[1] Hom. ii. 19.   [2] *Ibid.* ii. 51.
[3] *Ibid.* ii. 51, xviii. 20.   [4] *Ibid.* ii. 53.

"*It is thine, O man, said he, to prove my words, as silver and money are proved by the exchangers.*"[1]

"*Give none occasion to the evil one.*"[2]

Twice repeated we have the text, "*Thou shalt fear the Lord thy God, and him only shalt thou serve.*"[3]

In St. Matthew's Gospel (iv. 10.) it runs, "Thou shalt worship the Lord thy God, and him only shalt thou serve."

In the Clementines: "He alleged that it was right to present to him who strikes you on one cheek the other also, and to give to him who takes away your cloak your *hood* also, and to go two miles with him who compels you to go one."[4]   This differs from the account in St. Matthew, by using for the word χιτῶνα, "tunic," of the Canonical Gospel, the word μαφόριον, "hood."

There are other passages identical with, or almost identical with, the received text in St. Matthew's Gospel, which it is not necessary to enter upon separately.

They are: Matt. v. 3, 8, 17, 18, 34, 35, 37, 39, 40, 41, vi. 8, 13, vii. 7, 9, 10, 11, 13, 14, 21, viii. 11, 24, 25, 26, 27, 28, 29, 30, 31, ix. 13, x. 28, 34, xi. 25, 27, 28, xii. 7, 26, 34, 42, xiii. 17, 39, xv. 13, xvi. 13, 18, xix. 8, 17, xxii. 2, 32, xxiii. 25, xxiv. 45, 46, 47, 48, 49, 50, xxv. 41. In all, some fifty-five verses, almost and often quite the same as in St. Matthew's Gospel.

There is just one text supposed to be taken from St. Mark's Gospel, four from St. Luke's, and two from St. John's.   But I do not think we are justified in concluding that these quotations are taken from the three last-named Canonical Gospels.   That they are not taken

---

[1] Homil. ii. 61   [2] *Ibid.* xix. 2.

[3] *Ibid.* viii. 21. In the Hebrew תִּירָא, rendered by the LXX. φοβηθήσῃ. The word in St. Matthew is προσκυνήσεις.

[4] *Ibid.* xv. 5.

from St. Luke we may be almost certain, for that Gospel was not received by the Judaizing Christians. When we examine the passages, the probability of their being quotations from the Canonical Gospels disappears.

We find, "He, the true Prophet, said, *I am the gate of life; he that entereth through me entereth into life.*"[1] The words in St. John's Gospel are, "I am the door: by me if any man enter in, he shall be saved."[2] The idea is the same, but the mode of expression is different.

"Again he said, *My sheep hear my voice.*"[3]

The quotation from St. Mark is too brief for us to be able to form any well-founded opinion upon it. It is this: "But to those who were misled to imagine many gods, as the Scriptures say, he said, *Hear, O Israel; the Lord your God is one Lord.*"[4]

No prejudice would exist among the Ebionites against the Gospel of St. Mark, but the Christology of the Johannine Gospel, its doctrine of the Logos, would not accord with their low views of Christ. The Ebionites who denied the Godhead of Jesus could hardly acknowledge as canonical a Gospel which contained the words, "And the Word was with God, and the Word was God."

<table>
<tr><td>HOM. xix. 22.</td><td>JOHN ix. 1—3.</td></tr>
<tr><td>"Our Master replied to those who asked him concerning him that was born blind, and to whom he restored sight, if it was he or his parents who had sinned, in that he was born blind. *It is not that he hath sinned in anywise, nor his parents; but in order that*</td><td>"And as Jesus passed by, he saw a man which was blind from his birth.

"And his disciples asked him, saying, Master, who did sin, this man, or his parents, that he was born blind?

"Jesus answered, Neither hath this man sinned, nor his</td></tr>
</table>

[1] Homil. iii. 52.

[2] John x. 9.

[3] Homil. iii. 52; cf. John x. 16.

[4] *Ibid.* iii. 57; Mark xii. 29.

the power of God may be ma-
nifested, who healeth sins of
ignorance." [1]

parents : but that the works
of God should be made manifest in him."

The resemblance is striking. Nevertheless I do not
think we have a right to conclude that this passage in
the Clementine Homilies is necessarily a citation from
St. John.

The text is quoted in connection with the peculiar
Ebionite doctrine of seasons and days already alluded
to. When our Lord says that he heals the sins of ignorance, he is made in the Clementine Gospel to assert
that the blindness of the man was the result of disregard
by his parents of the new moons and sabbaths, not wilfully, but through ignorance. "The afflictions you mentioned," says St. Peter in connection with this quotation,
"are the result of ignorance, but assuredly not of wickedness. Give me the man who sins not, and I will show
you the man who suffers not."

But though this is the interpretation put on the words
of our Lord by the Clementine Ebionite, it by no means
flows naturally from them; it is rather wrung out of
them.

The words, I think, mean that the blindness of the
man is symbolical; its mystical meaning is ignorance.
Our Lord by opening the eyes of the blind exhibits himself as the spiritual enlightener of mankind. He is come
to unclose men's eyes to the true light that he sheds
abroad in the world.

In St. John's Gospel, after having declared that blindness was not the punishment of sin in the man or his

---

[1] Homil. ix. 27.

Οὔτε οὗτος τι ἥμαρτεν, οὔτε οἱ
γονεῖς αὐτοῦ, ἀλλ᾽ ἵνα δι᾽ αὐτοῦ
φανερωθῇ ἡ δύναμις τοῦ Θεοῦ τῆς
ἀγνοίας ἰωμένη τὰ ἁμαρτήματα.

Joan. ix. 3.

Οὔτε οὗτος ἥμαρτεν, οὔτε οἱ
γονεῖς αὐτοῦ, ἀλλ᾽ ἵνα φανερωθῇ
τὰ ἔργα τοῦ Θε ῦ ἐν αὐτῷ.

parents, our Lord continues, "I must work the works of Him that sent me, while it is day; the night cometh, when no man can work. As long as I am in the world, I am the light of the world."

Put this last declaration in connection with the saying, "I am come to heal the sins of ignorance," and the connection of ideas is at once apparent. The blindness of the man is symbolical of the ignorance of the world. "I am the light of the world, and I have come to dispel the darkness of the ignorance of the world." And so saying, "he spat on the ground, and made clay of the spittle, and he anointed the eyes of the blind man with the clay."

A few important words in Christ's teaching had escaped the memory of St. John. But they had been noted down by some other apostle, and the recollections of the latter were embodied in the Gospel in use among the Ebionites.

The texts resembling passages in St. Luke are four, but all of them are found in St. Matthew's Gospel as well.

"*Blessed is that man whom his Lord shall appoint to the ministry of his fellow-servants.*" [1]

"*The Queen of the South shall rise up with this generation, and shall condemn it; because she came from the extremities of the earth to hear the wisdom of Solomon; and behold, a greater than Solomon is here, and ye do not believe him.*

"*The men of Nineveh shall rise up with this generation and shall condemn it, for they heard and repented at the preaching of Jonas: and behold, a greater is here, and no one believes.*" [2]

---

[1] Homil. iii. 64 ; cf. Luke xii. 43, but also Matt. xxiv. 46.

[2] *Ibid.* xi. 33 ; cf. Luke xi. 31, 32, but also Matt. xii. 42, 41. The order in Matt. reversed.

L

The compiler of St. Matthew's Gospel had this striking passage in an imperfect condition.   St. Luke had it with both its members.   So had also the compiler of the Clementine Gospel.   The wording is not exactly identical with that in St. Luke, but the difference is not material.   "Ye do not believe him," "And no one believes," exist in the Ebionite, not in the Canonical text.

"For without the will of God, not even a sparrow can fall into a gin.   Thus even the hairs of the righteous are numbered by God." [1]

---

[1] Homil. xii. 31 ; cf. Matt. x. 29, 30 ; Luke xii. 6, 7.

III.

THE GOSPEL OF ST. PETER.

SERAPION, Bishop of Antioch, in 190, on entering his see, learned that there was a Gospel attributed to St. Peter read in the sacred services of the church of Rhosus, in Cilicia. Taking it for granted, as he says, that all in his diocese held the same faith, without perusing this Gospel, he sanctioned its use, saying, " If this be the only thing that creates difference among you, let it be read."

But he was speedily made aware that this Gospel was not orthodox in its tendency. It favoured the opinions of the Docetæ. It was whispered that if it had an apostolic parentage, it had heretical sponsors. Serapion thereupon borrowed the Gospel, read it, and found it was even as had been reported. " Peter," said he, " we receive with the other apostles as Christ himself," but this Gospel was, if not apocryphal as to its facts, at all events heretical as to its teaching.

Thereupon Serapion, regretting his precipitation in sanctioning the use of the Gospel, wrote a book upon it, " in refutation of its false assertions." [1]

· This book unfortunately has been lost, so that we are not able to learn much more about the Gospel. What was its origin ? Was it a forgery from beginning to end ? This is by no means probable.

The Gospel of St. Mark, as we have seen, was due to St. Peter, and by some went by the name of the Gospel

[1] Euseb. Hist. Eccl. vi. 12.

of St. Peter. It was a Gospel greatly affected by the
Docetæ and Elkesaites. " Those who distinguish Jesus
from Christ, and who say that Christ was impassible,
but that Jesus endured the sufferings of his passion,
prefer the Gospel of Mark," says Irenæus.[1]

It was likely that they should prefer it, for it began at
the baptism, and this event it stated, or was thought to
state, was the beginning of the Gospel; to Docetic minds
an admission, an assertion rather, that all that preceded
was of no importance; Jesus was but a man as are other
men, till the plenitude of the Spirit descended on him.
The early history might be matter of curiosity, but not
of edification.

That matter is evil is a doctrine which in the East
has proved the fertile mother of heresies. Those infected
with this idea—and it is an idea, like Predestinarianism,
which, when once accepted and assimilated, pervades the
whole tissue of belief and determines its form and complexion—could not acknowledge frankly and with conviction the dogma of the Incarnation. That God should
have part with matter, was as opposed to their notions
as a concord of light with darkness. Carried by the
current setting strongly that way, they found themselves
landed in Christianity. They set to work at once to
mould Christianity in accordance with their theory of
the inherent evil in matter. Christ, an emanation from
the Pleroma, the highest, purest wave that swept from
the inexhaustible fountain of Deity, might overshadow,
but could not coalesce with, the human Jesus. The
nativity and the death of our Lord were repugnant to
their consciences. They evaded these facts by considering that he was born and died as man, but that the

---

[1] "Qui Jesum separant a Christo et impassibilem perseverasse Christum,
passum vero Jesum dicunt, id quod secundum Marcum est præferunt Evangelium."—Iren. adv. Hæres. iii. 2. The Greek is lost.

bright overshadowing cloud of the Divinity, of the Christ, reposed on him for a brief period only; it descended at the baptism, it withdrew before the passion.

Such were the party—they were scarcely yet a sect—who used the Gospel of St. Peter. Was this Gospel a corrupted edition of St. Mark? Probably not. We have not much ground on which to base an opinion, but there is just sufficient to make it likely that such was not the case.

To the Docetæ, the nativity of our Lord was purely indifferent; it was not in their Gospel; that it was miraculous they would not allow. To admit that Christ was the Son of God when born of Mary, was to abandon their peculiar tenets. It was immaterial to them whether Jesus had brothers and sisters, or whether James and Jude were only his cousins. The Canonical Gospels speak of the brothers and sisters of Christ, and we are not told that they were not the children of Mary.[1] When the Memorabilia were committed to writing, there was no necessity for doing so. The relationship was known to every one. Catholics, maintaining the perpetual virginity of the mother of Jesus, asserted that they were children of Joseph by a former wife, or cousins. The Gospel of St. Peter declared them to be the children of Joseph by an earlier marriage. Origen says, "There are persons who assure us that the brothers of Jesus were the sons whom Joseph had by his first wife, before he married Mary. They base their opinion on either the Gospel entitled the Gospel of Peter, or on the Book of James (the Protevangelium)."[2]

Such a statement would not have been intruded into the Gospel by the Docetæ, as it favoured no doctrine of

---

[1] Matt. xii. 47, 48, xiii. 55; Mark iii. 32; Luke viii. 20; John vii. 5.

[2] Origen, Comment. in Matt. c. ix.

theirs. It must therefore have existed in the Gospel before it came into their hands.

We know how St. Mark's Gospel was formed. After the death of his master, the evangelist compiled all the fragmentary "Recollections" of St. Peter concerning our Lord. But these recollections had before this circulated throughout the Church. We have evidence of this in the incorporation of some of them into the Gospels of St. Matthew and St. Luke. Others, besides St. Mark, may have strung these fragments together. One such tissue would be the Gospel of St. Peter. It did not, perhaps, contain as many articles as that of St. Mark, but it was less select. Like those of St. Matthew and St. Luke, on the thread were probably strung memorabilia of other apostles and disciples, but also, perhaps, some of questionable authority.

This collection was in use at Rhosus. It may have been in use there since apostolic days; perhaps it was compiled by some president of the church there. But it had not been suffered to remain without interpolations which gave it a Docetic character.

Its statement of the relationship borne by the "brothers and sisters" to our Lord is most valuable, as it is wholly unprejudiced and of great antiquity. The Gospel, held in reverence as sacred in the second century at Rhosus, was probably brought thither when that church was founded, not perhaps in a consecutive history, but in paragraphs. The church was a daughter of the church of Antioch, and therefore probably founded by a disciple of St. Peter.

IV.

THE Gospel known by this name is mentioned by
several of the early Fathers.[1] It existed in the second
half of the second century; and as it was then in use
and regarded as canonical by certain Christian sects, it
must have been older. We shall not be far out if we
place its composition at the beginning of the second
century.

To form an idea of its tendency, we must have re-
course to two different sources, the second Epistle of
Clemens Romanus, the author of which seems to have
made use of no other Gospel than that of the Egyptians,
and Clement of Alexandria, who quotes three passages
from it, and refutes the theories certain heretics of his
time derived from them.

The second Epistle of St. Clement of Rome is a
Judaizing work, as Schneckenburg has proved incon-
testably.[2] It is sufficient to remark that the Chiliast
belief which transpires in . more than one place, the
analogy of ideas and of expressions which it bears to the
Clementine Homilies, and finally the selection of Clement of Rome, a personage as dear to the Ebionites as
the apostles James and Peter, to place the composition
under his venerated name, are as many indications of

[1] Τὸ αἰγύπτιον Εὐαγγέλιον; Epiphan. Hæres. lxii. 2; Evangelium
secundum Ægyptios; Origen, Hom. i. in luc.; Evangelium juxta Ægyptios;
Hieron. Prolog. in Comm. super Matth.

[2] Schneckenburg, Ueber das Evangelium der Ægypter; Berne, 1834.

the Judæo-Christian character and origin of this apocryphal work.

The Gospel cited by the author of this Epistle, except in two or three phrases which are not found in any of our Canonical Gospels, recalls that of St. Matthew. Nevertheless, it is certain that the quotations are from the Gospel of the Egyptians, for one of the passages cited in this Epistle is also quoted by Clement of Alexandria, who tells us whence it comes—from the Egyptian Gospel. We may conclude from this that the Gospel of the Egyptians presented great analogy to our first Canonical Gospel, without being identical with it, and consequently that it was related closely to the Gospel of the Hebrews.

If the second Epistle of Clement of Rome determines for us the family to which this Gospel belonged, the passages we shall extract from the Stromata of Clement of Alexandria will determine its order. There are three of these passages, and very curious ones they are.

The first is cited by both Clement of Rome and Clement of Alexandria, by one more fully than by the other.

" *The Lord, having been asked by Salome when his kingdom would come, replied, When you shall have trampled under foot the garment of shame, when two shall be one, when that which is without shall be like that which is within, and when the male with the female shall be neither male nor female.*"[1]

---

[1] CLEMENT OF ALEXANDRIA.
Stromat. iii. 12.

Πυνθανομένης τῆς Σαλωμῆς πότε γνωσθήσεται τὰ περὶ ὧν ἤρετο, ἔφη ὁ κύριος· ὅταν τὸ τῆς αἰσχύνης ἔνδυμα πατήσητε, καὶ ὅταν γένηται τὰ δύο ἕν, καὶ τὸ ἄρρεν μετὰ τῆς θηλείας οὔτε ἄρρεν οὔτε θῆλυ.

CLEMENT OF ROME.
2 Epist. c. 12.

Ἐπερωτηθεὶς γὰρ αὐτὸς ὁ κύριος ὑπό τινος πότε ἥξει αὐτοῦ ἡ βασιλεία; ὅταν ἔσται τὰ δύο ἕν, καὶ τὸ ἔξω ὡς ἔσω, καὶ τὸ ἄρσεν μετὰ τῆς θηλείας οὔτε ἄρσεν οὔτε θῆλυ.

The explanation of this singular passage by Clement of Rome is, "Two shall be one when we are truthful with each other, and when in two bodies there will be but one soul, without dissimulation and without disguise. That which is without is the body; that which is within is the soul. Just as your body appears externally, so should your soul manifest itself by good works." The explanation of the last member of the phrase is wanting, as the Epistle has not come down to us entire.

But this is certainly not the real meaning of the passage. Its true signification is to be found in the bloodless, passionless exaltation at which the ascetic aimed who held all matter to be evil, the body to be a clog to the soul, marriage to be abominable, meats to be abstained from. It points to that condition as one of perfection in which the soul shall forget her union with the body, and, sexless and ethereal, shall be supreme.

It was in this sense that the heretics took it. Julius Cassianus, "chief of the sect of the Docetæ,"[1] invoked this text against the union of the sexes. This interpretation manifestly embarrassed St. Clement of Alexandria, and he endeavours to escape from the difficulty by weakening the authority of the text.

He does this by pointing out that the saying of our Lord is found only in the Gospel of the Egyptians, and not in those four generally received. But as Julius Cassianus appealed at the same time to a saying of St. Paul, the authenticity of which was not to be contested, the Alexandrine doctor did not consider that he could avoid discussing the question; and he gives, on his side, an interpretation of the saying of Jesus in the Apocryphal Gospel, and of that of St. Paul, associated with it by Julius Cassianus. The words of St. Paul quoted by the

[1] Ὁ τῆς δοκήσεως ἰξάρχων.—Stromat. iii. 13.

heretic were those in Galatians (iii. 28): "There is neither Jew nor Greek, neither bond nor free, male or female." Cassianus paid no regard to the general sense of the passage, which is, that the privileges of the gospel are common to all of every degree and nation and sex, but fastening on the words "neither male nor female," contended that this was a prohibition of marriage. St. Clement pays every whit as little regard to the plain sense of the passage, and gives the whole an absurd mystic signification, as far removed from the thought of the apostle as the explanation of Julius Cassianus. "By male," says he, "understand anger, folly. By female understand lust; and when these are carried out, the result is penitence and shame."

It has been thought that the words "when two shall be one" recall the philosophic doctrine of the Pythagoreans on the subject of numbers and the dualism which was upheld by many of the Gnostics. St. Mark, according to Irenæus, taught that everything had sprung out of the monad and dyad.[1] But it is not so. The teaching was not philosophic, but practical. It may be thus paraphrased: "The kingdom of heaven shall have come when the soul shall have so broken with the passions and feelings of the body, that it will no longer be sensible of shame. The body will be lost in the soul, so that the two shall become one; the body which is without shall be like the soul within, and the male with the female shall be insensible to passion."

It was a doctrine which infected whole bodies of men later: the independence of the soul from the body led to wild asceticism and frantic sensuality running hand in hand. Holding this doctrine, the Fraticelli in the thirteenth century flung themselves into the most fiery temptations, placed themselves in the most perilous

[1] Adv. Hæres. i. 11.

positions; if they fell, it mattered not, the soul was not stained by the deeds of the body; if they remained unmoved, the body was indeed mastered, "the two had become one."

The garment of shame is to be trampled under foot. Julius Cassianus explains this singular expression. It is the apron of skins wherewith our first parents were clothed, when they blushed at their nakedness. They blushed because they were in sin; when men and women shall cease to blush at their nudity; then they have attained to the spiritual condition of unfallen man.

We see in embryo the Adamites of the Middle Ages, the Anabaptists of the Reformation.

But the garment of skin has a deeper signification. Philo taught[1] that it symbolized the human body that clothed the nakedness of the spirit. Gnosticism caught at the idea. Unfallen man was pure spirit. Man had fallen, and his fall consisted in being clothed in flesh. This garment of skin must be trodden under foot, that the soul may arise above it, be emancipated from its bonds.

The second passage is quite in harmony with the first: "*Salome having asked how long men should die, the Lord answered and said, As long as you women continue to bear children.*[2] *Then she said, I have done well, I have never borne a child. The Lord answered, Eat of every herb, but not of that containing in itself bitterness.*"[3]

Cassian appealed to this text also in proof that mar-

---

[1] "Ad mentem vero tunica pellicea symbolice est pellis naturalis, id est corpus nostrum. Deus enim intellectum condens primum, vocavit illum Adam; deinde sensum, cui vitæ (Eva) nomen dedit; tertio ex necessitate corpus quoque facit, tunicam pelliceam illud per symbolum dicens. Oportebat enim ut intellectus et sensus velut tunica cutis induerent corpus."—Philo: Quæst. et Solut. in Gen. i. 53, trans. from the Armenian by J. B. Aucher; Venice, 1826.

[2] Clem. Alex. Stromat. iii. 6.   [3] *Ibid.* 9.

riage was forbidden. But Clement of Alexandria refused to understand it in this sense. He is perhaps
right when he argues that the first answer of our Lord
means, that as long as there are men born, so long men
will die. But the meaning of the next answer entirely
escapes him. When our Lord says, " Eat of every herb
save that in which is bitterness," he means, says Clement,
that marriage and continence are left to our choice, and
that there is no command one way or the other; man
may eat of every tree, the tree of celibacy, or the tree
of marriage, only he must abstain from the tree of evil.

But this is not what was meant. Under a figurative
expression, the writer of this passage conveyed a warning against marriage. Death is the fruit of birth, birth
is the fruit of marriage. Abstain from eating of the
tree of marriage, and death will be destroyed.

That this is the real meaning of this remarkable saying is proved conclusively by another extract from the
Gospel of the Egyptians, also made by Clement of
Alexandria; it is put in the mouth of our Lord. "*I
am come to destroy the works of the woman; of the woman,
that is, of concupiscence, whose works are generation and
death.*"[1] This quotation bears on the face of it marks
of having been touched and explained by a later hand.
" Of the woman,—that is, concupiscence, whose works
are generation and death," are a gloss added by an
Encratite, which was adopted into the text received
among the Egyptian Docetæ. The words, " I am come
to destroy the works of the woman," *i.e.* Eve, may have
been spoken by our Lord. By Eve came sin and death
into the world, and these works Christ did indeed come
to destroy.

But the gloss, as is obvious, alters the meaning of the
saying. The woman is no longer Eve, but womankind

[1] Clem. Alex. Stromat. iii. 9.

in general; and by womankind, that is, by concupiscence, generation and death exist.

Clement of Alexandria was incapable of seizing the plain meaning of these words. He says, "The Lord has not deceived us, for he has indeed destroyed the works of concupiscence, viz. love of money, of strife, glory, of women . . . . now the birth of these vices is the death of the soul, for we die indeed by our sins."

We must look to Philo for the key. The woman, Eve, means, as he says, the sense; Adam, the intellectual spirit. The union of soul and body is the degradation of the soul, the fertile parent of corruption and death.[1] Out of Philo's doctrine grew a Manichæanism in the Christian community before Manes was born.

The work of Jesus was taught to be the emancipation of the soul, the rational spirit, Noῦς, from the restraints of the body, its restoration to its primitive condition. Death would cease when the marriage was dissolved that held the spirit fettered in the prison-house of flesh.

Philonian philosophy remained vigorous at Alexandria in the circle of enlightened Jews. It struck deep root, and blossomed in the Christian Church.

A Gospel, *which* we do not know—it may have been that of Mark—was brought into Egypt. The author of the Epistle to the Hebrews, an Epistle clearly addressed to the Alexandrine Jews, prepared their minds to fuse Philonism with Christianity. We see its influence in the Gospel of St. John. That evangelist adopted Philo's doctrine of the Logos; the author of the Gospel of the Egyptians, that of the bondage of the spirit in matter.

[1] "Sensus, quæ symbolice mulier est."—Philo: Quæst. et Solut. i. 52. "Generatio ut sapientum fert sententia, corruptionis est principium."—*Ibid.* 10.

The conceptions contained in the three passages which
Clement of Alexandria has preserved are closely united.
They all are referable to a certain theosophy, the exposition of which is to be found in the writings of Philo,
and which may be in vain sought elsewhere at that
period. Not only are there to be found here the theosophic system of the celebrated Alexandrine Jew, but
also, what is a still clearer index of the source whence
the Egyptian Gospel drew its mystic asceticism, we find
the quaint expressions and forms of speech which belonged to Philo, and to none but him. No one but
Philo had thought to find in the first chapters of Genesis
the history of the fall of the soul into the world of sense,
and to make of Eve, of the woman, the symbol of the
human body, and starting from this to explain how the
soul could return to its primitive condition, purely
spiritual, by shaking off the sensible to which in its
present state it is attached. When we shall have
trampled under foot our tunics of skins wherewith we
have been covered since the fall, this garment, given to
us because we were ashamed of our nakedness,—when
the body shall have become like the soul,—when the
union of the soul with the body, *i.e.* of the male and the
female, shall exist no more,—when the woman, that is
the body, shall be no more productive, shall no more
produce generation and death,—when its works are destroyed, then we shall not die any more; we shall be as
we were before our fall, pure spirits; and this will be
the kingdom of the Lord. And to prepare for this transformation, what is to be done? Eat of every herb,
nourish ourselves on the fruit of every tree of paradise,
—that is, cultivate the soul, and not occupy it with
anything but that which will make it live; but abstain
from the herb of bitterness,—the tree of the knowledge

of good and evil, that is,—reject all that can weave closer the links binding the soul to the body, retain it in its prison, its grave.[1]

It is easy to see how Philonian ideas continued to exert their influence in Egypt, when absorbed into Christianity. It was these ideas which peopled the deserts of Nitria and Scete with myriads of monks wrestling with their bodies, those prison-houses of their souls, struggling to die to the world of matter, that their ethereal souls might shake themselves free. Their spirits were like moths in a web, bound by silken threads; the spirit would be choked by these fetters, unless it could snap them and sail away.

[1] Nicolas : Etudes sur les Evangiles apocryphes, pp. 128—130. M. Nicolas was the first to discover the intimate connection that existed between the Gospel of the Egyptians and Philonian philosophy.

The relation in which Philo stood to Christian theology has not as yet, so far as I am aware, been thoroughly investigated. Dionysius the Areopagite, the true father of Christian theosophy, derives his ideas and terminology from Philo. Aquinas developed Dionysius, and on the Summa of the Angel of the Schools Catholic theology has long reposed.

PART III.

THE LOST PAULINE GOSPELS.

Under this head are classed such Gospels as have a distinct anti-Judaizing, Antinomian tendency. They were in use among the Churches of Asia Minor, and eventually found their way into Egypt.

This class may probably be subdivided into those which bore a strong affinity to the Canonical Gospel of St. Luke, and those which were independent compilations.

To the first class belongs—

1. The Gospel of the Lord.

To the second class—

1. The Gospel of Eve.
2. The Gospel of Perfection.
3. The Gospel of Philip.
4. The Gospel of Judas.

PART III.

THE LOST PAULINE GOSPELS.

I.

THE GOSPEL OF THE LORD.

The Gospel of the Lord, Ἐυαγγέλιον τοῦ Κυρίου, was the banner under which the left of the Christian army marched, as the right advanced under that of the Gospel of the Hebrews.

The Gospel of the Lord was used by Marcion, and apparently before him by Cerdo.[1]

In opposition to Ebionitism, with its narrow restraints and its low Christology, stood an exclusive Hellenism. Ebionitism saw in Jesus the Son of David, come to re-edit the Law, to provide it with new sanction, after he had winnowed the chaff from the wheat in it. Marcionism looked to the Atonement, the salvation wrought by Christ for all mankind, to the revelation of the truth, the knowledge (γνῶσις) of the mysteries of the Godhead made plain to men, through God the good and merciful, who sent His Son to bring men out of ignorance into

---

[1] Tert. De præscr. hæretica, c. 51. "Cerdon solum Lucæ Evangelium, nec tamen totum recipit."

light, out of the bondage of the Law into the freedom of the Gospel.[1]

The Gospel, in the eyes of Marcion and the extreme followers of St. Paul, represented free grace, overflowing goodness, complete reconciliation with God.

But such goodness stood contrasted with the stern justice of the Creator, as revealed in the books of the Old Testament; infinite, unconditioned forgiveness was incompatible with the idea of God as a Lawgiver and a Judge. The restraint of the Law and the freedom of the Gospel could no more emanate from the same source than sweet water and bitter.

Therefore the advanced Pauline party were led on to regard the God who is revealed in the Old Testament as a different God from the God revealed by Christ. Cerdo first, and Marcion after him, represented the God of this world, the Demiurge, to be the author of evil; but the author of evil only in so far as that his nature being incomplete, his work was incomplete also. He created the world, but the world, partaking in his imperfection, contains evil mixed with good. He created the angel-world, and part of it, through defect in the divinity of their first cause, fell from heaven.

The germs of this doctrine, it was pretended, were to be found in St. Paul's Epistles. In the second to the Corinthians, after speaking of the Jews as blinded to the revelation of the Gospel by the veil which is on their faces, the apostle says: "The God of this world hath blinded the minds of them which believe not, lest the light of the glorious gospel of Christ, who is the

[1] For an account of the doctrines of Marcion, the authorities are, The Apologies of Justin Martyr; Tertullian's treatise against Marcion, i.—v.; Irenæus against Heresies, i. 28; Epiphanius on Heresies, xlii. 1—3; and a "Dialogus de recta in Deum fide," printed with Origen's Works, in the edition of De la Rue, Paris, 1733, though not earlier than the fourth century.

image of God, should shine unto them."[1] St. Paul had no intention of representing the God of the Jews who veiled their eyes as opposed to Christ; but it is easy to see how readily those who followed his doctrine of antagonism between the Law and the Gospel would be led to suppose that he did identify the God of the Law with the principle of obstructiveness and of evil.

So also St. Paul's teaching that sin was produced by the Law, that it had no positive existence, but was called into being by the imposition of the Commandments, lent itself with readiness to Marcion's system. "The Law entered, that the offence might abound."[2] "The motions of sins are by the Law."[3] "I had not known sin, but by the Law: for I had not known lust, except the Law had said, Thou shalt not covet."[4]

This Law, imposed by the God of the Jews, is then the source of sin. It is imposed, not on the spirit, but on the flesh. In opposition to it stands the revelation of Jesus Christ, which repeals the Law of the Jews. "The Law of the spirit of life in Christ Jesus hath made me free from the law of sin and death."[5] "Therefore we conclude that a man is justified without the deeds of the Law."[6] "Before faith came, we were kept under the Law, shut up unto the faith which should afterwards be revealed. Wherefore the Law was our schoolmaster to bring us to Christ, that we might be justified by faith; but after that faith is come, we are no longer under a schoolmaster."[7]

We find in St. Paul's writings all the elements of Marcion's doctrine, but not compacted into a system, because St. Paul never had worked out such a theory,

[1] 1 Cor. iv. 4.
[2] Rom. v. 20.
[3] Rom. vi. 5.
[4] Rom. vii. 7.
[5] Rom. viii. 2.
[6] Rom. iii. 28.
[7] Gal. iii. 23—25.

and would have shrunk from the conclusions which might be drawn from his words, used in the heat of argument, for the purpose of opposing an error, not of establishing a dogmatic theory.

The whole world lay, according to Marcion, under the dispensation of the Demiurge, and therefore under a mixed government of good and evil. To the Jewish nation this Demiurge revealed himself. His revelation was stern, uncompromising, imperfect. Then the highest God, the God of love and mercy, who stood opposed to the inferior God, the Creator, the God of justice and severity, sent Jesus Christ for the salvation of all (ad salutem omnium gentium) to overthrow and destroy (arguere, redarguere, ἐλέγχειν, καταλεύειν) "the Law and the Prophets," the revelation of the world-God, the God of the Jews.

The highest God, whose realm and law were spiritual, had been an unknown God (deus ignotus) till Christ came to reveal Him. The God of this world and of the Jews had a carnal realm, and a law which was also carnal. They formed an antithesis, and true Christianity consisted in emancipation from the carnal law. The created world under the Demiurge was bad; matter was evil; spirit alone was pure. Thus the chain unrolled, and lapsed into Manichæism. Cerdo and Marcion stood in the same relation to Manes that Paul stood in to them. Manichæism was not yet developed; it was developing.

Gnosticism, with easy impartiality, affected Ebionitism on one side and Marcionism on the other, intensifying their opposition. It was like oxygen combining here to form an alkali, there to generate an acid.

The God of love, according to Marcion, does not punish. His dealings with man are all benevolence, communication of free grace, bestowal of ready forgiveness. For if sin be merely violation of the law of the God of this world, it is indifferent to the highest God, who is above the Demiurge, and regards not his vexatious restrictions on the liberty of man.

Yet Marcion was not charged by his warmest antagonists with immorality. They could not deny that the Marcionites entirely differed from other Pauline Antinomians in their moral conduct—that, for example, in their abhorrence of heathen games and pastimes they came fully up to the standard of the most rigid Catholic Christians. While many of the disciples of St. Paul, who held that an accommodation with prevailing errors was allowable, that no importance was to be attached to externals, found no difficulty in evading the obligation to become martyrs, the Marcionites readily, fearlessly, underwent the interrogations of the judges and the tortures of the executioner.[1]

Marcion, there is no doubt, regarded St. Paul as the only genuine apostle, the only one who remained true to his high calling. He taught that Christ, after revealing himself in his divine power to the God of this world, and confounding him unto submission, manifested himself to St. Paul,[2] and commissioned him to preach the gospel.

He rejected all the Scriptures now accounted canonical, except the Epistles of St. Paul, which formed with him an "Apostolicon," in which they were arranged in the following order:—The Epistle to the Galatians, the First and Second to the Corinthians, the Epistles to the Romans, the Thessalonians, Ephesians, Colossians, Philemon, and to the Philippians.[3]

Besides the Epistles of St. Paul, he made use of an

[1] Euseb. Hist. Eccles. iv. 15, vii. 12. De Martyr. Palæst. 10.
[2] Cf. 1 Col. ix. 1, xv. 8 ; 2 Cor. xii.
[3] Epiphan. Hæres. xlii. 11.

original Gospel, which he asserted was the evangelical record cited and used by Paul himself. The other Canonical Gospels he rejected as corrupted by Judaizers.

This Gospel bore a close resemblance to that of St. Luke. "Marcion," says Irenæus, "has disfigured the entire Gospel, he has reconstructed it after his own fancy, and then boasts that he possesses the true Gospel."[1]

Tertullian assures us that Marcion had cut out of St. Luke's Gospel whatever opposed his own doctrines, and retained only what was in favour of them.[2] This statement, as we shall see presently, was not strictly true.

Epiphanius is more precise. He goes most carefully over the Gospel used by Marcion, and discusses every text which, he says, was modified by the heretic.[3]

The charge of mutilating the Canonical Gospels was brought by the orthodox Fathers against both the Ebionites on one side, and the Marcionites and Valentinians on the other, because the Gospels they used did not exactly agree with those employed by the middle party in the Church which ultimately prevailed. But the extreme parties on their side made the same charge against the Catholics.[4] It is not necessary to believe these charges in every case.

If the Gospels[5] were compiled as in the manner I have contended they were, such discrepancies must have occurred. Every Church had its own collection of the

---

[1] Iren. adv. Hæres. iii. 11.

[2] "Contraria quæque sententiæ erasit, competentia autem sententiæ reservarit."—Tertul. adv. Marcion, iv. 6.

[3] Epiphan. Hæres. xlvii. 9—12.

[4] "Ego meum (Evangelium) dico verum, Marcion suum. Ego Marcionis affirmo adulteratum, Marcion meum. Quis inter nos disceptabit?"—Tert. adv. Marcion, iv. 4.

[5] Not St. John's Gospel; that is unique; a biography by an eye-witness, not a composition of distinct notices.

" Logia" and of the " Practhcnta" of Christ. The more voluminous of these collections, those better strung together, thrust the earlier, less complete, collections into the back-ground. And these collections were continually being augmented by the acquisition of fresh material; and this new material was squeezed into the existing text, often without much consideration for the chain of story or teaching which it broke and dislocated.

Marcion was too conscientious and earnest a man wilfully to corrupt a Gospel. He probably brought with him to Rome the Gospel in use at Sinope in Pontus, of which city, according to one account, his father was bishop. The Church in Sinope had for its first bishop, Philologus, the friend of St. Paul, if we may trust the pseudo-Hippolytus and Dorotheus. It is probable that the Church of Sinope, when founded, was furnished by St. Paul with a collection of the records of Christ's life and teaching such as he supplied to other " Asiatic " churches. And this collection was, no doubt, made by his constant companion Luke.

Thus the Gospel of Marcion may be Luke's original Gospel. But there is every reason to believe that Luke's Gospel went through considerable alteration, probably passed through a second edition with considerable additions to it made by the evangelist's own hand, before it became what it now is, the Canonical Luke.

He may have found reason to alter the arrangement of certain incidents; to insert whole paragraphs which had come to him since he had composed his first rough sketch; to change certain expressions where he found a difference in accounts of the same sayings, or to combine several.

Moreover, the first edition was published in the full heat of the Pauline controversy. Its strong Paulinianism lies on the surface. But afterwards, when this

M

excitement had passed away, and the popular misconception of Pauline sola-fidianism had become a general offence to morals and religion, then Luke came under the influence of St. John, and tempered his Gospel by adding to it incidents Paul did not care to have inserted in the Gospel he wished his converts to receive, or the accuracy of which, as disagreeing with his own views, he was disposed to question.

Of this I shall have more to say presently. It is necessary, in the first place, briefly to show that Marcion's Gospel contained a different arrangement of the narrative from the Canonical Luke, and was without many passages which it is not possible to believe he wilfully excluded. For instance, in Marcion's Gospel: "And as he entered into a certain village, there met him ten men that were lepers, which stood afar off: and they lifted up their voices, and said, Jesus, Master, have mercy on us. And when he saw them, he said unto them, Go, show yourselves unto the priests. And it came to pass, that as they went, they were cleansed. And many lepers were in Israel in the time of Eliseus the prophet; and none of them was cleansed saving Naaman the Syrian. And one of them, when he saw that he was healed," &c. Here the order is Luke xvii. 12, 13, 14, iv. 27, xvii. 15. Such a disturbance of the text in the Canonical Gospel could serve no purpose, would not support any peculiar view of Marcion, and cannot therefore have been a wilful alteration. And in the first chapter of Marcion's Gospel this is the sequence of verses whose parallels in St. Luke are: iii. 1, iv. 31, 32, 33, 34, 35, 36, 37, 38, 39, 16, 20, 21, 22, 23, 28, 29, 30, 40, 41, 42, 43, 44.

Thus the order of events is different in the two Gospels. Christ goes first to Capernaum in the "Gospel of the Lord," and afterwards to Nazareth, an inversion of the order as given in the Gospel of St. Luke. Again, in this instance, no purpose was served by this transposition. It is unaccountable on the theory that Marcion corrupted the Gospel of Luke; but if we suppose that Luke revised the arrangement of his Gospel after its first publication, the explanation is simple enough.

But what is far more conclusive of the originality of Marcion's Gospel is, that his Gospel was without several passages which occur in St. Luke, and which do apparently favour his views. Such are Luke xi. 51, xiii. 30 and 34, xx. 9—16. These contain strong denunciations of the Jews by Jesus Christ, and a positive declaration that they had fallen from their place as the elect people. Marcion insisted on the abrogation of the Old Covenant; it was a fundamental point in his system; he would consequently have found in these passages powerful arguments in favour of his thesis. He certainly would not have excluded them from his Gospel, had he tampered with the text, as Irenæus and Tertullian declare.

Yet Marcion would not scruple to use the knife upon a Gospel that came into his hands, if he found in it passages that wholly upset his doctrine of the Demiurge and of asceticism. For when the Church was full of Gospels, and none were as yet settled authoritatively as canonical, private opinion might, unrebuked, choose one Gospel and reject the others, or subject any Gospel to critical supervision. The manner in which the Gospels were composed laid them open to criticism. Any Church might hesitate to accept a saying of our Lord, and incorporate it with the Gospel with which it was acquainted, till satisfied that the saying was a genuine apostolic tradition. And how was a Church to be satisfied? By internal evidence of genuineness, when the apostles themselves had passed away. Consequently, each Church was obliged to exert its critical faculty in the composition of its Gospel. And that the churches did exert their judgment freely is evidenced by the mass of apocryphal matter which remains, the dross after the refining, piled up in the Gospels of Nicodemus, of the Infancy of Thomas, and of Joseph the Carpenter. All of which was deliberately rejected as resting on no apostolic authority, as not found in any Church to be read at the sacred mysteries, but as mere folk-tales buzzed about, nowhere producing credentials of authenticity.

Marcion, following St. Paul, declared that the Judaizing Church had "corrupted the word of God,"[1] meaning such "logia" as, "I am not come to destroy the Law or the Prophets." "Till heaven and earth pass, one jot or one tittle shall in no wise pass from the Law, till all is fulfilled."[2] These texts would naturally find no place in the original Pauline Gospels used by the Churches he had founded. In St. Luke's Gospel, accordingly, the Law and the Prophets are said to have been until John, and since then the Gospel, "the kingdom of God."[3] But the following verse in St. Luke's Gospel is, "It is easier for heaven and earth to pass, than one tittle of the Law to fail"—a contradiction of the immediately preceding verse, which declares that the Law has ceased with the proclamation of the Gospel. This verse, therefore, cannot have existed in its present form in the original Gospel of St. Luke, and must have been modified when a reconciliation had been effected between Petrine and Pauline Christianity.

It is not to be wondered at, therefore, that the verse should read differently in Marcion's Gospel, which contains the uncorrupted original passage, and runs thus "It is easier for heaven and earth to pass, than for one

---

[1] 2 Cor. ii. 17, and iv. 2. [2] Matt. v. 17, 18.

[3] Luke xvi. 16.

tittle of my words to fail;" or perhaps, "It is easier for heaven and earth to pass, than one tittle of the words of the Lord to fail;" for in this instance we have not the exact words.[1]

But though Marcion certainly endured the presence of texts in his Gospel which militated against his system, he may have cut out other passages. Passages, or words only, which he thought had crept into the text without authority. This can scarcely be denied when the texts are examined which are wanting in his Gospel. No strong conservative attachment to any particular Gospels had grown up in the Church as yet; no texts had been authoritatively sanctioned. As late as the end of the second century (A.D. 190), the Church of Rhossus was using its own Gospel attributed to Peter, till Serapion, bishop of Antioch, thinking that it contained Docetic errors, probably because of omissions, suppressed it,[2] and substituted for it, in all probability, one of the more generally approved Gospels.

The Church of Rhossus was neither heretical nor schismatical; it formed part of the Catholic Church, and no objection was raised against its use of a Gospel of its own, till it was suggested that this Gospel contained errors of doctrine. No question was raised whether it was an authentic Gospel by Peter or not; the standard by which it was measured was the traditional faith of the Church. It did not agree with this standard, and was therefore displaced. St. Epiphanius and St. Jerome assert, probably unjustifiably, that the orthodox did not hesitate to amend their Gospels, if they thought there were passages in them objectionable or doubtful. Thus

---

[1] Tert.: "Transeat cœlum et terra citius quam unus apex verborum Domini;" but Tertullian is not quoting directly, so that the words may have been, and probably were, $\tau\hat{\omega}\nu$ $\lambda\acute{o}\gamma\omega\nu$ $\mu o\upsilon$, not $\tau\omega\nu$ $\lambda\acute{o}\gamma\omega\nu$ $\tau o\hat{\upsilon}$ $\theta\epsilon o\hat{\upsilon}$.

[2] Euseb. Hist. Eccl. vi. 12; Theod. Fabul. hæret. ii. 2.

they altered the passage in which Jesus is said to have wept over Jerusalem (Luke xix. 41). St. Epiphanius frankly tells us so. "The orthodox," says he, "have eliminated these words, urged to it by fear, and not feeling either their purpose or force."[1] But it is more likely that the weeping of Jesus over Jerusalem was inserted by Luke in his Gospel at the time of reconciliation under St. John, so as to make the Pauline Gospel exhibit Jesus moved with sympathy for the holy city, the head-quarters of the Law. The passage is not in Marcion's Gospel; and though it is possible he may have removed it, it is also possible that he did not find it in the Pauline Gospel of the Church at Sinope.

St. Jerome says that Luke xxii. 43, 44, were also eliminated from some copies of the Canonical Gospel. "The Greeks have taken the liberty of extracting from their texts these two verses, for the same reason that they removed the passage in which it is said he wept. . . . . This can only come from superstitious persons, who think that Jesus Christ could not have become as weak as is represented."[2] St. Hilary says that these verses were not found in many Greek texts, or in some Latin ones.[3]

But here, also, the assertion of St. Jerome and St. Hilary cannot be taken as a statement of fact, but rather as a conclusion drawn by them from the fact that all copies of the Gospel of St. Luke did not contain these two verses. They are wanting in the Gospel of our Lord, and may be an addition made to the Gospel of St. Luke, after it had been first circulated. There is reason to suppose that after St. Luke had written his Gospel, additional matter may have been provided him, and that he published a second, and enlarged, edition of his

[1] Epiphan. Ancor. 31.   [2] Hieron. adv. Pelag. ii.
[3] Hilar. De Trinit. x.

Gospel. Thus some Churches would be in possession of the first edition, and others of the second, and Jerome and Epiphanius, not knowing this, would conclude that those in possession of the first had tampered with their text.

The Gospel of Marcion has been preserved to us almost in its entirety. Tertullian regarded Marcionism as the most dangerous heresy of his day. He wrote against it, and carefully went through the Marcionite Gospel to show that it maintained the Catholic faith, though it differed somewhat from the Gospel acknowledged by Tertullian, and that therefore Marcion's doctrine was untenable.[1] He does not charge Marcion with having interpolated or curtailed a Canonical Gospel, for Marcion was ready to retort the charge against the Gospel used by Tertullian.[2]

It is not probable that Tertullian passed over any passage in the "Gospel of the Lord" which could by any means be made to serve against Marcion's system. This is the more probable, because Tertullian twists the texts to serve his purpose which in the smallest degree lend themselves to being so treated.[3]

St. Epiphanius has gone over much the same ground as Tertullian, but in a different manner. He attempts to show how wickedly Marcion had corrupted the Word of God, and how ineffectual his attempt had been, inasmuch as passages in his corrupted Gospel served to destroy his system.

With these two purposes he went through the whole of the "Gospel of the Lord," and accompanied it with a string of notes, indicating all the alterations and omis-

---

[1] " Christus Jesus in evangelio tuo meus est."

[2] See note 4 on p. 240.

[3] As xix. 10 : " Filius hominis venit, salvum facere quod periit . . . . elisa est sententia hæreticorum negantium *carnis* salutem ;—pollicebatur (Jesus) *totius* hominis salutem."

sions he found in it. Each text from Marcion's Gospel,
or Scholion, is accompanied by a refutation. Epiphanius is very particular. He professes to disclose "the
fraud of Marcion from beginning to end." And the
pains he took to do this thoroughly appear from the
minute differences between the Gospels which he notices.[1] At the same time, he does not extract long passages entire from the Gospel, but indicates their subject,
where they agreed exactly with the received text. It
is possible, therefore, that other slight differences may
have existed which escaped his eye, but the differences
can only have been slight.

The following table gives the contents of the Gospel
of Marcion. It contains nothing that is not found in
St. Luke's Gospel. But some of the passages do not
agree exactly with the parallel passages in the Canonical
Gospel.

THE GOSPEL (Τὸ Εὐαγγέλιον).[2]

Chap. i.[3]

1. Now in the fifteenth year of the reign of Tiberius Cæsar,
Pontius Pilate ruling in Judea, Jesus came down to Capernaum, a city of Galilee, and straightway on the Sabbath days,
going into the synagogue, he taught.[4]

2. And they were astonished at his doctrine : for his word
was with power.

---

[1] Sch. 4, ἐν αὐτοῖς for μετ' αὐτῶν. Sch. 1, ὑμῖν for αὐτοῖς. Sch. 26,
κλῆσιν for κρίσιν. Sch. 34, πάτερ for πάτερ ὑμῶν, &c.

[2] Marcion called his Gospel "The Gospel," as the only one he knew and
recognized, or "The Gospel of the Lord."

[3] The division into chapters is, of course, arbitrary.

[4] Ἐν ἔτει πεντεκαιδεκάτῳ τῆς ἡγεμονίας Τιβερίου Καίσαρος, ἡγεμονεύοντος (St. Luke, ἐπιτροπεύοντος), Ποντίου Πιλάτου τῆς Ἰουδαίας, κατῆλθεν
ὁ Ἰησοῦς εἰς Καπερναούμ, πόλιν τῆς Γαλιλαίας· καὶ εὐθέως τοῖς σάββασιν
εἰσελθὼν εἰς τὴν συναγωγὴν ἐδίδασκε (St. Luke, καὶ διδάσκων αὐτοὺς ἐν
τοῖς σάββασιν).

3. And in the synagogue there was a man, which had a spirit of an unclean devil, and cried out with a loud voice,

4. Saying, Let us alone; what have we to do with thee, Jesus?[1] Art thou come to destroy us? I know thee who thou art; the Holy One of God.

5. And Jesus rebuked him, saying, Hold thy peace, and come out of him. And when the devil had thrown him in the midst, he came out of him, and hurt him not.

6. And they were all amazed, and spake among themselves, saying, What a word is this! for with authority and power he commandeth the unclean spirits, and they come out.

7. And he arose out of the synagogue,[2] and entered into Simon's house. And Simon's wife's mother was taken with a great fever; and they besought him for her.

8. And he stood over her, and rebuked the fever, and it left her: and immediately she arose and ministered unto them.

9. And the fame of him went out into every place of the country round about.

10. And he taught in their synagogues, being glorified of all.[3]

11. And he came to Nazareth;[4] and, as his custom was, he went into the synagogue on the Sabbath day,[5] and he began to preach to them.[6]

12. And all bare him witness, and wondered at the gracious words which proceeded out of his mouth.[7]

13. And he said unto them, Ye will surely say unto me

---

[1] Ναζαρηνέ omitted.

[2] St. Luke iv. 37 omitted here, and inserted after iv. 39.

[3] Luke iv. 15 inserted here.

[4] οὗ ἦν τεθραμμένος omitted.

[5] ἀνέστη ἀναγνῶναι omitted, and Luke iv. 17—20.

[6] καὶ ἤρξατο κηρύσσειν αὐτοῖς. St. Luke has, Ἤρξατο δὲ λέγειν πρὸς αὐτούς· ὅτι σήμερον πεπλήρωται ἡ γραφὴ αὕτη ἐν τοῖς ὠσὶν ὑμῶν.

[7] The rest of the verse (22) omitted.

M 3

this proverb, Physician, heal thyself: whatsoever we have heard done in Capernaum, do also here.[1]

14. But I tell you of a truth, many widows were in Israel in the days of Elias, when the heaven was shut up three years and six months, when great famine was throughout the land;

15. But unto none of them was Elias sent, save unto Sarepta, a city of Sidon, unto a woman that was a widow.

16. And many lepers were in the time of Eliseus the prophet in Israel,[2] and none of them was cleansed, saving Naaman the Syrian.

17. And all they in the synagogue, when they heard these things, were filled with wrath,

18. And rose up, and thrust him out of the city, and led him unto the brow of the hill whereon their city was built, that they might cast him down headlong.

19. But he passing through the midst of them, went his way to Capernaum.[3]

20. And when the sun was setting, all they that had any sick with divers diseases brought them unto him, &c. (as St. Luke iv. 40—44).

Chap. ii.

Same as St. Luke v.

Verse 14 differed slightly. For εἰς μαρτύριον αὐτοῖς, Marcion's Gospel had ἵνα τοῦτο ᾖ μαρτύριον ὑμῖν, "that this may be a testimony to you."

Chap. iii.

Same as St. Luke vi.

Verse 17, for μετ᾽ αὐτῶν, Marcion read ἐν αὐτοῖς; "among them" for "with them."

Chap. iv.

Same as St. Luke vii.

Verses 29—35 omitted.

[1] ἐν τῇ πατρίδι σου omitted.

[2] ἐν τῷ Ἰσραήλ after ἐπὶ Ἐλισσαίου τοῦ προφήτου.

[3] ἐπορεύετο εἰς Καπερναούμ. St. Luke has, ἐπορεύετο καὶ κατῆλθεν εἰς Καπερναούμ.

Chap. v.

Same as St. Luke viii.

But verse 19 was omitted by Marcion.

And verse 21 read: "And he answering, said unto them, Who is my mother, and who are my brethren?[1] My mother and my brethren are these which hear the word of God, and do it."

Chap vi.

Same as St. Luke ix.

But verse 31 was omitted.

Chap. vii.

Same as St. Luke x.

But verse 21 read: "In that hour he rejoiced in the Spirit, and said, I praise and thank thee, Lord of Heaven, that those things which were hidden from the wise and prudent thou hast revealed to babes: even so, Father; for so it seemed good in thy sight."[2]

And verse 22 ran: "All things are delivered to me of my Father, and no man hath known the Father save the Son, nor the Son save the Father, and he to whom the Son hath revealed;"[3] in place of, "All things are delivered to me of my Father; and no man knoweth who the Son is, but the Father; and who the Father is, but the Son, and he to whom the Son will reveal him."

And verse 25: "Doing what shall I obtain life?" "eternal," αἰώνιον, being omitted.

Chap. viii.

Same as St. Luke xi.

---

[1] τίς μου ἡ μήτηρ καὶ οἱ ἀδελφοί.

[2] Εὐχαριστῶ καὶ ἐξομολογοῦμαί σοι, κύριε τοῦ οὐρανοῦ, ὅτι ἅτινα ἦν κρυπτὰ σοφοῖς καὶ συνετοῖς ἀπεκάλυψας, &c. St. Luke has, ἐξομολογοῦμαί σοι, πάτερ, κύριε τοῦ οὐρανοῦ καὶ τῆς γῆς, ὅτι ἀπέκρυψας ταῦτα ἀπὸ σοφῶν καὶ συνετῶν καὶ ἀπεκάλυψας, &c.

[3] οὐδεὶς ἔγνω τὸν πατέρα εἰ μὴ ὁ υἱός, οὐδὲ τὸν υἱόν τις γινώσκει εἰ μὴ ὁ πατήρ, καὶ ᾧ ἂν ὁ υἱὸς ἀποκαλύψῃ.

But verse 2: "When ye pray, say, Father, may thy Holy Spirit come to us, thy kingdom come," &c., in place of "Hallowed be thy name."[1]

Verse 29: in Marcion's Gospel it ended, "This is an evil generation: they seek a sign; and there shall no sign be given it." What follows in St. Luke's Gospel, "but the sign of Jonas the prophet," and verses 30—32, were omitted.

Verse 42: "Woe unto you, Pharisees! ye tithe mint and rue and all manner of herbs, and pass over the calling[2] and the love of God," &c.

Verses 49—51 were omitted by Marcion.

Chap. ix.

Same as St. Luke xii.

But verses 6, 7, and "τῶν ἀγγέλων" in 8 and 9 omitted.

Verse 32 read: "Fear not, little flock; for it is the Father's good pleasure to give you the kingdom."[3]

And verse 38 ran thus: "And if he shall come in the evening watch, and find thus, blessed are those servants."[4]

Chap. x.

Same as St. Luke xiii. 11—28.

Marcion's Gospel was without verses 1—10.

Verse 28: for "Abraham and Isaac and Jacob and all the prophets," Marcion read, "all the righteous,"[5] and added "held back" after "cast."[6]

Verses 29—35 of St. Luke's chapter were not in Marcion's Gospel.

---

[1] In some of the most ancient codices of St. Luke, "which art in heaven" is not found. Πάτερ, ἐλθέτω πρὸς ἡμᾶς τὸ ἅγιον πνεῦμά σου.

[2] κλῆσιν instead of κρίσιν.   [3] ὑμῶν omitted.

[4] τῇ ἑσπερινῇ φυλακῇ, for ἐν τῇ δευτέρᾳ φυλακῇ καὶ ἐν τῇ τρίτῃ φυλακῇ.

[5] πάντας τοὺς δικαίους.

[6] ἐκβαλλομένους καὶ κρατουμένους ἔξω.

Chap. xi.

Same as St. Luke xiv.

Verses 7—11 omitted.

Chap. xii.

Same as St. Luke xv. 1—10.

Verses 11—32 omitted.

Chap. xiii.

Same as St. Luke xvi.

But verse 12: " If ye have not been faithful in that which is another man's, who will give you that which is mine ?"[1]

And verse 17: for "One tittle of the Law shall not fall," Marcion read, " One tittle of my words shall not fall."[2]

Chap. xiv.

Same as St. Luke xvii.

But verse 2: $\epsilon i \ \mu \eta \ \dot{\epsilon}\gamma\epsilon\nu\nu\dot{\eta}\theta\eta, \ \dot{\eta} \ \mu\dot{\nu}\lambda o\varsigma \ \dot{o}\nu\iota\kappa\dot{o}\varsigma,$[3] "if he had not been born, or if a mill-stone," &c.

Verses 9, 10 : Marcion's Gospel had, " Doth he thank that servant because he did the things that were commanded him ? I trow not. So likewise do ye, when ye shall have done all those things that are commanded you." Omitting, " Say, We are unprofitable servants ; we have done that which was our duty to do."

Verse 14 : " And he sent them away, saying, Go show yourselves unto the priests," &c., in place of, " And when he saw them, he said unto them," &c.[4]

Verse 18 ran : " These are not found returning to give glory to God. And there were many lepers in the time

---

[1] ἐμόν for ὑμέτερον.

[2] ἢ τῶν λόγων μου μίαν κεραίαν πεσεῖν.

[3] Some codices of St. Luke have, λίθος μυλικός ; others, μύλος ὀνικός.

[4] Ἀπέστειλεν αὐτοὺς λέγων.

I shall now make a few remarks on some of the
passages absent from Marcion's Gospel, or which, in it,
differ from the Canonical Gospel of St. Luke.

1. It was not attributed to St. Luke. It was Τὸ
Εὐαγγέλιον, not κατὰ Λουκᾶν. Tertullian explicitly says,
"Marcion inscribes no name on his Gospel,"[1] and in the
"Dialogue on the Right Faith" it is asserted that he
protested his Gospel was *the* Gospel, the only one; and
that the multiplicity of Gospels used by Catholics, and
their discrepancies, were a proof that none of these other
Gospels were genuine. He even went so far as to assert
that his Gospel was written by Christ,[2] and when closely
pressed on this point, and asked whether Christ wrote
the account of his own passion and resurrection, he said
it was so, but afterwards hesitated, and asserted that it
was probably added by St. Paul.

This shows plainly enough that Marcion had received
the Gospel, probably from the Church of Sinope, where
it was the only one known, and that he had heard
nothing about St. Luke as its author; indeed, knew
nothing of its origin. He treated it with the utmost
veneration, and in his veneration for it attributed its
authorship to the Lord himself; supposing the words of
St. Paul, "the Gospel of Christ,"[3] "the Gospel of his
Son,"[4] "the Gospel of God,"[5] to mean that Jesus Christ
was the actual author of the book.

Marcion, it may be remarked, would have had no
objection to acknowledging St. Luke as the compiler of

[1] Tert. adv. Marcion, iv. 2. "Marcion evangelio scilicet suo nullum
adscribit nomen."

[2] Ἔν ἐστι τὸ εὐαγγέλιον, ὃ ὁ Χριστὸς ἔγραψεν.

[3] Rom. i. 16, xv. 19, 29; 1 Cor. ix. 12, 18; 2 Cor. iv. 4, ix. 18;
Gal. i. 7.

[4] Rom. i. 9.

[5] Rom. i. 1, xv. 16; 1 Thess. ii. 2, 9; 1 Tim. i. 11.

the Gospel, as that evangelist was a devoted follower of St. Paul. If he did not do so, it was because at Sinope the Gospel read in the Church was not known by his name.

2. Marcion's Gospel was without the Preface, Luke i. 1—4.

This Preface is certainly by St. Luke, but was added, we may conjecture, after the final revision of his Gospel, when he issued the second edition. Its absence from Marcion's Gospel shows that it did not accompany the first edition.

3. The narrative of the nativity, Luke i. ii., is not in Marcion's Gospel.

It has been supposed by critics that he omitted this narrative purposely, because his Christ was descended from the highest God, had no part with the world of the Demiurge, and had therefore no earthly mother.[1] But if so, why did Marcion suffer the words, "Thy mother and thy brethren stand without desiring to see thee" (Luke viii. 20), to remain in his Gospel?

And it does not appear that Marcion denied the incarnation *in toto*, and went to the full extreme of Docetic doctrine. On the contrary, he taught that Christ deceived the God of this World, by coming into it as a man. The Demiurge trusted he would be his Messiah, to confirm the Law for ever. But when he saw that Christ was destroying the Law, he inflicted on him death. And this was only possible, because Christ was, through his human nature, subject to his power.

It is a less violent supposition that in the Church of Sinope the Gospel was, like that of St. Mark, without a narrative of the nativity and childhood of Jesus. It is probable, moreover, that the first two chapters of St. Luke's Gospel were added at a later period. The

---

[1] Volckmar: Das Evangelium Marcions; Leipzig, 1852, p. 54.

account of the nativity and childhood is taken from the
mouths of the blessed Virgin Mary, of eye-witnesses, or
contemporaries. "Mary kept all these things and pon-
dered them in her heart," and "His mother kept all
these sayings in her heart."[1] This is our guaranty that
the story is true. Mary kept them in memory, and the
evangelist appeals to her memory for them. So with
regard to the account of the nativity of the Baptist,
"All they that heard these things laid them up in their
hearts."[2] To their recollections also the evangelist
appeals as his authority.

Now it is not probable that St. Luke or St. Paul were
brought in contact with the Virgin and the people about
Hebron, relatives of the Baptist. Their lives were spent
in Asia Minor. But St. John, we know, became the
guardian of the blessed Virgin after the death of Christ.[3]
Greek ecclesiastical tradition declares that she accompanied him to Ephesus. But be that as it may, St. John
almost certainly would have tenderly and reverently
collected the "memorabilia" of the blessed Mother concerning her Divine Son's birth and infancy.

St. John had the organizing and disciplining of the
"Asiatic" churches founded by St. Paul after the removal of the Apostle of the Gentiles. When he came
to Ephesus, and went through the Churches of Asia
Minor, he found a Gospel compiled by St Luke in
general use. To this he added such particulars as were
expedient to complete it, amongst others the "recollections" of St. Mary, and the relatives of the Baptist. It
is most probable that he gave them to St. Luke to work
into his narrative, and thus to form a second edition
of his Gospel.[4] That the Gospel of St. Luke was re-

---

[1] Luke ii. 19, 51.   [2] Luke i. 66.   [3] John xix. 26.

[4] This was some time prior to the composition of St. John's Gospel.
The first two chapters of St. Luke's Gospel were written apparently by the

touched after the abatement of the anti-legal excitement can hardly be doubted. We shall see instances as we proceed.

4. The section relating to the Baptist (Luke iii. 2— 19), with which the most ancient Judaizing Gospels opened, was absent from that of Marcion.

John belonged to the Old Covenant; he could not therefore be regarded as revealing the Gospel of the unknown God. This is thought by Baur, Hilgenfeld and Volckmar, to be the reason of the omission. But the explanation is strained. I think it probable, as stated above, that St. Luke when with St. Paul had not got the narrative of those who had heard and seen the birth of the Baptist and his preaching beyond Jordan. Had Marcion, moreover, objected to the Baptist as belonging to the Old Covenant, he would not have suffered the presence in his Gospel of the passage, Luke vii. 24— 28, containing the high commendation of John, "This is he of whom it is written, Behold, I send my messenger before thy face, which shall prepare the way before thee."

5. There is no mention in Marcion's Gospel of the baptism of our Lord (Luke iii. 21, 22). This is given very briefly in St. Luke's Gospel. To the Nazarene Church this event was of the utmost importance; it was regarded as the beginning of the mission of Jesus, the ratification by God of his Messiahship, and therefore the Gospels of Mark and of the Hebrews opened with it. But the significance was not so deeply felt by the

same hand which wrote the rest. Similarities, identity of expression, almost prove this. Compare i. 10 and ii. 13 with viii. 37, ix. 37, xxiii. 1; also i. 10 with xiv. 17, xxii. 14; i. 20 with xxii. 27, and i. 20 with xii. 3, xix. 44; i. 22 with xxiv. 23; i. 44 with vii. 1, ix. 44; also i. 45 with x. 23, xi. 27, 28; also i. 48 with ix. 38; i. 66 with ix. 44; i. 80 with ix. 51; ii. 6 with iv. 2; ii. 9 with xxiv. 4; ii. 10 with v. 10; ii. 14 with xix. 18; ii. 20 with xix. 37; ii. 25 with xxiii. 50; ii. 26 with ix. 20.

Gentile converts, and therefore the circumstance is despatched in a few words.

6. The genealogy of Joseph is not given (Luke iii. 23—38). This is not to be wondered at. It is an evidently late interpolation, clumsily foisted into the sacred text, rudely interrupting the narrative.

(21): "Now when all the people were baptized, it came to pass that Jesus also being baptized, and praying, the heaven opened, (22) and the Holy Ghost descended in a bodily shape like a dove upon him, and a voice came from heaven, which said, Thou art my beloved Son; in thee I am well pleased. (iv. 1): And Jesus being full of the Holy Ghost returned from Jordan, and was led by the Spirit into the wilderness." Such is the natural order. But it is interrupted by the generation of Joseph, the supposed father of Jesus, from Adam. This generation does not concern Jesus at all, but it came through some Jewish Christians into the hands of the Church in Asia Minor, and was forced between the joints of the sacred text, to the interruption of the narrative and the succession of ideas.[1] Marcion had it not in the Gospel brought from Pontus.

7. The narrative of the Temptation is not in Marcion's Gospel. It can have been no omission of his, for it would have tallied admirably with his doctrine. He held that the God of this world believed Christ at first to be the Messiah, but finally was undeceived. In the narrative of the Temptation the devil offers Christ all the kingdoms of the world and the glory of them. He takes the position which in Marcion's scheme was occupied by the Demiurge. Had he possessed the record of

---

[1] The descent of the Holy Ghost in bodily shape explains why in iv. 1 he is said to have been full of the Holy Ghost. I suspect the narrative of the unction occurred here. This was removed to cut off occasion to Docetic error, and the gap was clumsily filled with an useless genealogy.

the Temptation, it would have mightily strengthened his position.

8. The "Gospel of our Lord" opens with the words, "In the fifteenth year of Tiberius Cæsar, Pontius Pilate ruling in Judæa (ἡγεμονεύοντος in place of ἐπιτροπεύοντος, an unimportant difference), Jesus came down to Capernaum, a city of Galilee, and straightway on the Sabbath days, going into the synagogue, he taught" (εἰσελθὼν εἰς τὴν συναγωγὴν ἐδίδασκε in place of καὶ διδάσκων αὐτοὺς ἐν τοῖς σάββασιν), again an unimportant variation.

9. The words "Jesus of Nazareth"[1] are in Marcion's Gospel simply "Jesus." This may have been done by Marcion on purpose. But there is no evidence that it was omitted in xxiv. 19.

10. The order of events, as given in Luke iv., is changed. Jesus, in Marcion's Gospel, goes first to Capernaum, and then to Nazareth, reversing the order in St. Luke.

THE GOSPEL OF THE LORD.	THE GOSPEL OF ST. LUKE, iv. 14—40.
9. Christ goes to Capernaum, and enters the synagogue to teach.	1. Christ comes into Galilee, and the fame of him goes round about (14).
10. All are astonished at his doctrine and power.	2. He teaches in the synagogues of Galilee, being glorified of all (15).
11. He heals the demoniac.	
12. All are amazed at his power.	3. He comes to Nazareth, and goes into the synagogue (16).
14. He enters Simon's house, and heals his wife's mother.	4. He opens Esaias, and interprets his prophecy (17—21).
13. His fame spreads.	
2. He teaches in the synagogues, being glorified of all.	5. All bare him witness, and wonder at his gracious words, but ask if he is not Joseph's son (22).
3. He comes to Nazareth, and goes into the synagogue.	
5. All bare him witness, and wonder at his gracious words.	6. Christ quotes a proverb, and combats it (23—27).

[1] Ναζωραῖος for Ναζαρηνός omitted.

6. Christ quotes a proverb, and combats it.

7. The Nazarenes seek to throw him down a precipice.

8. He escapes, and goes to Capernaum.

15. At sunset he heals the sick.

7. The Nazarenes seek to throw him down a precipice (28, 29).

8. He escapes, and goes to Capernaum (30, 31).

9. He teaches in the synagogue at Capernaum (31).

10. All are astonished at his doctrine and power (32).

11. He heals the demoniac (33—35).

12. All are amazed at his power (36).

13. His fame spreads (37).

14. He enters Simon's house, and heals his wife's mother (38, 39).

15. At sunset he heals the sick (40).

By placing the subject-matter of the two narratives side by side, and numbering that of St. Luke consecutively, and giving the corresponding paragraphs, with their numbers as in Luke's order, arranged in the Marcionite succession, the reader is able at once to see the difference. No doctrinal question was touched by this transposition. The only explanation of it which is satisfactory is that each Gospel contained fragments which were pieced together differently. One block consisted of paragraphs 2—8; another, of paragraphs 9—14; another 15. Besides these blocks, there were chips, splinters, the paragraphs 1, 13, 15. Marcion's Gospel was without 1 and 4.

Par. 2, verse 15: "He taught in their synagogues, being glorified of all," was common to both Gospels. In Marcion's, most appropriately, it came after Christ has performed miracles; less judiciously in Luke's does it come before the performance of miracles.

Par. 13: "And the fame of him went out into every place of the country round about." St. Luke put this after Christ had taught in Nazareth and Capernaum ; in Marcion's Gospel it was before he had been to Nazareth, but immediately after the healing of Simon's wife's mother. It ought probably to occupy the place assigned it in Marcion's text. The fame of Christ spreads. They in Nazareth hear of it, and say, "What we have heard done in Capernaum, do also here."

Par. 15 : "Now when the sun was setting, all they that had any sick with divers diseases brought them unto him," &c., as in St. Luke iv. 40, 41. This Marcion's Gospel has immediately after the healing of the sick wife of Simon, as though the rumour of the miracle attracted all who had sick relations to bring them to Christ. No doubt the paragraph should rightly stand in connection with this miracle of healing the fevered woman.

But there are omissions supposed to have been made purposely by Marcion. In verse 16 of St. Luke's Gospel, c. iv.: "He came to Nazareth, where he had been brought up," in the "Gospel of the Lord" ran, "He came to Nazareth" only. But it is not improbable that "where he had been brought up" was a gloss which crept into the text after the addition of the narrative of the early years of Christ had been added to the Canonical Gospel.

All the reading from the prophet Esaias, and the exposition of the prophecy (Luke iv. 17—21) was omitted, there can be small question, by Marcion, because it mutilated against his views touching the prophets as ministers, not of the God of Christ, but of the God of this world.

Luke iv. 23 : "Do also here in thy country," changed into, "Do also here." It is possible that "in thy country" may be a gloss which has crept into a later text of St. Luke's Gospel, or was inserted by Luke in his second edition.

11. Luke vii. 29—35 are wanting in Marcion's Gospel.

That verses 29—32 should have been purposely excluded, it is impossible to suppose, as they favoured
Marcion's tenets. It has been argued that the rest of
the verses, 33—35, were cut out by Marcion because in
verse 34 it is said, "The Son of Man is come eating and
drinking; and ye say, Behold a gluttonous man and a
winebibber." But the "Gospel of the Lord" contained
Luke v. 33: "Why do the disciples of John fast often,
and make long prayers, and likewise the disciples of the
Pharisees; but thine eat and drink;" and the example
of Christ going to the feast prepared by Levi is retained
(v. 29).

12. Luke viii. 19: "Then came to him his mother
and his brethren," &c., omitted; but the next verse,
"And it was told him by certain which said, Thy mother
and thy brethren stand without, desiring to see thee."
This cannot be admitted as a mutilation by Marcion.
Had he cut out verse 19, he would also have removed
verse 20. Rather is verse 19 an amplification of the
original text. The "saying" of Jesus was known in
the "Asiatic" churches; and when Luke wove it into
the text of his Gospel, he introduced it with the words,
"Then came to him his mother and his brethren, and
could not come at him for the press," words not necessary, but deducible from the preserved text, and useful
as introducing it.

13. Luke x. 21: "In that hour he rejoiced in the
spirit, and said, I praise and thank thee, Lord of heaven,
that those things which are hidden from the wise and
prudent thou hast revealed to babes." The version in
Luke's Gospel may have been tampered with by Marcion, lest God should appear harsh in hiding "those
things from the wise and prudent." But it is more
likely that Marcion's text is the correct one. Why
should Christ thank God that he has hidden the truth

from the wise and prudent? The reading in Marcion's Gospel is not only a better one, but it also appears to be an independent one. He has, "I praise and thank thee." The received text differs in different codices; in some, Jesus rejoices "in the Spirit;" in others, "in the Holy Spirit."

14. Luke x. 22: "All things are delivered to me of my Father, and no man hath known the Father save the Son, nor the Son save the Father, and he to whom the Son hath revealed him." No doctrinal purpose was effected by the change. It is therefore probable that the Sinope Gospel ran as in Marcion's text.

15. Luke x. 25: "Doing what shall I obtain life?" "eternal" being omitted, it is thought, lest Jesus should seem to teach that eternal life was to be obtained by fulfilling the Law.[1] But Marcion did not alter the same question when asked by the ruler, in Luke xviii. 18; for then Christ, after he has referred him to the Law, goes on to impose on him a higher law—that of love. But "eternal" may be an addition to Luke's text in the second edition.

16. The first petition in the Lord's Prayer differs in Marcion's Gospel from that in St. Luke. Marcion has, "Father! may thy Holy Spirit come to us, Thy kingdom come," &c., instead of, "Father! (which art in heaven—not in the most ancient copies of St. Luke). Hallowed be thy name," &c. No purpose was served by this difference, and we must not attribute to Marcion in this instance wilful alteration of the sacred text. It is apparent that several versions of the Lord's Prayer existed in the first age of the Church, and that this was the form in which it was accepted and used in Pontus, perhaps throughout Asia Minor.

[1] Tertul. adv. Marcion, iv. c. 25, "ut doctor de ea vita videatur consuluisse, quæ in lege promittitur longæva."

That the Lord's Prayer in St. Luke's Gospel stood originally as in Marcion's Gospel is made almost certain by verse 13. After giving the form of prayer, xi. 2—4, Christ instructs his disciples on the readiness of God to answer prayer. "And," he continues, "if ye then, being evil, know how to give good gifts unto your children; how much more shall your heavenly Father give the Holy Spirit to them that ask him?" How ready will He be to give that which you have learned to ask in the first petition of the prayer I have just taught you! The petition was altered in the received text later, to accommodate it to the form given in St. Matthew's Gospel.

17. Luke xi. 29: "There shall no sign be given." What follows in St. Luke's Gospel, "but the sign of the prophet Jonas," and verses 30—32, were not found in Marcion's Gospel. Perhaps all this was inserted in the second edition of St. Luke's Gospel. But also perhaps the allusions to the Ninevites and the Queen of the South were omitted, because of the condemnation pronounced on the generation which received not Christ through them; and Jesus was not the manifestation of the God of judgment, but of the God of mercy.

18. So also "judgment" was turned into "calling," in verse 42; and also the verses 49—51, in which the blood of the prophets is said to be "required of this generation."

19. Luke xii. 38: "The evening watch" is perhaps an earlier reading than the received one: "If he shall come in the second watch, or come in the third watch;" which has the appearance of an expansion of the simpler text.

The evening watch was the first watch. The Christians in the first age thought that our Lord would come again immediately. But as he did not return again in glory in the first watch, they altered the text to "the second watch or the third watch." · Consequently Marcion's text is the original unaltered one.

20. Luke xii. 6, 7 : "Are not five sparrows sold for two farthings, and not one of them is forgotten before God? But even the very hairs of your head are all numbered. Fear not therefore ; ye are of more value than many sparrows." Perhaps Marcion omitted this because he did not hold that the Supreme God concerned Himself with the fate of men's bodies.

But more probably the passage did not occur in the original Pauline Gospel, but was grafted into it afterwards when St. Matthew's Gospel came into the hands of the Asiatic Christians, when it was transferred from it (x. 29—31) verbatim to Luke's Gospel.

21. Marcion's Gospel was without Luke xiii. 1—10.

The absence of the account of the Galilæans, whose blood Pilate had mingled with their sacrifices, and of those on whom the tower in Siloam fell, which occurs in the received text, removes a difficulty. St. Luke says, "There were present at that season some that told him of the Galilæans, whose blood," &c., as though it were a circumstance which had just taken place, whereas this act of barbarity was committed when Quirinus, not Pilate, was governor, twenty-four years before the appearance of Jesus. And no tower in Siloam is mentioned in any account of Jerusalem. The mention of the Galilæans in the canonical text has the appearance of an anachronism, and probably did not exist in the Gospel which Marcion received, and was a late addition to the Gospel of Luke.

The parable of the fig-tree which follows may, however, have been removed by Marcion lest the Supreme God should appear as a God of judgment against those who produced no fruit, *i.e.* did no works. But it is

more probable that this parable, which has an anti-
Pauline moral, was not in the original edition of Luke's
Gospel.

22. Luke xiii. 28: "There shall be weeping and
gnashing of teeth, when ye shall see Abraham, and
Isaac, and Jacob, and all the prophets, in the kingdom
of God, and you yourselves thrust out," altered into,
" when ye shall see all the righteous in the kingdom of
God, and ye yourselves cast and held back without."[1]

The change of "the righteous" into "Abraham, and
Isaac, and Jacob," in the deutero-Luke, clearly disturbs
the train of thought. Ye Jews shall weep when ye see
the δικαίοι, those made righteous through faith, by the
righteousness which is *not* of the Law, Gentiles from East
and West, in the kingdom, and ye yourselves cast out.

Hilgenfeld thinks that the account of the Judgment
by St. Matthew and St. Luke is couched in terms
coloured by the respective parties to which the evangelists belonged, and that the sentences on the lost are
sharpened to pierce the antagonistic party. Thus, in the
Gospel of St. Luke, Christ dooms to woe those who are
workers of unrighteousness, ἐργάται ἀδικίας,[2] using the
Pauline favourite expression to designate those who are
cast out to weeping and gnashing of teeth, as men who
have not received the righteousness which is of faith;
whereas, in St. Matthew it is the workers of anomia,
οἱ ἐργαζόμενοι τὴν ἀνομίαν,[3] by which Hilgenfeld thinks
the Pauline anti-legalists are not obscurely hinted at,
who are hurled into outer darkness. In St. Luke it is
curious to notice how the lost are described as Jews:
" We have eaten and drunk in thy presence, and thou
hast taught in our streets;" whereas the elect who

---

[1] ὅταν ὄψησθε πάντας τοὺς δικαίους ἐν τῇ βασιλείᾳ τοῦ θεοῦ, ὑμᾶς δὲ
ἐκβαλλομένους καὶ κρατουμένους ἔξω.—Epiph. Schol. 40; Tertul. c. 30.

[2] Luke xiii. 25—30.   [3] Matt. vii. 13.

"sit down in the kingdom of God" come "from the east and from the west, and from the north and from the south," that is to say, are Gentiles.

In Marcion's text we have therefore the ἀδικαίοι shut and cast out, and the δικαίοι sitting overthroned in the kingdom of God. It can scarcely be doubted that this is the correct reading, and that "Abraham, Isaac and Jacob," was substituted for δικαίοι at a later period with a conciliatory purpose.

The rest of the chapter, 31—35, is not to be found in Marcion's Gospel. The first who are to be last, and the last first, not obscurely means that the Gentiles shall precede the Jews. This was in the "Gospel of the Lord," which was, however, without the warning given to Christ, "Get thee out, and depart hence; for Herod will kill thee," and the lamentation of the Saviour over the holy city, "O Jerusalem, Jerusalem, which killest the prophets," &c. Why Marcion should omit this is not clear. It was probably not in the Gospel of Sinope.

23. Luke xiv. 7—11. The same may be said of the parable put forth to those bidden to a feast, when Christ marked how they chose out the chief rooms. It has been supposed by critics that Marcion omitted it, lest Jesus should seem to sanction feasting; but this reason is far-fetched, and it must be remembered that he did retain Luke v. 29 and 33.

24. Luke xv. 11—32. The parable of the Prodigal Son is omitted. That it is left out, as is suggested by some critics, because the elder son signifies mystically the Jewish Church, and the prodigal son represents the Heathen world, is to transfer such allegorical interpretations back to an earlier age than we are justified in doing. Marcion was not bound to admit such an interpretation of the parable, if received in his day. Marcion,

moreover, opposed allegorizing the sayings of Scripture, and insisted on their literal interpretation. Neander says, "The other Gnostics united with their theosophical idealism a mystical, allegorizing interpretation of the Scriptures. Marcion, simple in heart, was decidedly opposed to this artificial method of interpretation. He was a zealous advocate of the literal interpretation which prevailed among the antagonists of Gnosticism."[1] It is therefore most improbable that a popular interpretation of this parable, if such an interpretation existed at that time, should have induced Marcion to omit the parable.

25. Luke xvi. 12 : "If ye have not been faithful in that which is another man's, who will give you that which is mine ?" Surely a reading far preferable to that in the Canonical Gospel, "who will give you that which is your own ?"

26. Luke xvi. 17 : "One tittle of my words shall not fall," in place of, "One tittle of the Law shall not fall." As has been already remarked, the reading in St. Luke is evidently corrupt, altered deliberately by the party of conciliation. Marcion's is the genuine text.

27. Luke xvii. 9, 10. The saying, "We are unprofitable servants; we have done that which was our duty to do," was perhaps omitted by Marcion, lest the Gospel should seem to sanction the idea that any obligation whatever rested on the believer. The received text is thoroughly Pauline, inculcating the worthlessness of man's righteousness. Hahn and Ritschl argue that the whole of the parable, 7—10, was not in Marcion's Gospel; and this is probable, though St. Epiphanius only says that Marcion cut out, "We are unprofitable servants ; we have done that which was our duty to

---

[1] Hist. of the Christian Religion, tr. Bohn, ii. p. 131.

do."[1] The whole parable has such a Pauline ring, that it would probably have been accepted in its entirety by , Marcion, if his Gospel had contained it; and the parable is divested of its point and meaning if only the few words are omitted which St. Epiphanius mentions as deficient.

28. Luke xvii. 18 : "There are not found returning to give glory to God. And there were many lepers in the time of Eliseus the prophet in Israel ; and none of them was cleansed, saving Naaman the Syrian."   In the Gospel of the Lord, this passage concerning the lepers in the time of Eliseus occurs *twice ;* once in chap. i. v. 15, as already given, and again here. It has been preserved in St. Luke's Gospel in only one place, in that corresponding with Marcion i. 15, viz. Luke iv. 27.

It is clear that this was a fragmentary saying of our Lord drifting about, which the compiler of the Sinope Gospel inserted in two places where it thought it would fit in with other passages. When St. Luke's Gospel was revised, it was found that this passage occurred twice, and that it was without appropriateness in chap. xvii. after verse 18, and was therefore cut out.   But in Marcion's Gospel it remained, a monument of the manner in which the Gospels were originally constructed.

29. Luke xviii. 19.   Marcion had : "Jesus said to him, Do not call me good ; one is good, the Father ;" another version of the text, not a deliberate alteration.

30. Luke xviii. 31—34. The prophecies of the passion omitted by Marcion.

31. Luke xix. 29—46. The ride into Jerusalem on an ass, and the expulsion of the buyers and sellers from the Temple, are omitted.

Why the Palm-Sunday triumphal entry should have

[1] παρέκοψε τό· λέγετε, ἀχρεῖοι δοῦλοί ἐσμεν· ὃ ὠφείλομεν ποιῆσαι πεποιήκαμεν, Sch. 47.

been excluded does not appear. In St. Luke's Gospel
Jesus is not hailed as "King of the Jews" and "Son of
David." Had this been the case, these two titles, we
may conclude, would have been eliminated from the
narrative; but we see no reason why the whole account
should be swept away. It probably did not exist in the
original Gospel Marcion obtained in Pontus.

Did Marcion cut out the narrative of the expulsion of
the buyers and sellers from the Temple? I think not.
St. John, in his Gospel, gives that event in his second
chapter as occurring, not at the close of the ministry of
Christ, but at its opening.

St. John is the only evangelist who can be safely relied upon for giving the chronological order of events.
St. Matthew, as has been already shown, did not write
the acts of our Lord, but his sayings only; and St. Mark
was no eye-witness.

A Pauline Gospel would not contain the account of
the purifying of the Temple, and the saying, "My
house is the house of prayer." But when St. Matthew's
Gospel, or St. Mark's, found its way into Asia Minor,
this passage was extracted from one of them, and interpolated in the Lucan text, in the same place where it
occurred in those Gospels—at the end of the ministry,
and therefore in the wrong place.

32. Luke xx. 9—18. The parable of the vineyard
and the husbandmen. This Marcion probably omitted
because it made the Lord of the vineyard, who sent
forth the prophets, the same as the Lord who sent his
son. The lord of the vineyard to Marcion was the
Demiurge, but the Supreme Lord sent Christ.

33. Luke xx. 37, 38, omitted by Marcion, because a
reference to Moses, and God, as the God of Abraham,
Isaac and Jacob.

34. Luke xxi. 18: "There shall not an hair of your

head perish," omitted, perhaps, lest the God of heaven, whom Christ revealed, should appear to concern himself about the vile bodies of men, under the dominion of the God of this world ; but more probably this verse did not exist in the original text. The awkwardness of its position has led many critics to reject it as an interpolation,[1] and the fact of Marcion's Gospel being without it goes far to prove that the original Luke Gospel was without it.

35. Luke xxi. 21, 22. The warning given by our Lord to his disciples to flee from Jerusalem when they see it encompassed with armies. Verse 21 was omitted no doubt because of the words, "These be the days of vengeance, that all things which are written may be fulfilled." This jarred with Marcion's conception of the Supreme God as one of mercy, and of Jesus as proclaiming blessings and forgiveness, in place of the vengeance and justice of the World-God.

36. Luke xxii. 16—18. The distribution of the paschal cup among the disciples is omitted.

37. Luke xxii. 28—30. The promise that the apostles should eat and drink in Christ's kingdom and judge the twelve tribes, was omitted by Marcion, as inconsistent with his views of the spiritual nature of the heavenly kingdom ; and that judgment should be committed by the God of free forgiveness to the apostles, was in his sight impossible. Why Luke xxiii. 43, 47—49, were not in Marcion's Gospel does not appear; they can hardly have been omitted purposely.

38. Luke xxiii. 2. In Marcion's Gospel it ran : " And they began to accuse him, saying, We found this one perverting the nation, and destroying the Law and the Prophets, and forbidding to give tribute to Cæsar, and leading away the women and children." ·

---

[1] Baur calls it an "ungeschickte Zusatz."

It is not possible that Marcion should have forced the words "destroying the Law and the Prophets" into the text, for these are the accusations of *false* witnesses. And this is precisely what Marcion taught that Christ had come to do. Both this accusation and that other, that he drew away after him the women and children from their homes and domestic duties and responsibilities, most probably did exist in the original text. It is not improbable that they were both made to disappear from the authorized text later, when the conciliatory movement began.

39. Luke xxiv. 43. In Marcion's Gospel, either the whole of the verse, "Verily, I say unto thee, To-day shalt thou be with me in Paradise," was omitted, or more probably only the words "in Paradise." Marcion would not have purposely cut out such an instance of free acceptance of one who had all his life transgressed the Law, but he may have cancelled the words "in Paradise."

40. Luke xxiv. 25 stood in Marcion's Gospel, "O fools, and in heart slow to believe all that he spake unto you;" and 27 and 45, which relate that Jesus explained to the two disciples out of Moses and the Prophets how he must suffer, and that he opened their understanding to understand the Scriptures, were both absent.

41. Luke xxiv. 46. Instead of Christ appealing to the Prophets, Marcion made him say, "These are the words which I spake unto you, while I was yet with you, that thus it behoved Christ to suffer, and to rise from the dead the third day." This was possibly Marcion's doing.

The other differences between Marcion's Gospel and the Canonical Gospel of St. Luke are so small, that the reader need not be troubled with them here. For a fuller and more particular account of Marcion's Gospel he is referred to the works indicated in the foot-note.[1]

It will be seen from the list of differences between the "Gospel of our Lord" and the Gospel of St. Luke, that all the apparent omissions cannot be attributed to Marcion. The Gospel he had he regarded with supreme awe; it was because his Gospel was so ancient, so hallowed by use through many years, that it was invested by him with sovereign authority, and that he regarded the other Gospels as apocryphal, or at best only deutero-canonical.

It is by no means certain that even where his Gospel has been apparently tampered with to suit his views, his hands made the alterations in it. What amplifications St. Luke's Gospel passed through when it underwent revision for a second edition, we cannot tell.

The Gospel of our Lord, if not the original Luke Gospel—and this is probable—was the basis of Luke's compilation. But that it was Luke's first edition of his Gospel, drawn up when St. Paul was actively engaged in founding Asiatic Churches, is the view I am disposed to take of it. As soon as a Church was founded, the need of a Gospel was felt. To satisfy this want, Paul employed Luke to collect memorials of the Lord's life, and weave them together into an historical narrative.

The Gospel of our Lord contains nothing which is not found in that of St. Luke. The arrangement is so similar, that we are forced to the conclusion that it was

[1] The Gospel is printed in Thilo's Codex Apocryph. Novi Testamenti, Lips. 1832, T.I. pp. 401—486. For critical examinations of it see Ritschl: Das Evangelium Marcions und das Kanonische Ev. Lucas, Tübingen, 1846. Baur: Kritische Untersuchungen über die Kanonischen Evangelien, Tübingen, 1847, p. 393 sq. Gratz: Krit. Untersuchungen über Marcions Evangelium, Tübing. 1818. Volckmar: Das Evangelium Marcions, Leipz. 1852. Nicolas: Etudes sur les Evangiles Apocryphes, Paris, 1866, pp. 147—160.

either used by St. Luke, or that it was his original composition. If he used it, then his right to the title of
author of the third Canonical Gospel falls to the ground,
as what he added was of small amount. Who then
composed the Gospel ? We know of no one to whom
tradition even at that early age attributed it.

St. Luke was the associate of St. Paul; ecclesiastical
tradition attributes to him a Gospel. That of " Our
Lord" closely resembles the Canonical Luke's Gospel,
and bears evidence of being earlier in composition,
whilst that which is canonical bears evidence of later
manipulation. All these facts point to Marcion's Gospel
as the original St. Luke—not, however, quite as it came
to Marcion, but edited by the heretic.

That the first edition of Luke bore a stronger Pauline
impress than the second is also probable. The Canonical
Luke has the Pauline .stamp on it still, but beside it is
the Johannite seal. More fully than any other Gospel
does it bring out the tenderness of Christ towards sinners, a feature which has ever made it exceeding precious
to those who have been captives and blind and bruised,
and to whom that Gospel proclaims Christ as their deliverer, enlightener and healer.[1]

It is not necessary here to point out the finger-mark
of Paul in this Gospel; it has been often and well done
by others. It is an established fact, scarcely admitting
dispute, that to him it owes its colour, and that it
reflects his teaching.[2]

And it was this Gospel, in its primitive form, before
it had passed under the hands of St. John, or had been

---

[1] Luke iv. 18.

[2] Luke iv. 28 ; compare vi. 13 with Matt. x. and Luke x. 1—16, vii.
36—50, x. 38—42, xvii. 7—10, xvii. 11—19, x. 30—37, xv. 11—32;
Luke xiii. 25—30, compared with Matt. vii. 13 ; Luke vii. 50, viii. 48,
xviii. 42, &c.

recast by its author, that I think we may be satisfied Marcion possessed. That he made a few erasures is probable, I may almost say certain; but that he ruthlessly carved it to suit his purpose cannot be established.

Of the value of Marcion's Gospel for determining the original text of the third Gospel, it is difficult to speak too highly.

II.

THE GOSPEL OF TRUTH.

VALENTINE, by birth an Egyptian, probably of Jewish descent, it may be presumed received his education at Alexandria. From this city he travelled to Rome (circ. A. D. 140); in both places he preached the Catholic faith, and then retired to Cyprus.[1] A miserable bigotry which refused to see in a heretic any motives but those which are evil, declared that in disgust at not obtaining a bishopric which he coveted, and to which a confessor was preferred, Valentine lapsed into heresy. We need no such explanation of the cause of his secession from orthodoxy. He was a man of an active mind and ardent zeal. Christian doctrine was then a system of facts; theology was as yet unborn. What philosophic truths lay at the foundation of Christian belief was unsuspected. Valentine could not thus rest. He strove to break through the hard facts to the principles on which they reposed. He was a pioneer in Christian theology.

And for his venturous essay he was well qualified. His studies at Alexandria had brought him in contact with Philonism and with Platonism. He obtained at Cyprus an acquaintance with the doctrines of Basilides. His mind caught fire, his ideas expanded. The Gnostic seemed to him to open gleams of light through the facts of the faith he had hitherto professed with dull, unintelligent submission; and he placed himself under the inspiration and instruction of Basilides.

[1] He died about A.D. 160.

But he did not follow him blindly. The speculations of the Gnostic kindled a train of ideas which were peculiarly Valentine's own.

The age was not one to listen patiently to his theorizing. Men were called on to bear testimony by their lives to facts. They could endure the rack, the scourge, the thumbscrew, the iron rake, for facts, not for ideas. That Jesus had lived and died and mounted to heaven, was enough for their simple minds. They cared nothing, they made no effort to understand, what were the causes of evil, what its relation to matter.

Consequently Valentine met with cold indifference, then with hot abhorrence. He was excommunicated. Separation embittered him. His respect for orthodoxy was gone; its hold upon him was lost; and he allowed himself to drift in the wide sea of theosophic speculation wherever his ideas carried him.

Valentine taught that in the Godhead exerting creative power were manifest two motions—a positive, the evolving, creative, life-giving element; and the negative, which determined, shaped and localized the creative force. From the positive force came life, from the negative the direction life takes in its manifestation.

The world is the revelation of the divine ideas, gradually unfolding themselves, and Christ and redemption are the perfection and end of creation. Through creation the idea goes forth from God; through Christ the idea perfected returns to the bosom of God. Redemption is the recoil wave of creation, the echo of the fiat returning to the Creator's ear.

The manifestation of the ideas of God is in unity; but in opposition to unity exists anarchy; in antagonism with creation emerges the principle of destruction. The representative of destruction, disunion, chaos, is Satan. The work of creation is infinite differentiation in perfect harmony. But in the midst of this emerges discord, an element of opposition which seeks to ruin the concord in the manifestation of the divine ideas. Therefore redemption is necessary, and Christ is the medium of redemption, which consists in the restoration to harmony and unity of that which by the fraud of Satan is thrown into disorder and antagonism.

But how comes it that in creation there should be a disturbing element? That element must issue in some manner from the Creator; it must arise from some defect in Him. Therefore, Valentinian concluded, the God who created the world and gave source to the being of Satan cannot have been the supreme, all-good, perfect God.

But if redemption be the perfecting of man, it must be the work of the only perfect God, who thereby counteracts the evil that has sprung up through the imperfection of the Demiurge.

Therefore Jesus Christ is an emanation from the Supreme God, destroying the ill effects produced in the world by the faulty nature of the Creator, undoing the discord and restoring all to harmony.

Jesus was formed by the Demiurge of a wondrously constituted ethereal body, visible to the outward sense. This Jesus entered the world through man, as a sunbeam enters a chamber through the window. The Demiurge created Jesus to redeem the people from the disorganizing, destructive effects of Satan, to be their Messiah.

But the Supreme God had alone power perfectly to accomplish this work; therefore at the baptism of Christ, the Saviour (Soter) descended on him, consecrating him to be the perfect Redeemer of mankind, conveying to him a mission and power which the Demiurge could not have given.

In all this we see the influence of Marcion's ideas.

We need not follow out this fundamental principle of his theosophy into all its fantastic formularies. If Valentine was the precursor of Hegel in the enunciation of the universal antinomy, he was like Hegel also in involving his system in a cloud of incomprehensible terminology, in producing bewilderment where he sought simplicity.

Valentine accepted the Old Testament, but only in the same light as he regarded the great works of the heathen writers to be deserving of regard.[1] Both contained good, noble examples, pure teaching; but in both also was the element of discord, contradictory teaching, and bad example. Ptolemy, the Valentinian who least sacrificed the moral to the theosophic element, scarcely dealt with the Old Testament differently from St. Paul. He did not indeed regard the Old Testament as the work of the Supreme God; the Mosaic legislation seemed to him to be the work of an inferior being, because, as he said, it contained too many imperfections to be the revelation of the Highest God, and too many excellences to be attributed to an evil spirit. But, like the Apostle of the Gentiles, he saw in the Mosaic ceremonies only symbols of spiritual truth, and, like him, he thought that the symbol was no longer necessary when the idea it revealed was manifested in all its clearness. Therefore, when the ideas these symbols veiled had reached and illumined men's minds, the necessity for them—husks to the idea, letters giving meaning to the thought—was at an end.

Like St. Paul, therefore, he treated the Old Testament as a preparation for the New one, but as nothing more. We ascertain Ptolemy's views from a letter of his to

---

[1] Clem. Alex. Strom. vi.

Flora, a Catholic lady whom he desired to convert to Valentinianism.[1]

In this letter he laboured to show that the God of this world (the Demiurge) was not the Supreme God, and that the Old Testament Scriptures were the revelation of the Demiurge, and not of the highest God. To prove the first point, Ptolemy appealed to apostolic tradition—no doubt to Pauline teaching—which had come down to him, and to the words of the Saviour, by which, he admits, all doctrine must be settled. In this letter he quotes largely from St. Paul's Epistles, and from the Gospels of St. Matthew and St. John.

Like Marcion, Ptolemy insisted that the Demiurge, the God of this world, was also the God who revealed himself in the Old Testament, and that to this God belonged justice, wrath and punishment; whereas to the Supreme Deity was attributed free forgiveness, absolute goodness. The Saviour abolished the Law, therefore he abolished all the system of punishment for sin, that the reign of free grace might prevail.

According to Ptolemy, therefore, retributive justice exercised by the State was irreconcilable with the nature of the Supreme God, and the State, accordingly, was under the dominion of the Demiurge.

To the revelation of the old Law belonged ordinances of ceremonial and of seasons. These also are done away by Christ, who leads from the bondage of ceremonial to spiritual religion.

Another Valentinian of note was Heracleon, who wrote a Commentary on the Gospel of St. John, of which considerable fragments have been preserved by Origen; and perhaps, also, a Commentary on the Gospel of St. Luke. Of the latter, only a single fragment, the exposi-

---

[1] Epiphan. Hæres. xxx. 3—7.

tion of Luke xii. 8, has been preserved by Clement of Alexandria.[1]

Heracleon was a man of deep spiritual piety, and with a clear understanding. He held Scripture in profound reverence, and derived his Valentinian doctrines from it. So true is the saying:

> "Hic liber est in quo quærit sua dogmata quisque,
> Invenit pariter dogmata quisque sua."

His interpretation of the narrative of the interview of the Saviour with the woman of Samaria will illustrate his method of dealing with the sacred text.

Heracleon saw in the woman of Samaria a type of all spiritual natures attracted by that which is heavenly, godlike; and the history represents the dealings of the Supreme God through Christ with these spiritual natures (πνευματικοί).

For him, therefore, the words of the woman have a double meaning: that which lies on the surface of the sacred record, with the intent and purpose which the woman herself gave to them; and that which lay beneath the letter, and which was mystically signified. "The water which our Saviour gives," says he, "is his spirit and power. His gifts and grace are what can never be taken away, never exhausted, can never fail to those who have received them. They who have received what has been richly bestowed on them from above, communicate again of the overflowing fulness which they enjoy to the life of others."

But the woman asks, "Give me this water, that I thirst not, neither come hither to draw"—hither—that is, to Jacob's well, the Mosaic Law from which hitherto she had drunk, and which could not quench her thirst, satisfy her aspirations. "She left her water-pot behind

---

[1] Strom. iv.

her" when she went to announce to others that she had
found the well of eternal life. That is, she left the
vessel, the capacity for receiving the Law, for she had
now a spiritual vessel which could hold the spiritual
water the Saviour gave.

It will be seen that Valentinianism, like Marcionism,
was an exaggerated Paulinism, infected with Gnosticism,
clearly antinomian. Though the Valentinians are not
accused of licentiousness, their ethical system was plainly
immoral, for it completely emancipated the Christian
from every restraint, and the true Christian was he who
lived by faith only. He had passed by union with
Christ from the dominion of the God of this World, a
dominion in which were punishments for wrong-doing,
into the realm of Grace, of sublime indifference to right
and wrong, to a region in which no acts were sinful, no
punishments were dealt out.

If Valentinianism did not degenerate into the frantic
licentiousness of the earlier Pauline heretics, it was
because the doctrine of Valentine was an intellectual,
theosophical system, quite above the comprehension of
vulgar minds, and therefore only embraced by exalted
mystics and cold philosophers.

The Valentinians were not accused of mutilating the
Scriptures, but of evaporating their significance. "Marcion," says Tertullian, "knife in hand, has cut the Scriptures to pieces, to give support to his system; Valentine
has the appearance of sparing them, and of trying rather
to accommodate his errors to them, than of accommodating them to his errors. Nevertheless, he has curtailed,
interpolated more than did Marcion, by taking from the
words their force and natural value, to give them forced
significations."[1]

The Pauline filiation of the sect can hardly be mis-

[1] Tertul. De Præscrip. 49.

taken. The relation of Valentine's ideas to those of Marcion, and those of Marcion to the doctrines of St. Paul, are fundamental. But, moreover, they claimed a filiation more obvious than that of ideas—they asserted that they derived their doctrines from Theodas, disciple of the Apostle of the Gentiles.[1] The great importance they attributed to the Epistles of St. Paul is another evidence of their belonging to the anti-judaizing family of heretics, if another proof be needed.

The Valentinians possessed a number of apocryphal works. "Their number is infinite," says Irenæus.[2] But this probably applies not to the first Valentinians, but to the Valentinian sects, among whom apocryphal works did abound. Certain it is, that in all the extracts made from the writings of Valentine, Ptolemy and Heracleon, by Origen, Epiphanius, Tertullian, &c., though they abound in quotations from St. Paul's Epistles and from the Canonical Gospels, there are none from any other source.

Nevertheless, Irenæus attributes to them possession of a " Gospel of Truth " (Evangelium Veritatis). " This Scripture," says he, " does not in any point agree with our four Canonical Gospels."[3] To this also, perhaps, Tertullian refers, when he says that the Valentinians possessed " their own Gospel in addition to ours."[4]

Epiphanius, however, makes no mention of this Gospel; he knew the writings of the Valentinians well, and has inserted extracts in his work on heresies.

[1] Tertul. De Præscrip. 38.   [2] Iren. Adv. Hæres. i. 20.
[3] Ibid. iii. 11.
[4] "Suum præter hæc nostra."—Tertull. de Præscrip. 49.

THE GOSPEL OF EVE.

THE immoral tendency of Valentinianism broke out in coarse, flagrant licentiousness as soon as the doctrines of the sect had soaked down out of the stratum of educated men to the ranks of the undisciplined and vulgar.

Valentinianism assumed two forms, broke into two sects,—the Marcosians and the Ophites.

Mark, who lived in the latter half of the second century, came probably from Palestine, as we may gather from his frequent use of forms from the Aramæan liturgy. But he did not bring with him any of the Judaizing spirit, none of the grave reverence for the moral law, and decency of the Nazarene, Ebionite and kindred sects sprung from the ruined Church of the Hebrews.

He was followed by trains of women whom he corrupted, and converted into prophetesses. His custom was, in an assembly to extend a chalice to a woman saying to her, "The grace of God, which excels all, and which the mind cannot conceive or explain, fill all your inner man, and increase his knowledge in you, dropping the grain of mustard-seed into good ground."[1] A scene like a Methodist revival followed. The woman was urged to speak in prophecy ; she hesitated, declared her inability; warm, passionate appeals followed closely one on another, couched in equivocal language, exciting the

[1] Epiphan. Hæres. xxxiv. 1 ; Iren. Hær. i. 9.

religious and natural passions simultaneously. The end was a convulsive fit of incoherent utterings, and the curtain fell on the rapturous embraces of the prophet and his spiritual bride.

Mark possessed a Gospel, and "an infinite number of apocryphal Scriptures," says Irenæus. The Gospel contained a falsified life of Christ. One of the stories from it he quotes. When Jesus was a boy, he was learning letters. The master said, "Say Alpha." Jesus repeated after him, "Alpha." Then the master said, "Say Beta." But Jesus answered, "Nay, I will not say Beta till you have explained to me the meaning of Alpha."[1] The Marcosians made much of the hidden mysteries of the letters of the alphabet, showing that Mark had brought with him from Palestine something akin to the Cabbalism of the Jewish rabbis.

This story is found in the apocryphal Gospel of St. Thomas. It runs somewhat differently in the different versions of that Gospel, and is repeated twice in each with slight variations.

In the Syriac :

"Zacchæus the teacher said to Joseph, I will teach the boy Jesus whatever is proper for him to learn. And he made him go to school. And he, going in, was silent. But Zacchæus the scribe began to tell him (the letters) from Alaph, and was repeating to him many times the whole alphabet. And he says to him that he should answer and say after him; but he was silent. Then the scribe became angry, and struck him with his hand upon his head. And Jesus said, A smith's anvil, being beaten, can (not) learn, and it has no feeling ; but I am able to say those things, recited by you, with knowledge and understanding (unbeaten)."[2]

---

[1] Iren. i. 26.

[2] Wright : Syriac Apocrypha, Lond. 1865, pp. 8—10.

In the Greek:

"Zacchæus said to Joseph . . . Give thy son to me, that he may learn letters, and with his letters I will teach him some knowledge, and chiefly this, to salute all the elders, and to venerate them as grandfathers and fathers, and to love those of his own age. And he told him all the letters from Alpha to Omega. Then, looking at the teacher Zacchæus, he said to him, Thou that knowest not Alpha naturally, how canst thou teach Beta to others? Thou hypocrite! if thou knowest, teach Alpha first, and then we shall believe thee concerning Beta." [1]

Or, according to another Greek version, after Jesus has been delivered over by Joseph to Zacchæus, the preceptor

"—wrote the alphabet in Hebrew, and said to him, Alpha. And the child said, Alpha. And the teacher said again, Alpha. And the child said the same. Then again a third time the teacher said, Alpha. Then Jesus, looking at the instructor, said, Thou knowest not Alpha; how wilt thou teach another the letter Beta? And the child, beginning at Alpha, said of himself the twenty-two letters. Then he said again, Hearken, teacher, to the arrangement of the first letter, and know how many accessories and lines it hath, and marks which are common, transverse and connected. And when Zacchæus heard such accounts of one letter, he was amazed, and could not answer him." [2]

Another version of the same story is found in the Gospel of the pseudo-Matthew:

"Joseph and Mary coaxing Jesus, led him to the school, that he might be taught his letters by the old man, Levi. When he entered he was silent; and the master, Levi, told one letter to Jesus, and beginning at the first, Aleph, said to

---

[1] Tischendorf: Codex Apocr. N. T.; Evang. Thom. i. c. 6, 14.
[2] *Ibid.* ii. c. 7; Latin Evang. Thom. iii. c. 6, 12.

him, Answer. But Jesus was silent, and answered nothing. Wherefore, the preceptor Levi, being angry, took a rod of a storax-tree, and smote him on the head. And Jesus said to the teacher Levi, Why dost thou smite me? Know in truth that he who is smitten teacheth him that smiteth, rather than is taught by him. . . . And Jesus added, and said to Levi, Every letter from Aleph to Tau is known by its order; thou, therefore, say first what is Tau, and I will tell thee what Aleph is. And he added, They who know not Aleph, how can they say Tau, ye hypocrites? First say what Aleph is, and I shall then believe you when you say Beth. And Jesus began to ask the names of the separate letters, and said, Let the teacher of the Law say what the first letter is, or why it hath many triangles, scalene, acute-angled, equilinear, curvi-linear," &c.[1]

At the root of Mark's teaching there seems to have been a sort of Pantheism. He taught that all had sprung from a great World-mother, partook of her soul and nature; but over against this female principle stood the Deity, the male element.

Man represents the Deity, woman the world element; and it is only through the union of the divine and the material that the material can be quickened into spiritual life. In accordance with this theory, they had a ceremonial of what he called spiritual, but was eminently carnal, marriage, which is best left undescribed.

Not widely removed from the Marcosians was the Valentinian sect of the Ophites. Valentinianism mingled with the floating superstition, the fragments of the wreck of Sabianism, which was to be found among the lower classes.

The Ophites represented the Demiurge in the same way as did the Valentinians. They called the God of this world and of the Jews by the name of Jaldaboth.

[1] Pseud. Matt. c. 31.

O

He was a limited being, imposing restraint on all his creatures; he exercised his power by imposing law. As long as his creatures obeyed law, they were subject to his dominion. But above Jaldaboth in the sublime region without limit reigns the Supreme God. When Adam broke the Law of the World-God, he emancipated himself from his bondage, he passed out of his·realm, he placed himself in relation to the Supreme God.

The world is made by Jaldaboth, but in the world is infused a spark of soul, emanated from the highest God. This divine soul strives after emancipation from the bonds imposed by connection with matter, created by the God of this world. This world-soul under the form of a serpent urged Eve to emancipate herself from thraldom, and pass with Adam, by an act of transgression, into the glorious liberty of the sons of the Supreme God.

The doctrine of the Ophites with respect to Christ was that of Valentine. Christ came to break the last chains of Law by which man was bound, and to translate him into the realm of grace where sin does not exist.

The Ophites possessed a Gospel, called the " Gospel of Eve." It contained, no doubt, an account of the Fall from their peculiar point of view. St. Epiphanius has preserved two passages from it. They are so extraordinary, and throw such a light on the doctrines of this Gospel, that I quote them. The first is:

"I was planted on a lofty mountain, and lo! I beheld a man of great stature, and another who was mutilated. And then I heard a voice like unto thunder. And when I drew near, he spake with me after this wise: I am thou, and thou art I. And wheresoever thou art, there am I, and I am dispersed through all. And wheresoever thou willest, there canst thou gather me; but in gathering me, thou gatherest thyself."[1]

The meaning of this passage is not doubtful. It expresses the doctrine of absolute identity between Christ and the believer, the radiation of divine virtue through all souls, destroying their individuality, that all may be absorbed into Christ. Individualities emerge out of God, and through Christ are drawn back into God.

The influence of St. Paul's ideas is again noticeable. We are not told that the perfect man who speaks with a voice of thunder, and who is placed in contrast with the mutilated man, is Christ, and that the latter is the Demiurge, but we can scarcely doubt it. It is greatly to be regretted that we have so little of this curious book preserved.[2] The second passage, with its signification, had better repose in a foot-note, and in Greek. It allows us to understand the expression of St. Ephraem, " They shamelessly boast of their Gospel of Eve."[3]

---

[1] Epiph. Hæres. xxvi. 3.

[2] The second passage and its meaning are : Εἶδον δένδρον φέρον δώδεκα καρποὺς τοῦ ἐνιαυτοῦ, καὶ εἰπέ μοι· τοῦτό ἐστι τὸ ξύλον τῆς ζωῆς, ὃ αὐτοὶ ἀλληγορουσιν εἰς τὴν κατὰ μῆνα γινομένην γυναικείαν ῥύσιν. Μισγόμενοι δὲ μετ' ἀλλήλων τεκνοποιίαν ἀπαγορεύουσιν. οὐ γὰρ εἰς τὸ τεκνοποιῆσαι παρ' αὐτοῖς ἡ φθορὰ ἐσπούδασται, ἀλλ' ἡδονῆς χάριν.—Epiph. Hæres. xxvi. 5.

[3] Epiphan. Hæres. xxvi. 2. He says, moreover: οὐκ αἰσχυνόμενοι αὐτοῖς τοῖς ῥήμασι τὰ τῆς πορνείας διηγεῖσθαι πάλιν ἐρωτικὰ τῆς κύπριδος ποιητούματα.

IV

THE GOSPEL OF PERFECTION.

THE Gospel of Perfection was another work regarded as sacred by the Ophites. St. Epiphanius says: "Some of them (*i.e.* of the Gnostics) there are who vaunt the possession of a certain fictitious, far-fetched poem which they call the Gospel of Perfection, whereas it is not a Gospel, but the perfection of misery. For the bitterness of death is consummated in that production of the devil. Others without shame boast their Gospel of Eve."

St. Epiphanius calls this Gospel of Perfection a poem, ποίημα. But M. Nicolas justly observes that the word ποίημα is used here, not to describe the work as a poetical composition, but as a fiction. In a passage of Irenæus,[1] of which only the Latin has been preserved, the Gospel of Judas is called "confictio," and it is probable that the Greek word rendered by "confictio" was ποίημα.[2]

Baur thinks that the Gospel of Perfection was the same as the Gospel of Eve.[3] But this can hardly be. The words of St. Epiphanius plainly distinguish them: "Some vaunt the Gospel of Perfection . . . . others boast . . . . the Gospel of Eve;" and elsewhere he speaks of their books in the plural.[4]

---

[1] Iren. Hæres. i. 35.

[2] Nicolas: Etudes sur les Evangiles Apocryphes, p. 168.

[3] Baur: Die Christliche Gnosis, p. 193.

[4] ἐν ἀποκρύφοις ἀναγινώσκοντες.—Hæres. xxvi. 5.

V.

THE GOSPEL OF ST. PHILIP.

THIS Gospel belonged to the same category as those of Perfection and of Eve, and belonged, if not to the Ophites, to an analogous sect, perhaps that of the Prodicians. St. Philip passed, in the early ages of Christianity, as having been, like St. Paul, an apostle of the Gentiles,[1] and perhaps as having agreed with his views on the Law and evangelical liberty. But tradition had confounded together Philip the apostle and Philip the deacon of Cæsarea, who, after having been a member of the Hellenist Church at Jerusalem, and having been driven thence after the martyrdom of Stephen, was the first to carry the Gospel beyond the family of Israel, and to convert the heathen to Christ.[2] His zeal and success caused him to be called an Evangelist.[3] In the second century it was supposed that an Evangelist meant one who had written a Gospel. And as no Gospel bearing his name existed, one was composed for him and attributed to him or to the apostle—they were not distinguished.

St. Epiphanius has preserved one passage from it:

" The Lord has revealed to me the words to be spoken by the soul when it ascends into heaven, and how it has to answer each of the celestial powers. The soul must say, I have known myself, and I have gathered myself from all parts. I have not borne children to Archon (the prince of

---

[1] Euseb. Hist. Eccl. ii. 1.   [2] Acts viii. 5, 13, 27—39, xxi. 8.
[3] Acts xxi. 8.

this world); but I have plucked up his roots, and I have gathered his dispersed members. I have learned who thou art; for I am, saith the soul, of the number of the celestial ones. But if it is proved that the soul has borne a son, she must return downwards, till she has recovered her children, and has absorbed them into herself."[1]

It is not altogether easy to catch the meaning of this singular passage, but it apparently has this signification. The soul trammelled with the chains of matter, created by the Archon, the Creator of the world, has to emancipate itself from all material concerns. Each thought, interest, passion, excited by anything in the world, is a child borne by the soul to Archon, to which the soul has contributed animation, the world, form. The great work of life is the disengagement of the soul from all concern in the affairs of the world, in the requirements of the body. When the soul has reached the most exalted perfection, it is cold, passionless, indifferent; then it comes before the Supreme God, passing through the spheres guarded by attendant æons or angels, and to each it protests its disengagement. But should any thought or care for mundane matters be found lurking in the recesses of the soul, it has to descend again, and remain in exile till it has re-absorbed all the life it gave, the interest it felt, in such concerns, and then again make its essay to reach God.

The conception of Virtues guarding the concentric spheres surrounding the Most High is found among the Jews. When Moses went into the presence of God to receive the tables of stone, he met first the angel Kemuel, chief of the angels of destruction, who would have slain him, but Moses pronounced the incommunicable Name, and passed through. Then he came to the sphere governed by the angel Hadarniel, and by virtue

[1] Epiphan. Hæres. xxvi. 13.

of the Name passed through. Next he came to the sphere over which presided the angel Sandalfon, and penetrated by means of the same Name. Next he traversed the river of flame, called Riggon, and stood before the throne.[1]

St. Paul held the popular Rabbinic notion of the spheres surrounding the throne of God, for he speaks of having been caught up into the third heaven.[2] In the apocryphal Ascension of Isaiah there are seven heavens that the prophet traverses.

The Rabbinic ideas on the spheres were taken probably from the Chaldees, and from the same source, perhaps, sprang the conception of the soul making her ascension through the angel-guarded spheres, which we find in the fragment of the Gospel of St. Philip.

Unfortunately, we have not sufficient of the early literature of the Chaldees and Assyrians to be able to say for certain that it was so. But a very curious sacred poem has been preserved on the terra-cotta tablets of the library of Assurbani-Pal, which exhibits a similar belief as prevalent anciently in Assyria.

This poem represents the descent of Istar into the Immutable Land, the nether world, divided into seven circles. The heavenly world of the Chaldees was also divided into seven circles, each ruled by a planet. The poem therefore exhibits a descent instead of an ascent. But there is little reason to doubt that the passage in each case would have been analogous. We have no ancient Assyrian account of an ascent; we must therefore content ourselves with what we have.

Istar descends into the lower region, and as she traverses each circle is despoiled of one of her coverings

---

[1] Jalkut Rubeni, fol. 107. See my "Legends of Old Testament Characters," II. pp. 108, 109.

[2] 2 Cor. xii. 2.

worn in the region above, till she stands naked before Belith, the Queen of the Land of Death.

i. " At the first gate, as I made her enter, I despoiled her; I took the crown from off her head.

" ' Hold, gatekeeper ! Thou hast taken the crown from off my head.'

" ' Enter into the empire of the Lady of the Earth, to this stage of the circles.'

ii. " At the second gate I made her enter; I despoiled her, and took from off her the earrings from her ears.

" ' Hold, keeper of the gate ! Thou hast despoiled me of the earrings from my ears.'

" ' Enter into the empire of the Lady of the Earth, to this stage of the circles.'

iii. " At the third gate I made her enter; I despoiled her of the precious jewels on her neck.

" ' Hold, keeper of the gate ! Thou hast despoiled me of the jewels of my neck.'

" ' Enter into the empire of the Lady of the Earth, to this stage of the circles.'

iv. " At the fourth gate I made her enter; I despoiled her of the brooch of jewels upon her breast.

" ' Hold, keeper of the gate ! Thou hast despoiled me of the brooch of jewels upon my breast.'

" ' Enter into the empire of the Lady of the Earth, to this stage of the circles.'

v. " At the fifth gate I made her enter; I despoiled her of the belt of jewels about her waist.

" ' Hold, keeper of the gate ! Thou hast despoiled me of the belt of jewels about my waist.'

" ' Enter into the empire of the Lady of the Earth, to this stage of the circles.'

vi. " At the sixth gate I made her enter ; I despoiled her of her armlets and bracelets.

" ' Hold, keeper of the gate ! Thou hast despoiled me of my armlets and bracelets.'

" 'Enter into the empire of the Lady of the Earth, to this stage of the circles.'

vii. "At the seventh gate I made her enter; I despoiled her of her skirt."

" 'Hold, keeper of the gate! Thou hast despoiled me of my skirt.'

" 'Enter into the empire of the Lady of the Earth, to this degree of circles.'"[1]

We have something very similar in the judgment of souls in the Egyptian Ritual of the Dead. From Chaldæa or from Egypt the Gnostics who used the Gospel of St. Philip drew their doctrine of the soul traversing several circles, and arrested by an angel at the gate of each.

The soul, a divine element, is in the earth combined with the body, a work of the Archon. But her aspirations are for that which is above; she strives to "extirpate his roots." All her "scattered members," her thoughts, wishes, impulses, are gathered into one uptapering flame. Then only does she "know (God) for what He is," for she has learned the nature of God by introspection.

Such, if I mistake not, is the meaning of the passage quoted by St. Epiphanius. The sect which used such a Gospel must have been mystical and ascetic, given to contemplation, and avoiding the indulgence of their animal appetites. It was that, probably, of Prodicus, strung on the same Pauline thread as the heresies of Marcion, Nicolas, Valentine, Marcus, the Ophites, Carpocratians and Cainites.

Prodicus, on the strength of St. Paul's saying that all Christians are a chosen generation, a royal priesthood, maintained the sovereignty of every man placed under

[1] The cuneiform text in Lenormant, Textes cuneiformes inédits, No. 30. The translation in Lenormant : Les premières civilisations, I. pp. 87—89.

the Gospel. But a king is above law, is not bound by law. Therefore the Christian is under no bondage of Law, moral or ceremonial. He is lord of the Sabbath, above all ordinances. Prodicus made the whole worship of God to consist in the inner contemplation of the essence of God.

External worship was not required of the Christian; that had been imposed by the Demiurge on the Jews and all under his bondage, till the time of the fulness of the Gospel had come.[1]   The Prodicians did not constitute an important, widely-extended sect, and were confounded by many of the early Fathers with other Pauline-Gnostic sects.

---

[1] Clem. Alex. Stromata, i. f. 304 ; iii. f. 438 ; vii. f. 722.

VI

THE Pauline Protestantism of the first two centuries of the Church had not exhausted itself in Valentinianism. The fanatics who held free justification and emancipation from the Law were ready to run to greater lengths than Marcion, Valentine, or even Marcus, was prepared to go.

Men of ability and enthusiasm rose and preached, and galvanized the latent Paulinian Gnosticism into temporary life and popularity, and then disappeared; the great wave of natural common-sense against which they battled returned and overwhelmed their disciples, till another heresiarch arose, made another effort to establish permanently a religion without morality, again to fail before the loudly-expressed disgust of mankind, and the stolid conviction inherent in human nature that pure morals and pure religion are and must be indissolubly united.

Carpocrates was one of these revivalists. Everything except faith, all good works, all exterior observances, all respect for human laws, were indifferent, worse than indifferent, to the Christian: these exhibited, where found, an entanglement of the soul in the web woven for it by the God of this world, of the Jews, of the Law. The body was of the earth, the soul of heaven. Here, again, Carpocrates followed and distorted the teaching of St. Paul; the body was under the Law, the soul was free. Whatsoever was done in the body did not affect the soul. "It is no more I that do it, but sin that dwelleth in me." [1]

"All depends upon faith and love," said Carpocrates; "externals are altogether matters of indifference. He who ascribes moral worth to these makes himself their slave, subjects himself to those spirits of the world from whom all religious and political ordinances have proceeded; he cannot, after death, pass out of the sphere of the metempsychosis. But he who can abandon himself to every lust without being affected by any, who can thus bid defiance to the laws of those earthly spirits, will after death rise to the unity of that Original One, with whom he has, by uniting himself, freed himself, even in this present life, from all fetters." [2]

Epiphanes, the son of Carpocrates, a youth of remarkable ability, who died young, exhausted by the excesses to which his solifidianism exposed him, wrote a work on Justification by Faith, in which he said:

"All nature manifests a striving after unity and fellowship; the laws of man contradicting these laws of nature, and yet unable to subdue the appetites implanted in human nature by the Creator himself—these first introduced sin." [3]

With Epiphanes, St. Epiphanius couples Isidore, and quotes from his writings directions how the Faithful are to obtain disengagement from passion, so as to attain union with God. Dean Milman, in his "History of Christianity," charitably hopes that the licentiousness attributed to these sects was deduced by the Fathers from their writings, and was not actually practised by them. But the extracts from the books of Isidore, Epiphanes and Carpocrates, are sufficient to show that

---

[1] Rom. vii. 17. [2] Iren. Hæres. i. 25.

[3] Compare Rom. iii. 20. Epiphanes died at the age of seventeen. Epiphan. Hæres. xxxii. 3.

their doctrines were subversive of morality, and that, when taught as religious truths to men with human passions, they could not fail to produce immoral results. An extract from Isidore, preserved by Epiphanius, giving instructions to his followers how to conduct themselves, was designed to be put in practice. It is impossible even to quote it, so revolting is its indecency. In substance it is this : No man can approach the Supreme God except when perfectly disengaged from earthly passion. This disengagement cannot be attained without first satisfying passion ; therefore the exhaustion of desire consequent on the gratification of passion is the proper preparation for prayer.[1]

To the same licentious class of Antinomians belonged the sect of the Antitactes. They also held the distinction between the Supreme God and the Demiurge, the God of the Jews,[2] of the Law, of the World. The body, the work of the God of creation, is evil ; it " serves the law of sin ;" nay, it is the very source of sin, and imprisons, degrades, the soul entangled in it. Thus the soul serves the law of God, the body the law of sin, *i.e.* of the Demiurge. But the Demiurge has imposed on men his law, the Ten Commandments. If the soul consents to that law, submits to be in bondage under it, the soul passes from the liberty of its ethereal sonship, under the dominion of a God at enmity with the Supreme Being. Therefore the true Christian must show his adherence to the Omnipotent by breaking the laws of the Decalogue,—the more the better.[3]

---

[1] Epiphan. xxxii. 4. [2] Clem. Strom. iii. fol. 526.

[3] It is instructive to mark how the enunciation of the same principles led to the same results after the lapse of twelve centuries. The proclamation of free grace, emancipation from the Law, justification by faith only, in the sixteenth century quickened into being heresies which had lain dead through long ages. Bishop Barlow, the Anglican Reformer, and one of the

Was religious fanaticism capable of descending lower?
Apparently it was so. The Cainites exhibit Pauline antinomianism in its last, most extravagant, most grotesque
expression. Their doctrine was the extreme development of an idea in itself originally containing an element
of truth.

Paul had proclaimed the emancipation of the Christian from the Law. Perhaps he did not at first sufficiently distinguish between the moral and the ceremonial law; he did not, at all events, lay down a broad,
luminous principle, by which his disciples might distinguish between moral obligation to the Decalogue and
bondage to the ceremonial Law. If both laws were
imposed by the same God, to upset one was to upset the
other. And Paul himself broke a hole in the dyke when
he opposed the observance of the Sabbath, and instituted
instead the Lord's-day.

Through that gap rushed the waves, and swept the
whole Decalogue away.

compilers of our Prayer-book, thus describes the results of the enunciation
of these doctrines in Germany and Switzerland, results of which he was
an eye-witness: "There be some which hold opinion that all devils and
damned souls shall be saved at the day of doom. Some of them persuade
themselves that *the serpent which deceived Eve was Christ.* Some of them
grant to every man and woman two souls. Some affirm lechery to be no
sin, and that one may use another man's wife without offence. Some take
upon them to be soothsayers and prophets of wonderful things to come, and
have prophesied the day of judgment to be at hand, some within three
months, some within one month, some within six days. Some of them,
both men and women, at their congregations for a mystery show themselves
naked, affirming that they be in the state of innocence. Also, some hold
that no man ought to be punished or suffer execution for any crime or trespass, be it ever so horrible" (A Dyalogue describing the orygynall ground
of these Lutheran faccyons, 1531). We are in presence once more of Marcosians, Ophites, Carpocratians. Had these sects lingered on through twelve
centuries? Possibly only; but it is clear that the dissemination of the
same doctrines caused the production of these obscene sects by inevitable
logical necessity, whether an historical filiation be established or not.

Some, to rescue jeoparded morality, maintained that the Law contained a mixture of things good and bad; that the ceremonial law was bad, the moral law was good. Some, more happily, asserted that the whole of the Law was good, but that part of it was temporary, provisional, intended only to be temporary and provisional, a figure of that which was to be; and the rest of the Law was permanent, of perpetual obligation.

The ordinances of the Mosaic sanctuary were typical. When the fulfilment of the types came, the shadows were done away. This was the teaching of the author of the Epistle to the Hebrews, called forth by the disorders which had followed indiscriminating denunciation of the Law by the Pauline party.

But a large body of men could not, or would not, admit this distinction. St. Paul had proclaimed the emancipation of the Christian from the Law. They, having been Gentiles, had never been under the ceremonial Law of Moses. How then could they be set at liberty from it? The only freedom they could understand was freedom from the natural law written on the fleshy tables of their hearts by the same finger that had inscribed the Decalogue on the stones in Sinai. The God of the Jews was, indeed, the God of the world. The Old Testament was the revelation of his will. Christ had emancipated man from the Law. The Law was at enmity to Christ; therefore the Christian was at enmity to the Law. The Law was the voice of the God of the Jews; therefore the Christian was at enmity to the God of the Jews. Jesus was the revelation of the All-good God, the Old Testament the revelation of the evil God.

Looking at the Old Testament from this point of view, the extreme wing of the Pauline host, the Cainites, naturally came to regard the Patriarchs as being under the protection, the Prophets as being under the inspiration, of the God of the Jews, and therefore to hold them in abhorrence, as enemies of Christ and the Supreme Deity. Those, on the other hand, who were spoken of in the Old Testament as resisting God, punished by God, were true prophets, martyrs of the Supreme Deity, forerunners of the Gospel. Cain became the type of virtue; Abel, on the contrary, of error and perversity. The inhabitants of Sodom and Gomorrah were pioneers of Gospel freedom; Corah, Dathan and Abiram, martyrs protesting against Mosaism.

In this singular rehabilitation, Judas Iscariot was relieved from the anathema weighing upon him. This man, who had sold his Master, was no longer regarded as a traitor, but as one who, inspired by the Spirit of Wisdom, had been an instrument in the work of redemption. The other apostles, narrowed by their prejudices, had opposed the idea of the death of Christ, saying, " Be it far from thee, Lord; this shall not be unto thee."[1] But Judas, having a clearer vision of the truth, and the necessity for the redemption of the world by the death of Christ, took the heroic resolution to make that precious sacrifice inevitable. Rising above his duties as disciple, in his devotion to the cause of humanity, he judged it necessary to prevent the hesitations of Christ, who at the last moment seemed to waver; to render inevitable the prosecution of his great work. Judas therefore went to the chiefs of the synagogue, and covenanted with them to deliver up his Master to their will, knowing that by his death the salvation of the world could alone be accomplished.[2]

Judas therefore became the chief apostle to the Cain-

---

[1] Matt. xvi. 21, 22; Mark vii. 31.

[2] Ideas reproduce themselves singularly. There is an essay by De Quincy advocating the same view of the character and purpose of Judas.

ites. They composed a Gospel under his name, τὸ Εὐαγγέλιον τοῦ Ἰούδα.[1] Irenæus also mentions it;[2] it must therefore date from the second century. Theodoret mentions it likewise. But none of the ancient Fathers quote it. Not a single fragment of this curious work has been preserved.

"It is certainly to be regretted," says M. Nicolas, "that this monument of human folly has completely disappeared. It should have been carefully preserved as a monument, full of instruction, of the errors into which man is capable of falling, when he abandons himself blindly to theological dogmatism."[3]

In addition to the Gospel of Judas, the Cainites possessed an apocryphal book relating to that apostle whom they venerated scarcely second to Judas, viz. St. Paul. It was entitled the "Ascension of Paul," Ἀναβατικὸν Παύλου,[4] and related to his translation into the third heaven, and the revelation of unutterable things he there received.[5]

An "Apocalypse of Paul" has been preserved, but it almost certainly is a different book from the Anabaticon. It contains nothing favouring the heretical views of the Cainites, and was read in some of the churches of Palestine. This Apocalypse in Greek has been published by Dr. Tischendorf in his Apocalypses Apocryphæ (Lips. 1866), and the translation of a later Syriac version in the Journal of the American Oriental Society, Vol. VIII. 1864.[6]

---

[1] Epiphan. Hæres. xxxviii. 1. [2] Iren. Adv. Hæres. i. 31.

[3] Etudes, p. 176.

[4] Epiphan. Hæres. xxxviii. 2. [5] 2 Cor. xii. 4.

[6] Reprinted in the Journal of Sacred Literature and Biblical Record, p. 372.

LONDON:
PRINTED BY C. GREEN AND SON,
178, STRAND.

Catalogue of some Works

PUBLISHED BY

WILLIAMS & NORGATE.

———✦———

Ali (Syed Ameer)—Life of Mohammed. A Critical Exa-
mination of the Life and Teachings of Mohammed, from a Moham-
medan Standpoint ; including Chapters on Polygamy, Slavery, Moslem
Rationalism, Moslem Mysticism, &c. By SYED AMEER ALI, Moulvie,
M.A., LL.B. of the Inner Temple, Barrister-at-Law, &c. Crown 8vo,
cloth, 9s.

Apocryphal Gospels, and other Documents relating to the
History of Christ. Translated from the Originals in Greek, Latin,
Syriac, &c.; with Notes, References, and Prolegomena. By B. HARRIS
COWPER. Third Edition. 8vo, cloth, 6s.

Baur (F. C.)—Paul, the Apostle of Jesus Christ, his Life
and Works, his Epistles and Teaching. A Contribution to a Critical
History of Primitive Christianity. Translated from the Second Edition, edited by E. ZELLER. Vol. I. 8vo, cloth, 10s. 6d.

Beard (Rev. Charles)—Port Royal. A Contribution to the
History of Religion and Literature in France. Cheaper Edition.
2 vols. crown 8vo, 12s.

Belsham (T.)—Memoirs of the Rev. Theophilus Lindsey,
M.A. The Centenary Volume. 8vo, cloth, 5s.

Bible (The) for Young People.—A Critical, Historical, and
Moral Handbook to the Old and New Testaments. By Dr. H. OORT
and Dr. J. HOOYKAAS, with the assistance of Dr. KUENEN. Translated from the Dutch by the Rev. P. H. WICKSTEED. Vol. I. Introduction and the Generations before Moses. Crown 8vo, cloth, 4s.

Channing (Rev. Dr.)—The Perfect Life. A Series of Un-
published Discourses of William Ellery Channing, D.D. Edited by
the Rev. W. H. CHANNING. Crown 8vo, 6s.

Channing and Lucy Aikin. — Correspondence of William
Ellery Channing, D.D., and Lucy Aikin, from 1826 to 1842. Edited
by Anna Letitia Le Breton. Crown 8vo, cloth, 9s.

Cobbe (Miss F. P.)—The Hopes of the Human Race, Here-
after and Here. Essays on the Life after Death and the Evolution of
the Social Sentiment. Crown 8vo, cloth, 7s. 6d.

Cobbe (Miss F. P.)—Essays. Darwinism in Morals, and
(13) other Essays (Religion in Childhood, Unconscious Cerebration,
Dreams, the Devil, Auricular Confession, &c. &c.) 400 pp. 8vo,
cloth (published at 10s.), 5s.

Cobbe (Miss F. P.)—Religious Duty. 8vo, cloth (published
at 7s. 6d.), 5s.

Cobbe (Miss F. P.)—Broken Lights. An Inquiry into the
Present Condition and Future Prospects of Religious Faith. New
Edition. 8vo, cloth, 5s.

Cobbe (Miss F. P.)—Dawning Lights. An Inquiry con-
cerning the Secular Results of the New Reformation. 8vo, cloth, 5s.

Cobbe (Miss F. P.)—Alone to the Alone. Prayers for
Theists, by several Contributors. New Edition. Crown 8vo, cloth, 5s.

Cobbe (Miss F. P.)—Studies, New and Old, of Ethical and
Social Subjects. 8vo, cloth (published at 10s. 6d.), 5s.

Cobbe (Miss F. P.)—Italics. Brief Notes on Politics, People
and Places in Italy in 1864. 8vo, cloth (published at 12s. 6d.), 5s.

Cobbe (Miss F. P.)—Hours of Work and Play. 8vo,
cloth, 2s. 6d.

Davidson (Dr. S.)—On a Fresh Revision of the English
Old Testament. By SAMUEL DAVIDSON, D.D. Crown 8vo, cloth, 5s.

Echoes of Holy Thoughts : arranged as Private Meditations
before a First Communion. Second Edition, with a Preface by the
Rev. J. HAMILTON THOM, of Liverpool. Printed with red lines.
Crown 8vo, cloth, 2s. 6d.

Flower (J. W.)—Adam's Disobedience, and the Results attributed to it, as affecting the Human Race. Second Edition, enlarged and corrected. 8vo, cloth, 6s. 6d.

Higginson (Rev. E.)—Ecce Messias; or, The Hebrew Messianic Hope and the Christian Reality. By EDWARD HIGGINSON. 8vo, cloth (published at 10s. 6d.), 6s.

Jesus (The) of History. By the Hon. Sir Richard Hanson, Chief Justice of South Australia. 8vo, cloth, 12s.

Keim (Dr. T.)—History of Jesus of Nazara. Considered in its connection with the National Life of Israel, and related in detail. Translated from the German. Vol. I. 8vo, cloth, 10s. 6d.

Kuenen (Dr. A.)—The Religion of Israel to the Fall of the Jewish State. Translated from the Dutch by A. H. MAY. 8vo, cloth, 10s. 6d.

Letters to and from Rome in the Years A.D. 61, 62, and 63. Translated by C. V. S. Crown 8vo, cloth, 2s. 6d.

Mackay (R. W.)—Progress of the Intellect, as exemplified in the Religious Development of the Greeks and Hebrews. 2 vols. 8vo, cloth, 24s.

Mackay (R. W.)—Sketch of the Rise and Progress of Christianity. 8vo, cloth (published at 10s. 6d.), 6s.

Man's (A) Belief: an Essay on the Facts of Religious Knowledge. Crown 8vo, sewed, 2s.

Martineau (Rev. Dr. James). — Religion as affected by Modern Materialism. Third Edition. 8vo, sewed, 1s.

Martineau (Rev. Dr. James). — New Affinities of Faith; a Plea for Free Christian Union. 12mo, 1s.

Multum in Parvo.—Thoughts for every Day in the Year. Selected from the Writings of Spiritually-minded Persons. By the Author of "Visiting my Relations." Crown 8vo, cloth, 2s. 6d.

Must God annihilate the Wicked? A Reply to Dr. Jos. Parker. 12mo, 1s.

Review of the Four Gospels. Part I. Their Evidentiary Value. 8vo, 1s.

Reville (Rev. Dr. A.).—The Song of Songs, commonly called the Song of Solomon, or the Canticle. Translated from the French. Crown 8vo, cloth, 1s. 6d.

Reville (Rev. Alb.)—The Devil: his Origin, Greatness, and Decadence. Translated from the French of the Rev. ALBERT REVILLE, D.D. 12mo, cloth, 5s.

Samuelson (James).—Views of the Deity, Traditional and Scientific; a Contribution to the Study of Theological Science. By JAMES SAMUELSON, Esq., of the Middle Temple, Barrister-at-Law, Founder and former Editor of the Quarterly Journal of Science. Crown 8vo, cloth, 4s. 6d.

Spencer (Herbert).—Essays, Scientific, Political, and Specu- lative. (Being the First and Second Series re-arranged, and containing an additional Essay.) Cheaper Edition. 2 vols. 8vo, cloth, 16s.
    A *Third* Volume of Essays (Second Edition), 7s. 6d.

Strauss (Dr. D. F.)—New Life of Jesus. The Authorized English Edition. 2 vols. 8vo, cloth, 24s.

Taine (H.)—On John Stuart Mill. English Positivism. A Study. Translated by T. D. HAYE. Second Edition. Crown 8vo, cloth, 3s.

Tayler (Rev. John James).—Letters, embracing his Life, of John James Tayler, Professor of Ecclesiastical History and Biblical Theology; and Principal of Manchester New College, London. Edited by the Rev. JOHN HAMILTON THOM. 2 vols. crown 8vo, with Portrait, in one volume cloth, 10s. 6d.

Tayler (Rev. J. J.)—An Attempt to ascertain the Character of the Fourth Gospel, especially in its relation to the Three First. New Edition. 8vo, cloth, 5s.

Theological Review: a Journal of Religious Thought and Life. Published Quarterly. Each No. 8vo, 2s. 6d.
    Annual Subscription, 10s. post free.

Williams (Dr. Rowland).—The Hebrew Prophets. Trans- lated afresh, and Illustrated for English Readers. 2 vols. 8vo, loth, 22s. 6d.

63023083R10192

Made in the USA
Columbia, SC
07 July 2019